ROSSEL ISLAND

ROSSEL ISLAND

An Ethnological Study

BY

W. E. ARMSTRONG, M.A.

*formerly Assistant Government Anthropologist,
Territory of Papua*

WITH
AN INTRODUCTION BY

A. C. HADDON, Sc.D., F.R.S.

CAMBRIDGE
AT THE UNIVERSITY PRESS
1928

CAMBRIDGE UNIVERSITY PRESS
Cambridge, New York, Melbourne, Madrid, Cape Town,
Singapore, São Paulo, Delhi, Tokyo, Mexico City

Cambridge University Press
The Edinburgh Building, Cambridge CB2 8RU, UK

Published in the United States of America by Cambridge University Press, New York

www.cambridge.org
Information on this title: www.cambridge.org/9781107600256

© Cambridge University Press 1928

First published 1928
First paperback edition 2011

A catalogue record for this publication is available from the British Library

ISBN 978-1-107-60025-6 Paperback

To P. C.

PREFACE

THIS volume was primarily intended as a general survey of Rossel Island culture; but it will be clear to the reader that many important aspects of the subject have been rather summarily treated. The discovery of an unusual system of currency led me to concentrate on the attempt to elucidate what turned out to be a very complex monetary system; and consequently other approaches to the study of this anomalous culture have been somewhat neglected.

In the course of my investigations, before the full importance of the monetary system had become apparent, I had been devoting special attention to the study of the system of relationships. This clearly bears a general similarity to certain relationship-systems that I had been investigating among the Massim—systems belonging to the type known as classificatory; and as Dr Rivers' treatment of the classificatory system appears unsatisfactory when subjected to close analysis, I have added an appendix of purely theoretical character which may help to make clear the working of the particular variety of this system found on Rossel. Similar considerations have led me in Chapter III to emphasise certain theoretical points in the course of my description of social organisation—points that are of particular importance in the case of Melanesian societies, and the neglect of which by anthropologists seems to have led to some confusion of thought and terminology.

The material used was collected in 1921 during a stay of about two months on Rossel Island. Although this visit was primarily a consequence of my holding temporarily the position of Assistant Anthropologist to the Papuan Government, it was also in no small degree made possible by grants previously allocated by various learned societies for the purpose of enabling me to visit New Guinea and carry out ethnological studies among its peoples. These grants included an Anthony Wilkin studentship from Cambridge University, a substantial sum from the Percy Sladen Trust Fund, and assistance from the Royal Society, as well as from Sidney Sussex College, Cambridge (which has also generously contributed to the cost of producing the present volume). To Dr A. C. Haddon and the late Dr W. H. R. Rivers my thanks are particularly due for fathering this expedition and to Dr Haddon for encouragement and help in the production of this particular volume. I should like also to mention my more indirect debt to Prof. Seligman and Dr Malinowski for advice as to procedure in a part of New Guinea generally familiar to them, and for encouragement in other ways.

It is only possible in a general way to express my thanks to government officials, missionaries, and other residents, who gave me the help and hospitality, without which ethnological research in this remote region would have been almost an impossibility. On Rossel itself, but for the generous hospitality of the Osbornes, particularly in the provision of transport, my difficulties would have been acute.

In the work of preparing the manuscript and reading the proofs I am indebted to Dr L. Alston for much valuable criticism, and also to my father for help of a similar character. My thanks are due to Miss C. H. Wedgwood for preparing the diagrams and to Mr J. R. Armstrong for compiling the Index.

W. E. ARMSTRONG

CAMBRIDGE
August 1927

CONTENTS

ILLUSTRATIONS

PLATES[1]

[1] The photographs IX, X, XI, XII, XX are of objects, collected in 1921, now in the Museum of Archaeology and Ethnology, Cambridge. The remaining photographs were taken on Rossel in 1921. I have to thank the Editor of *Man* for permission to reproduce Plate XX, which appeared in *Man*, November, 1924.

MAPS AND DIAGRAMS

INTRODUCTION

ROSSEL ISLAND, or Yela, was first discovered about 160 years ago, but it passed into oblivion until some 68 years ago when a French sailing vessel, *St Paul*, was wrecked there on her way to Australia with 327 Chinese coolies on board, who were seeking their fortunes in the gold mines of Australia. All but two or three of them were killed and eaten by the Rossel islanders, and one was rescued by the *Styx* in 1859. Many years later I heard that this man subsequently had got into trouble somewhere in South Australia, but on learning about him, the magistrate let him off on account of his terrible experiences in Rossel. The sensational account of the fate of the Chinese has more than once been denied and later reaffirmed, and now Mr Armstrong gives us all the available evidence and this disputed incident may be regarded as settled finally. Mr Armstrong points out that cannibalism is the necessary adjunct to the funeral rites of a chief, though he also suggests that there may have been other occasions for the practice. At all events, it seems pretty clear that at the time of the shipwreck of the *St Paul*, a certain 'chief' named Muwo was a wild disorderly person, and the dumping of this cargo of live stock came very opportunely for him and seems also to have been the means of aggravating his craving for anthropophagy. It was, to say the least of it, unfortunate that the shipwreck took place when that particular man was powerful, or the fate of the Chinese might have been very different.

It is not only in the above matter that we find contradictory accounts about the natives of Rossel, and it is therefore particularly satisfactory that 'this most unalluring fastness of the Giant Despair—the Ultima Thule of the Louisiade Archipelago', as the Hon. John Douglas termed it, should have been studied by a competent ethnologist. Prejudices and errors have been removed, but it is evident that there is yet more to learn about these interesting people, but, indeed, the same may be said of almost all ethnographical investigations, unless the observer has lived for a long time among his people and has special ability and great perseverance.

THE PHYSICAL ANTHROPOLOGY OF
THE MASSIM AREA

In the following observations measurements made on males are solely dealt with, as those made on females are too few to be of any value at present. My thanks are due to Prof. C. G. Seligman, Mr E. W. P. Chinnery and Mr Armstrong for allowing me to utilise their unpublished measurements.

Mr Armstrong has made a series of interesting measurements of men of certain mainland Massim groups, consisting of 24 from the village of Isudau, Fife Bay, who, he says, are representative of the Daui area which extends from Mullins Harbour to Baxter Harbour; 19 Bohutu, a bush tribe between Mullins Harbour and the head of Milne Bay; 25 Gibara, adjacent to and north of the Bohutu and near to the Maiwara; 17 Maiwara at the head of Milne Bay; and 4 from Tawala district, Milne Bay, but these last are too few in number to be of comparative value. Seligman measured 10 men at Wagawaga and 4 others from Milne Bay; 5 from South Cape and its vicinity. Armstrong measured 6 men from Bohilai (Basilaki or Moresby Island) and 10 at Tubetube (Engineer group), Seligman also measured 10 men at Tubetube, and he gives measurements of 9 men from various islands in the Louisiades. Armstrong measured 7 men at Misima, 14 at Sudest (Tagula) and Sabari (Calvados Chain), 23 at Rossel and 10 at Bunama, a district on the south coast of Normanby, D'Entrecasteaux group. Seligman measured 5 Normanby men, 14 from Fergusson and 8 Goodenough men. Chinnery measured 24 Fergusson and 38 Goodenough men, and obtained the stature of 27 other men from the D'Entrecasteaux. Seligman measured 20 men at Boioa, Trobriands, 5 at Kwaiawata and 10 at Gawa, Marshall Bennets, and 6 men at Suloga village, Murua (Woodlarks).

In a comparison of the cephalic index, nasal index, and stature of the inhabitants of the Massim area certain broad features can be made out, but as the data at present available consist of only some 327 men, they are too few to lead to reliable results, especially as in many cases very few individuals have been measured at any one spot. Although measurements have a definite value in giving precision to descriptions, observations on the living, such as those given

Table of measurements in percentages.

	C.I.				N.I.				Stature		
	Dol.	Mes.	Br.	Lept.	Mes.	Ch.	H.ch.	Pygmy	Short	Medium	Tall
24 Isudau	50	41·7	8·3	—	29·1	58·3	12·3	—	50	45·8	4·1
19 Bohutu	42	37	21	—	15·8	63·2	21	5·2	52·6	42·1	—
25 Gibara	36	40	24	—	12	56	32	16	48	32	4
17 Maiwara	82·3	17·6	—	—	17·6	47	35·3	—	64·7	29·4	5·9
10 Wagawaga	80	20	50	—	30	60	10	—	40	50	10
4 Milne Bay	—	—	—	—	25	75	—	50	25	75	—
4 ", Tawala	100	50	—	—	—	75	25	—	50	—	—
5 South Cape	20	80	—	—	40	40	20	—	—	100	—
6 Bohilai	83·3	16·6	—	—	33·3	50	16·6	—	33·3	66·6	—
10 Tubetube A.	70	30	—	—	30	50	20	10	90	10	—
10 ", S.	80	20	—	20	40	40	—	25	70	20	—
9 Louisiades	22	44	33	11	33	44	11	—	50	25	—
7 Misima	100	—	—	—	28·5	57·1	14·3	—	28·5	57·1	14·3
14 Sabari + Sudest	21·4	35·7	42·8	—	35·7	57·1	7·1	14·2	57·1	28·5	—
23 Rossel	21·7	56·5	21·7	—	34·7	60·8	4·3	13	52·1	34·7	—
10 Normanby A.	90	10	—	10	50	40	—	50	50	—	—
5 ", S.	60	40	—	—	60	40	—	—	80	20	—
14 Fergusson S.	71·4	7·1	21·9	—	28·5	57·2	14·3	30·7	61·5	7·7	—
24 ", C.	62·5	29·1	8·3	—	—	—	—	12·5	41·6	45·8	—
8 Goodenough S.	65·7	37·5	—	—	37·5	62·5	—	—	42·8	57	—
38 ", C.	45	31·5	2·6	—	—	—	—	10·5	47·3	42·1	—
20 Trobriands	—	40	15	—	60	40	—	—	25	65	10
5 Kwaiawata	—	80	20	—	80	—	20	—	40	60	—
10 Gawa	20	40	40	20	50	20	10	—	30	70	—
6 Murua	—	83·3	16·6	—	83·3	16·6	—	—	33·3	16·6	33·3 Very tall 16·6

by Seligman, are most important, as they can be made on a
greater number of persons than can measurements, and they
can be made on those whom it is not possible to measure,
since measurements are, as a rule, taken on the common
people and not on the chiefly class, where such exists.

The following grouping has been here adopted: Cephalic
Index: dolichocephalic, –77; mesocephalic, 77–82; brachycephalic, 82 +. Nasal Index: leptorrhine, –70; mesorrhine,
78–85; chamaerrhine, 85–100; hyperchamaerrhine, 100 +.
Stature: pygmy, –1·48 m.; short, 1·48–1·58 m.; medium,
1·58–1·68 m.; tall, 1·68–1·72 m.; very tall, 1·72 m. +.

In the following synopsis the more extreme indices or
measurements are mainly considered, as they presumably
indicate the more distinct racial elements.

Cephalic Index. Dolichocephaly occurs everywhere, but
in varying proportions. In Milne Bay and at Bohilai (Basilaki,
or Moresby Island) the percentage is 80 or more and there
are no brachycephals. In the districts of Gibara and Bohutu,
inland of Milne Bay, the percentage is about half of this and
there are over 20 per cent. of brachycephals. At Isudau, or
Fife Bay, in the Daui district 50 per cent. are dolicho- and
8 per cent. brachycephals. Seligman (1901, p. 271) was informed that the natives of Tubetube (Engineer group) claim
to have come from Normanby Island, the cephalic index is
similar in both places, and is not very different from that of
Milne Bay.[1] The nine observations from the western Louisiades show 33 per cent. of brachycephals, the seven Misima
men measured by Armstrong are all dolichocephalic. The
Sabari + Sudest and the Rossel islanders are nearly 22 per
cent. dolichocephalic, the former are nearly 43 per cent.
brachycephalic and the latter nearly 22 per cent. As we have
seen, the cephalic index of the southernmost of the D'Entrecasteaux Islands (Normanby) agrees closely with Milne Bay,[1]
but in Fergusson Island there is a noticeable strain of brachycephaly which weakens considerably in Goodenough. In the
Trobriands and Murua there is a distinct brachycephalic
element varying from 15 to 40 per cent. It would thus seem
that the brachycephaly in Sabari + Sudest and Rossel has
spread from Murua and not from the mainland Massim area.

Nasal Index. In Milne Bay[1] and Bohilai there is a pre-

[1] Maiwara and Wagawaga.

ponderance of chamaerrhines and a large proportion of hyper-chamaerrhines, and the same may be said for Gibara, Bohutu and Isudau, and Armstrong's 10 Tubetube men agree very well with these, but of the 10 men measured by Seligman 20 per cent. are leptorrhine and none are hyperchamaerrhine. Of the 9 Louisiade men 11 per cent. are either lepto- or hyperchamaerrhine. There are no leptorrhines in the three most easterly islands and the percentage of hyperchamaer-rhines descends from 14·3 in Misima to 4·3 in Rossel. Arm-strong's measurements on Normanby (10) give 10 per cent. of leptorrhines, but in Seligman's (5) there are none, both give 40 per cent. of chamaerrhines and no hyperchamaer-rhine. Thus so far as the N.I. is concerned, Armstrong's measurements at Normanby agree pretty closely with Selig-man's at Tubetube. There are no leptorrhine measurements for the other D'Entrecasteaux Islands, and hyperchamaer-rhines are recorded only on Fergusson, 14 per cent. out of 14. Only at Gawa in the Marshall-Bennets are leptorrhines re-corded, 20 per cent. out of 10, and there is a noticeable hyperchamaerrhine element which, however, is absent from Murua (6). The absence of leptorrhiny in the three most easterly islands of the Louisiade group agrees with the evidence from the district about Milne Bay, but the hyper-chamaerrhiny is distinctly less.

Stature. Throughout the whole region the stature is short or medium, but in some areas there is an element which has pygmy stature, and in others there are some individuals who are distinctly tall.

The pygmy statures occur among the Bohutu and Gibara, being respectively 5·2 and 16 per cent. Of 4 men measured by Armstrong at Tawala in Milne Bay 2 are pygmy and 2 are short, but other measurements from Milne Bay do not show pygmies; Seligman found 1 out of 10 in Tube-tube, which may be due to the Normanby stock. There seem to be a few in the Louisiades, but there are none recorded by Armstrong from Misima, though he found 14·2 per cent. out of 14 in Sabari + Sudest, and 13 per cent. out of 23 in Rossel. When we turn to the D'Entrecasteaux, the propor-tion of those with pygmy stature is quite marked, indeed it has been observed for a long time that there are numerous very short people in that group, but no measurements were available till Seligman measured 27 men, Armstrong measured 10 and Chinnery 62. Of Armstrong's 10 Normanby men half were of pygmy stature, but out of 5 Seligman did not record any. The combined observations (37) of Seligman and Chinnery for Fergusson give 18·9 per cent. pygmy, 48·6 per cent. short and 32·4 per cent. medium, and those (46) for Goodenough give 8·8 per cent. pygmy, 46·6 per cent. short, and 44·4 per cent. medium. Another series of Chinnery's from the D'Entrecasteaux (islands not specified) of 127 persons (1·321–1·613 m.) gives 26 per cent. pygmy, 70 per cent. short and 4 per cent. medium. There are no pygmy statures recorded for the Trobriands, Marshall Bennets, and Woodlarks.

The tall statures occur where the pygmy stature appears to be absent, as, for example, at Isudau in Fife Bay, and at Maiwara and Wagawaga in Milne Bay, but strangely enough at Gibara Armstrong measured 1 very tall man, 1·810 m., who made 4 per cent. of tall men (exactly as at Isudau), though we have seen there are also 16 per cent. of pygmy stature. Tall people appear to be absent from the Louisiades except on Misima, where Armstrong found 14·3 per cent. out of 7 men. Tallness is also absent from the D'Entrecasteaux, but reappears in the Trobriands, 10 per cent. out of 20 Boioa men, no tall men have been recorded by Seligman from the Marshall Bennets, though doubtless they occur there, and of 6 men at Murua 2 are short, 1 medium, 2 tall, and 1 very tall.

Taking the Massim as a whole it appears that there is:

1. A dolichocephalic stock which is distinctly chamaerrhine and, though short, has a tendency to medium stature.

2. A strain of pygmy stature which is mesocephalic and on the whole low chamaerrhine.

3. A tall strain which is dolichocephalic and very chamaerrhine.

4. A tall strain which is mesocephalic and mesorrhine.

5. A brachycephalic stock which is mesochamaerrhine and of short stature.

The Isudau appear to belong to 1 with a small proportion of 5 and a still smaller of 3.

The Bohutu on the whole belong to 1, but have a distinct trace of 5 and a small proportion of 2 and none of 3.

The Gibara have less 1 and more of 5, and an appreciable amount of 2, and the same amount of 3 as the Isudau.

The Maiwara appear to belong almost entirely to 1, with a trace of 3, as probably do the Milne Bay natives as a whole.

The Bohilai appear to be nearly pure 1.

The Tubetube are mainly 1, but there is an element of 2.

Scattered observations of 9 Louisiade men indicate a mixture of 1, 2 and 5.

The Misima are mainly 1, but with a distinct strain of 3.

The Sabari + Sudest appear to be a mixture of 1, 2 and 5.

The Rossel closely resemble the latter; but here those of pygmy stature are brachycephalic and meso-chamaerrhine.

The Normanby are a mixture of 1 and 2, and on the whole resemble the Tubetube, sporadic leptorrhiny occurs in both.

The Fergusson and Goodenough are a mixture of 1, 2 and 5.

The Trobriands are a mixture of 1, 4 and 5.

The Marshall-Bennets are probably the same, though 4 has not been recorded, leptorrhiny occurs at Gawa.

The Murua are apparently 4 and 5; stock 1 does not appear in the six measurements on the living, but it is very evident in the skulls.

Leptorrhiny in the Massim Area.

It is rather surprising to find six cases of leptorrhiny in the area: Tubetube, 2; Louisiade, 1; Normanby, 1; Marshall-Bennets, 2; the range is from 64 to 69. These fall into two groups: (A) dolichocephalic, av. C.I. 72, with an average short stature of 1·496 m. (59 in.), Tubetube and Normanby; and (B) mesocephalic, C.I. 80·3, with a low medium stature of 1·586 m. (62½ in.), Louisiades and Marshall-Bennets. Thus these very few cases are evenly distributed between two distinct types.

Tall men.

Only 10 tall men were noted by Armstrong and Seligman; they fall into two groups: (A) a dolichocephalic group: Isudau, 1; Maiwara, 1; Wagawaga, 1; Misima, 1, all of whom are chamaerrhine except the last, who is mesorrhine, the very tall Gibara man is mesocephalic (79·7) and hyper-chamaerrhine; (B) a mesocephalic group, of these the two

Trobrianders are very low chamaerrhine and the three from Murua are mesorrhine.

The element of pygmy stature.

On the mainland, at Tubetube and in the D'Entrecasteaux, as well as at Sabari + Sudest and Rossel, there are persons of pygmy stature apparently mixed up with those of taller stature and not segregated so as to form a racial group. These may be classed as (I) a western (or northern) and (II) an eastern (or southern) group. An analysis of these two groups gives the following results.

I. The western group consists of (1) a mainland section (4 Gibara, C.I. 77·5–81·7, av. 79·8; N.I. 83–97·9, av. 90·6; 1 Bohutu, C.I. 84·5, N.I. 80·4) which on the whole is mesocephalic and low chamaerrhine; but at Tawala (Milne Bay) the two subjects are dolichocephalic and chamaerrhine; (2) an insular section (D'Entrecasteaux) which is dolichocephalic and chamaerrhine (C.I. 69–82·6, av. 74·9; N.I. 67·4–97·8, av. 86·8). The single Tubetube man agrees with the Normanby men.

At Bohutu and Gibara there is a distinct brachycephalic strain in the general population. At Tawala, Tubetube and Normanby the population is predominantly dolichocephalic and there are no brachycephals recorded, and the men of pygmy stature in these places are solely dolichocephals. At Fergusson and Goodenough there are respectively one mesocephal and one brachycephal of pygmy stature, and there are brachycephals in these two islands. Leptorrhiny has been noted in the D'Entrecasteaux group only in Normanby and one is of pygmy stature.

II. The eastern group consists of Sabari + Sudest and Rossel, C.I. 78·4–88, av. 82·1, 50 per cent. meso- and 50 per cent. brachycephalic; N.I. 73·1–97·7, av. 85·6, 33 per cent. meso- and 66 per cent. chamaerrhine; the average stature is 1·439 m. (56½ in.); the 3 pygmy men of Sabari + Sudest are mesocephalic and mesorrhine and the 3 from Rossel brachycephalic and meso-chamaerrhine. They are thus mesobrachycephals and meso-chamaerrhines. In these islands there is a strong brachycephalic strain in the general population, and only about 21·5 per cent. of dolichocephals.

This analysis of the people of pygmy stature seems to indicate that in their C.I. and N.I. they so closely resemble their taller fellow-countrymen that no distinct pygmy group can be isolated.

The brachycephalic element.

An analysis of the brachycephals, excluding those of pygmy stature of whom there are six, gives the following results. Those of the mainland (12) (Isudau, Bohutu, Gibara, and Milne Bay) and of the Louisiades (2, Seligman) are chamaer-rhine, av. of 14, N.I. 90·8, and of short stature, av. 1·555 m. (61¼ in.). Those of Sabari + Sudest and Rossel (8) and 3 of Fergusson (Seligman) are mesorrhine and of short stature. Those of the Trobriands (4) are mesorrhine and on the average of medium stature, while those of the Marshall-Bennets and Murua (5) are mesorrhine, av. of 20 (excluding the 2 from the Louisiades), N.I. 82·5, and of short stature, av. 1·559 m. (less than 61½ in.), but if the 4 Trobrianders be excluded the average is 1·551 m. Thus with the exception of the Trobrianders, the average stature of all of them is short, those of the mainland are chamaerrhine, while all the insular brachycephals are mesorrhine with the exception of two from the Louisiades measured by Seligman. The total number, 34, is small, but there does seem to be sufficient evidence to state that the insular brachycephals have distinctly narrower noses than the mainlanders, and all are of short stature except the 4 Trobrianders who have an average medium stature, though two of them are short. Chinnery measured a Suau (S. Cape) man of medium stature, C.I. 85·3.

Chinnery found 3 brachycephals in the D'Entrecasteaux Group, one from Goodenough is of pygmy stature, two from Fergusson are both of medium stature, av. 1·626 m. (64 in.), which is slightly higher than the average, 1·616 m. (63⅝ in.) of the two medium Trobrianders; he did not take nasal measurements.

These somewhat tedious statistics confirm in a general way the conclusions at which Dr Seligman arrived, and though these were based on fewer data they were the result of personal observations by a trained anthropologist ('A classification of the natives of British New Guinea', *J.R.A.I.* xxxix, 1909, pp. 246 and 314). He clearly distinguishes between the

Papuans on the one hand and the Western Papuo-Melanesians and the Massim, or Eastern Papuo-Melanesians on the other (pp. 250–255). He states 'that the tribes of the western division of the Papuo-Melanesians vary among themselves, both in physical and cultural characteristics, far more than the Massim who are comparatively homogeneous in cultural characteristics, and in physical characters show a more or less orderly change from west to east, from short-statured dolichocephaly to brachycephaly associated with increase of stature' (p. 315). The Massim are divided by him into a southern area and a northern area, which consists of the Trobriands, Marshall-Bennets and Murua. The former 'is inhabited by a short, predominantly dolichocephalic, rather broad-faced people with moderately dark skin and frizzly, or rarely curly, hair, and often a "snouty" mouth'. In the northern area 'the people are usually somewhat lighter in colour, and often have curly or wavy hair. Many of the men are taller, and they are as a rule less prognathous. Their skulls are rounder, and their noses often longer and narrower, while the bridge of the nose may be high and narrow. But these characters are shown only by a portion of the natives of these islands, and even in them the degree in which they occur is not constant. In fact, if skin colour be ignored, it is possible in the Trobriands to meet with individuals making a complete series from typical Papuo-Melanesians to tall, good-looking men who are quite Polynesian in feature' (p. 269). In the Marshall-Bennets and Murua two types occur, 'one long-faced and leptorrhine or mesorrhine, the other platyrrhine and generally broad-faced'; a similar distinction is seen in the Trobriand islanders. 'The Trobriand people seem rather taller and tend more to mesaticephaly, the average stature of 20 men being 1·609 m. (about 63½ in.) with an average cephalic index of 78 (72–84). Like the Marshall-Bennet islanders, their hair is often wavy...Although no measurements of Trobriand chiefs were taken, the two members of one of the royal houses that I met were obviously of the long-faced, tall type' (p. 273). Seligman found that in the Marshall-Bennets the more important and energetic men belonged to this type. Probably we shall not be far wrong in assuming that the bearers of the higher culture to the Massim area were mainly of this type; but it must not be overlooked that the northern area of the Massim has received a greater amount of foreign influence than the southern, and some of this presumably arrived at a later date. Seligman says 'we know nothing of the inhabitants of Yela (Rossel Island)' (p. 270). Thanks to Armstrong's investigations this is no longer the case, and we now know that the Rossel and Sudest islanders, while agreeing in many respects with Seligman's southern group of the Massim, have also a strong infusion of the northern group from Murua.

For some time it has been known that the Rossel islanders spoke a non-Melanesian language, and there were several characteristics of their culture that indicated that they were different from their neighbours. From this it was inferred that there was a large proportion of an old stock, which could in general terms be designated as Papuan, a stratum which elsewhere in the Massim area has been overwhelmed by migrations of Melanesian-speaking peoples. It is not yet possible to dissect out, as it were, the different culture-layers of the area, especially since our knowledge of the remaining islands of the Louisiades is so very defective, but the following very tentative conclusions may be hazarded.

The language may be regarded as belonging to the aboriginal inhabitants, but if not, it must almost certainly have been introduced by the earliest of subsequent invaders. Possibly to this stratum belong the houses built on the ground as opposed to the pile-dwellings, indeed the latter are acknowledged to have been borrowed from Sudest. The absence of drums, bows and arrows, and stone-headed clubs is remarkable and the lack of the two former, at least, may confidently be attributed to disuse. The absence of pottery-making probably characterises the oldest stratum of culture, as may the purchase of wives which does not occur among the Massim, and the position of women is far inferior to that among these latter people. There is no evidence of real warfare or head-hunting either in the past or in the present.

Belonging doubtless to a later stratum are houses built on terraces (though these are ground-houses). As the only recognised form of cannibalism is that associated with the death of a chief, it would seem that cannibalism came in with the chiefly class, and the victims, which are always young boys and girls, are eaten at the *jagega*, squatting places, circular groups of stones similar to the *gahana* of various places in the neighbourhood of Milne Bay and in the D'Entre-casteaux group, but these circles of flat stones are not re-served solely for cannibal feasts, and Armstrong thinks that they are more particularly associated with feasts connected with money operations. The monetary system, which is well described, is very complicated and calculations run into high numbers, neither of which is 'Papuan'. All these are common to a culture which has spread over the Massim area.

The mythology possesses many interesting characters. A hierarchy of gods which occurs in Rossel is not known in the rest of the Massim area, nor indeed among the Papuo-Melanesians. Seligman says, concerning the Southern Massim: 'No cult of a superior being nor of the heavenly bodies could be discovered. Nor could I discover any definite cult of ancestors or of the spirits of the dead, though I formed the opinion that in Milne Bay the shades were certainly con-sidered to know when *toreha* (and perhaps other feasts) were held...But though there is no cult of a superior intelligence, nor, so far as I could discover, any attempt to enter into personal relation with any spiritual beings, there is a sturdy belief in the existence of a large number of mythical beings'. (*The Melanesians of British New Guinea*, 1910, p. 646). A theology is, however, a marked feature in the Papuan Gulf, where it appears to have drifted down from the north.

Wonajö, the supreme deity, who is a snake by day, lives on the highest mountain of Rossel and made the land, clouds, and stars, but not the sun and moon. He invited a snake god, Mbasi of Sudest, who had a dark colour, to visit Rossel, and the islanders are his progeny by Könjini, an oviparous fair-skinned girl of Rossel. When Wonajö visited Sudest, or sent one of his snake friends, the voyage across was made in a wooden dish, as canoes were not then known; perhaps this refers to a dug-out without an outrigger, at all events, the *para nö* canoes (or *ndap* canoes) (p. 28) are attributed to him, these never carry sails and may be described as 'cere-monial canoes'. Mbasi, however, arrived in a sailing canoe, *lia nö* (p. 24) bringing with him the sun, moon, pig, dog and taro. The sun and moon being too close to the earth were raised by Wonajö with a pole to their present position.

Wonajö and Mbasi at a very early stage instituted exogamic clan-divisions and Mbasi gave each clan its particular totem, for totemism appears to have already existed among the gods, because Wonajö had two of each of the three linked totems (i.e. 2 plants, 2 birds and 2 fishes), he had also two homes on Rossel, two *dama* songs, and he made the two kinds of money, *nkö* and *ndap*. The plant totem of a god was assigned to each mortal, together with the appropriately associated bird and fish, an intimate relation with a particular god was also assigned to each person, which god is now often described as a fourth totem, but spoken of as if it were a species of snake. Matrilineal descent was established when the totems had been distributed.

Our information concerning the totemism of other parts of the Massim area is very imperfect, matrilineal descent is universal, as is clan exogamy. At Wagawaga in Milne Bay there are two clan-groups: Garuboi (with one clan, Garuboi) and Modewa (with two clans, Modewa and Hurana), each clan has at least one bird totem with, in each case, a linked fish, snake, and plant totem. Seligman regards the clan-groups as originally phratries. At Tubetube in the Engineer Group, according to the Rev. J. T. Field (*Ann. Rep. B.N.G.* 1898, p. 134 and *Eighth Meeting of the Australasian Assoc. Advanc. Sci.*, Melbourne, 1900 (1901), p. 301) there are six clans, each of which has a bird or fish totem; Seligman gives four clans with linked bird, fish and snake totems, but only one hamlet has a plant totem, which is not held in respect and this hamlet has a different origin from its neighbours. No dual grouping has been described.

In Bartle Bay Seligman investigated three communities: (1) at Gelaria there are two clan-groups, Garuboi (with two clans, Garuboi and Girimoa) and Elewa (with one clan, Elewa). The totems were given by the great snake Garuboi, when he separated mankind into clans. In Wamira and Wedau there are numerous clans, typically each clan has the usual three-linked totems, but some clans have linked bird and fish, bird and snake, or bird and a four-footed vertebrate.

In the Trobriands there are four clans, each with a supreme bird totem to which is linked a four-footed vertebrate, a fish, and a plant, besides a number of less important birds; there is reason to suppose that at one time snakes may have been totem animals. In the Marshall-Bennets there is much the same system, the snake totem is obviously òf little importance and some clans are said to have none; the plant totems are also unimportant. In Murua it is stated that the totems were originally distributed by an old man who gave a bird and fish to each clan. In the villages of Dekoias, although everyone has linked totems belonging to different orders of vertebrates, no one has plant totems; the bird seems to be the chief totem.

In the Louisiades at Panatinani (Joannet Island) everyone has a number of linked totems which may consist of one or more birds, with a fish, a snake, and often a tree. One of the bird totems is more important than the others, and the place of the fish totem may be taken by a turtle or crocodile, and that of the snake by a lizard. At Tagula (Sudest) a similar system obtains, in one instance the flying-fox replaces the chief bird. There does not appear to be a dual or multiple grouping of the clans. (The foregoing condensed information is derived from C. G. Seligman, *The Melanesians of British New Guinea*, Cambridge, 1910, in which other references will be found.)

This brief and very imperfect survey of the totemism of the Massim area shows that the totemism of Rossel belongs to the same general system, but the great importance of the plant totem and the snake-god are distinctive. The general impression seems to be that Rossel has retained more primitive features, which one would expect from its isolated position.

Mythology also refers, in the fight of snakes with fish, to a period before true men had appeared (p. 131). No information is given concerning the weapons of the fish, but the Wonajö snakes were armed with man-catchers (the man-catcher has not been recorded east of East Cape), but as *wyeli* it is said to be used in Rossel in children's games (f.n. p. 131); a similar implement but without the spike is used for catching pigs by the Buji and Marind of South-west New Guinea. The Mbasi snakes had tomahawk stones (apparently these were of the Massim ceremonial kind, now only used for purposes of currency and ceremonial). The Mbyung fought with stones (probably thrown from slings, which are common among the Massim). The Gadiu carried bows and arrows (the bow and arrow occurs now only as a toy or as a fleam in Rossel and elsewhere in South-east New Guinea, it does not now occur as a weapon among any of the Papuo-Melanesians), while the Nongwa used their fingers only. The snakes won; Wonajö, Mbasi and Mbyung retained their snake form, the others being turned to stone.

The god Ye, whose animal form is a huge fish-hawk, has a sacred place, *yaba*, in the island of Loa, and to him is attributed the origin of sorcery, the most evil thing in the world. Before there was death in the world, Ye committed incest with his sister at which a dog laughed. Ye killed his sister by the *ngwivi* method of sorcery and she and Kaijum, lord of Yuma, were the first to die by this method. Ye's sister was the first for whom a cannibal mortuary feast was made, Ye ate the man who was sacrificed on account of her death.

Ye and Wonajö are in continual conflict which is only half serious, and they play tricks on each other.

When the mythology of other Louisiade islanders is investigated, we shall probably obtain more light upon that of Rossel, which appears to consist of somewhat confused fragments and it certainly contains elements of widely spread mythical Oceanic narratives.

The fight between the snakes and the fish appears to be reminiscent of the conflict of invaders with the aboriginal population (the fish), but judging from their weapons the former were not a homogeneous people, since the bow and arrow, and probably the man-catcher, belong to a 'Papuan' stage of culture, but missile stones are 'Melanesian'.

Mbasi, although he was dark-coloured, was a culture hero-god, and it was not until he came and married a light-skinned woman (presumably of the snake race) that true men were born; for, as is usual, the superior invaders regarded the autochthonous population as not being proper men. He and the supreme Wonajö regulated the universe, introduced the dog, pig, and taro, and organised human society on the pattern of their own.

The playful antagonism of Wonajö and Ye has many parallels in Oceania and it is significant that the animal form of Ye is the fish-hawk. He also introduced sorcery, and through his conduct death came to mankind.

The main point which comes out clearly from the foregoing

is that the mythology belongs to a group or groups which introduced into Rossel a higher culture with a definite social system, and that it had the essential characteristics of that remarkable culture which has left such clear traces of progress throughout Melanesia and over a great part of New Guinea. It hardly appears probable that it spread over Melanesia in a single migratory movement, and, so far as New Guinea and its archipelagoes are concerned, it seems evident that there were several subsidiary cultural drifts and cross currents characterised by variations, or even by the absence, of certain elements in the higher culture. The existing evidence seems to point to successive spreads of a fairly uniform basic culture into Melanesia, and we may find that the more complete forms of it have survived in remote spots or in those more difficult of access, while in other areas it has been subject to partial disintegration owing to disturbing factors.

The evidence of the observations on the physical anthropology of the Massim made by Mr Armstrong supports the conclusion that the racial history of the whole area is intricate, and this complexity is also manifested in Rossel.

A. C. HADDON

CHAPTER I

Introduction

THE island of Rossel, the most easterly of the Louisiade group, Papua, occupies a position of peculiar isolation. Indeed, for the Rossel Islander, until recently, the outside world consisted of the island of Sudest, with its satellite, Piron, and a shadowy world of islands beyond, with the inhabitants of which he had only indirect communication through the people of Sudest. Even this island, 20 miles to the south-west, played no great part in his life. No doubt this was partly owing to the treacherous nature of the open sea separating the reefs of the two islands, but also partly because the tradition of voyaging and exchange characteristic of the Massim[1] area was absent, both from Rossel and from Sudest.

The culture of any one part of the Massim area cannot be completely described without reference to other parts of the area. This is to a certain extent true even of Sudest, which may, on the whole, be regarded as Massim in culture. The culture of Rossel on the other hand can be described with some completeness without reference to the relations of the islanders to the inhabitants of the remainder of the Archipelago. Throughout the rest of this Archipelago, with its adventurous navigators connecting up island with island, a single general type of language and culture prevails. Both language and culture on Rossel differ profoundly from this general type, and even the most daring raiders from the west, who made the Sudest beaches uninhabitable, avoided this mysterious island. Even to the casual visitor it seems to have a special quality of isolation. Sudest is not 20 but 100 miles away, and generally does not exist when the rain squalls drift monotonously west.

The island is small, about 100 square miles in area, its greatest length about 20 miles and its greatest breadth about

---

[1] The term Massim is used throughout this work in the sense defined by Prof. Seligman ('A Classification of the Natives of British New Guinea.' *Journal of the Royal Anthropological Institute*, vol. XXXIX, 1909), except that Rossel is definitely excluded.

10 miles, and has a population of about 1500 persons. It is surrounded by a coral reef, which encloses a large lagoon of some 100 square miles at the west end of the island, and one of about 20 square miles at the eastern extremity. On the edge of the latter lagoon, about five miles from the mainland, is the little island of Loa, near which no woman may go, and in connection with which there are a number of curious rites.

The island is of volcanic formation, the highest mountain reaching nearly 3000 feet. It is thickly wooded throughout, and contains the usual economic plants of this part of the tropics; for instance, the sago palm is plentiful. A peculiar feature is the abundance of orchids. The coast is much indented, and the mangrove flourishes along the shores and lower reaches of the numerous rivers. Sandy beaches are rare, and most of the villages are situated in the interior, many at a height of over 1000 feet. The fauna is more restricted than in the regions west of Rossel; for instance, there appear to be no poisonous snakes on the island. Crocodiles, on the other hand, are especially numerous and dangerous, and a millipede, only rarely encountered further west and considered dangerous there, is omnipresent. The mollusc *Spondylus*, from which are made the sapi-sapi beads used throughout a large part of New Guinea, is abundant, as well as other molluscs; of these latter the *Trochus* and pearl mussel are valuable to the white man. The mosquito and the sandfly divide the distinction of being the worst pests. The rainfall is considerable in both the south-east and the north-west seasons, and in the latter violent thunderstorms are common. The climate is probably more humid than anywhere else in South-East New Guinea[1].

Although remote from the present centres of government in Papua, Rossel Island was visited by Europeans a number of times before a settled government had been established in Papua, the visits being sometimes involuntary, as the evidences of former shipwrecks on the reef go to prove.[2]

Comparatively little was known of the island previous to

[1] See footnote below. The island is described by Macgillivray, App. I, pp. 189–191; Rochas, p. 201; Douglas, p. 205; Macgregor, p. 205.

[2] All visits to the island by Europeans recorded in the literature consulted are mentioned in App. I, 'History and Bibliography'. An attempt has also been made in this Appendix to quote all first-hand accounts of Rossel that have so far been published, if they are of the slightest anthropological or historical interest.

the present writer's visit. Much of the information extant is summed up in a few pages by the present Lieutenant-Governor in his volume on Papua.[1] The first European to land on the island and publish some account of the natives was M. de Rochas in 1859. He was a passenger on the *Styx*, a French vessel which had been sent from New Caledonia to rescue some 300 Chinese, who had been wrecked on Rossel a few months earlier. It was found on arrival that almost all these Chinamen had been eaten.[2] Naturally enough, M. de Rochas does not give us a very pleasing picture of the island, and he was not in a position to obtain much information about its inhabitants. This unpleasant incident seems to have unduly biassed the judgments of later visitors; for instance, the Hon. John Douglas, repatriating natives from the Queensland sugar plantations in 1887, refers to this ' most unalluring fastness of the Giant Despair ', with its ' revolting looking anthropophagi '.[3] But Sir Wm Macgregor, unfavourably impressed by the islanders in 1888, finds them in 1890 'perhaps the most harmless and inoffensive in the Possession ',[4] and in 1892 becomes convinced that they were not cannibals, and did not murder the castaways of the *St Paul*,[5] and also finds them most zealous in the securing of certain murderers for whom he was looking, even killing one in their zeal—zeal to get rid of an inconvenient witness, perhaps, although Macgregor does not take this view. Nevertheless, Macgregor's account gives us some valuable information as to material culture.[6] The nature of their cannibalism and homicidal customs is partially elucidated by subsequent observers, such as Mr Campbell in 1901,[7] and Mr Moreton a year or two later,[8] but no important addition

[1] J. H. P. Murray, *Papua or British New Guinea*, 1912, pp. 130–140.

[2] See M. de Rochas' account in App. I, pp. 192–203, and Chap. IX, pp. 108–112, for a further discussion of this incident.

[3] App. I, p. 205.   [4] App. I, p. 207.

[5] In spite of Macgregor, later writers return to a belief in this tragedy of the Chinamen, but the scene of the wreck is now the larger island of Loa (Adele Island), many miles from Heron Island, the actual place of the tragedy. As the story revives, with dramatic elaborations, so we find the Rossel Islander losing the gentle and lovable disposition which he enjoyed for a few years, and becoming again the most unspeakable in the Possession. The account of this incident that I obtained before discovering Rochas' confirmatory article is given in Chap. IX. Here references are given to all the earlier accounts, which are recorded in full in App. I.

[6] App. I, pp. 209–213.   [7] App. I, p. 216.   [8] App. I, pp. 217–218.

to previous information is made until 1908, when the Lieutenant-Governor, J. H. P. Murray, visited the island, and also Mr Bell. The Lieutenant-Governor takes the view in his report that the islanders are 'about as murderous a lot of people as you can find in Papua', and gives some interesting information about their habits.[1]

Mr Bell's report[2] contains a good deal of useful data concerning both material culture and social organisation, and to this information some important additions were made in 1911 by the Lieutenant-Governor.[3]

In recent years the island has been brought into more permanent, though still slender, contact with European influences, mainly by the Osbornes, who have been resident on the island for many years. They do not subscribe to the view that the Rossel Islander is particularly repulsive, or to the view that he is particularly lovable. No trace of missionary influence has yet reached the island, a recent attempt being a complete failure.

Physically, the inhabitants are similar to the Papuo-Melanesians of the Archipelago, though differing slightly in certain respects.[4] Measurements of 26 natives show that,

---

[1] App. I, pp. 218-220.   [2] App. I, pp. 221-228.   [3] App. I, pp. 228-229.

[4] Rochas refers to the dull black skin of 'ces affreux personnages', the flattened nose, big mouth, prominent cheek-bones, and receding forehead (App. I, pp. 202-203). Macgregor says that 'they distinctly belong to the Papuan race', and that 'they are the purest blooded Papuans we have in the Possession'. He attributes the ringworm, *Tinea desquamans*, which afflicts many of the natives, to recent communication with Sudest (App. I, p. 212). The first estimate of population was made by Macgregor in 1888, when he put it at 1000 to 1200 (App. I, p. 206). In 1899 Le Hunte gives an estimate of 2000 to 3000 (App. I, p. 214). If this number be correct, a rapid decrease must have set in, for Mr Osborne estimated the population at 1500 in 1908 (App. I, p. 218), which is also the figure given by Bell (App. I, p. 223). Since this date the population has remained about stationary, for in 1920 a census of the island gave the figure 1415 (App. I, p. 230). Nevertheless, in 1908, Mr Osborne stated that the people were decreasing (App. I, p. 223). The increase, if it really took place, from 1888 to 1899 may have been in part due to the cessation of raids of 'blackbirders', recruiting for the Queensland plantations; while the decrease from 1899 may have resulted from the renewal of recruiting, for Campbell refers in 1908 to the return by a recruiting ship of less than half the number of carriers that had been originally removed, the natives stating that of 54 natives taken to Mambare about 20 died and 10 deserted (App. I, p. 214). In 1908, according to Bell, the women outnumbered the men (App. I, p. 223), but the census of 1920 indicates a slight excess of males, although the figure for adult females is greater than that for adult males (App. I, p. 230).

PLATE I

(a) Mt Rossel from Heron Island.

(b) Mt Rossel from Heron Island, nearer view.

PLATE II

(*a*) Mt Mbwo.

(*b*) Wolunga Bay.

compared with the Southern Massim (on the basis of similar measurements in Daui), the Rossel Islander is slightly darker in skin colour, rather more broad-headed, and rather shorter.[1] No other appreciable differences were revealed by the measurements taken, although by general appearance they can as a rule be differentiated from the natives of the rest of the Archipelago. This cast of countenance may, however, be only a cultural feature; for the Rossel natives have not the gay disposition characteristic of the Massim, and it is highly probable that this difference of temperament reflects a difference of culture rather than of nature.

The language is uniform throughout the island, except for the usual dialectic variations.[2] The change of dialect as we pass, for instance, from west to east, is perhaps rather greater than is usual amongst the Massim, but the change is progressive, and the division of the language into two dialects, as here adopted, is quite arbitrary, indicating merely the extremes of variation of the one language. Comparing either of these dialects with the most easterly dialect of Sudest, we find that, although there are certain similarities in construction and grammar, the language of Sudest clearly belongs to a different family; in fact, from Sudest to the most distant point in the Massim area the change of dialect is gradual throughout, and it could be said with some approximation to the truth that difference of dialect between any two points is proportional to the distance separating them.

Unlike the Melanesian languages of the Massim, the Rossel language seemed to me peculiarly difficult. Even Mr Frank Osborne, who had resided on the island for perhaps 15 years, knew no more than a number of useful phrases, and I could discover no native of Sudest who knew very much more. Although I paid considerable attention to the language, I found that the phonetic values of the consonants

---

[1] See App. ii, 'Physical Measurements'.

[2] Macgregor noticed the non-Melanesian character of the language in 1892, and states that the provincial differences of language between north and south are so great 'that it (the language) is hardly comprehensible in both districts to one interpreter' (App. i, p. 213). Murray states in 1908 that 'the East and West speak different dialects, which, however, are now becoming assimilated', and that the language 'cannot be better described than as resembling the snarling of a dog interspersed with hiccoughs' (App. i, pp. 218–219). Bell in the same year finds the language to be only 'slightly different at both ends of the island' (App. i, p. 225).

and even to a certain extent of the vowels offered difficulties that I, lacking sufficient phonetic training and with only a short time at my disposal. was unable to overcome. The vocabulary and grammar that I collected on the island are not published here, as being of doubtful value. A short vocabulary and grammar by the present writer have, however, been published by the Papuan Government,[1] and there is a more lengthy vocabulary and grammar (the name of the compiler is not given) in the *Annual Report on British New Guinea* for 1893–94.[2] But neither of these can be regarded as at all accurate. As regards the construction of the language, the chief points of interest are: (1) the indication of personal possession by prefixes— the Massim, and I think, all Melanesian languages use suffixes for this; (2) the absence of a distinction between the inclusive and exclusive first person plural—a distinction, generally, if not always, made in Melanesian languages; and (3) the irregularity of the verb, which appears to be conjugated partly by means of changes in the verbal particles in the typical Melanesian manner, and partly by means of suffixes or other inflexions, the verbal particles even being dispensed with in some cases. The vocabulary also reveals the underlying non-Melanesian character of the language, although there are a few recognisable Melanesian words.

English consonantal and Italian vowel values are to be given to the letters of native words in the text; *ö* is used for the very common vowel sound generally symbolised in English by 'er', as in 'fern' and 'longer'.

The map (p. 8) gives approximately those districts on the island that the rough geography of common language recognises and some of the principal villages and other localities. The districts corresponding to the numbers on the map are given below. The termination *we* means 'district of', and may be added to a village name to indicate a vaguely defined locality in the neighbourhood of the village. As would be expected, a district name has usually a more limited extension when used by inhabitants of the neighbourhood of the district than

[1] *Annual Report, Papua*, 1921–22, pp. 31–37, reprinted in *Papua, Native Taxes Ordinance*, 1917–22; *Reports on Anthropology*, No. 2, pp. 12–31.
[2] *Annual Report on British New Guinea*, 1893–94, pp. 116–120.

when used by those living at a distance. The map represents a compromise between these different points of view, and, though roughly drawn, is all that is required for our purposes.

In the following list the numbers without a suffixed letter indicate coastal districts, while those with a suffixed letter are used for interior districts:

1. Milewe.
   1 a. Ngöwe.
2. Dyödowaiwe.
   2 a. Kwmarawe.
3. Dyindyöwe.
   3 a. Yeliuwe.
   3 b. Gwabowe.
   3 c. Ngwöwe.
4. Wadugedawe.
   4 a. Tunubawe.
5. Lawe.
   5 a. Munowe.
6. Yabuwe.
   6 a. Chalibawe.
7. Peawe.
   7 a. Maguwe.
8. Piamadawe.
   8 a. Piuwonggowe.
9. Yilinowawe.
   9 a. Lileuwe.
10. Bewe.
    10 a. Milewe.
11. Dongwe.
    11 a. Mboiuwe.
12. Könawe.
    12 a. Kwabawe.
    12 b. Beangwe.
13. Dimogolowe.
    13 a. Yebowe.
14. Denöwe.
    14 a. Mbomuwe.
    14 b. Wöböwe.
15. Gwolowe.
    15 a. Piangowe.

16. Ponguyawe.
    16 a. Ngunöwe.
17. Kwedabowe.
    17 a. Kamboiuwe.
18. Pwabenuwe.
    18 a. Kwabawe.
19. Tumuwe.
    19 a. Boboiuwe.
20. Bwabuwe.
    20 a. Ngöwe.
21. Kwobuwe.
    21 a. Yuluwe.
22. Borowe.
    22 a. Kwalewe.
23. Tawalewe.
    23 a. Tongowe.
24. Koliwe.
    24 a. Pomgawe.
25. Tamuwe.
    25 a. Dogowe.
26. Doowe.
    26 a. Pemewe.
27. Ngaguwe.
    27 a. Kwunewe.
28. Bambawe.
    28 a. Kadawe.
29. Bumawe.
    29 a. Piöwe.
30. Chomabewe.
    30 a. Yeowe.
31. Chajawe.
    31 a. Bubuwe.
32. Mbwaduwe.
    32 a. Iyangiuwe.

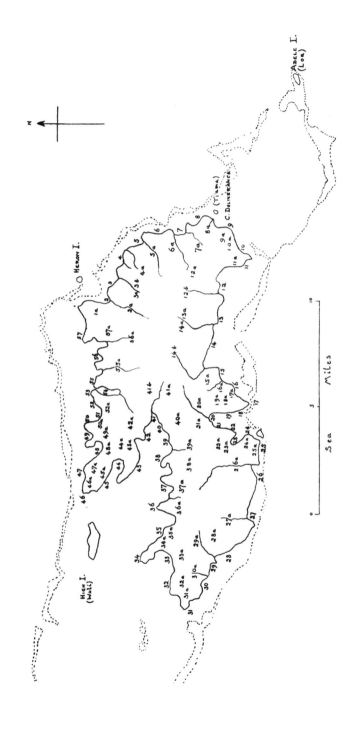

HERON I.

HIGH I.
(Wali)

ADELE I.
(Loa)

C. DELIVERANCE

O (Tiama)

N

Sea Miles

33. Mangowe.
    33 *a*. Kwebewe.
34. Yaniuwe.
    34 *a*. Mediuwe.
35. Piyorananowe.
    35 *a*. Kwinowe.
36. Biowe.
    36 *a*. Tabweangwe.
37. Tebewe.
    37 *a*. Kenyawe.
38. Gilewanawe.
    38 *a*. Dyinöwe.
39. Kwowe.
    39 *a*. Könönbowe.
40. Moiuwe.
    40 *a*. Pyungawe.
41. Yongöwe.
    41 *a*. Wöböwe.
    41 *b*. Bwogwowe.
42. Leiuwe.
    42 *a*. Mbawe.
43. Walewe.
    43 *a*. Walebongawe.
44. Mbowe.
    44 *a*. Tongowe.

45. Chabawe.
    45 *a*. Liangawe.
46. Mamiawe.
    46 *a*. Koowe.
47. Maiuwe.
    47 *a*. Mworobwongowe.
48. Ngawe.
    48 *a*. Mejumawe.
49. Kwalewe.
    49 *a*. Nowongwawe.
50. Dawawe.
    50 *a*. Bwangowe.
51. Mbulawe.
52. Malawe.
    52 *a*. Yomongowe.
53. Piöwadawe.
54. Wolungawe.
55. Pomowe.
    55 *a*. Mpwaliuwe.
56. Yamawe.
    56 *a*. Wulebiuwe.
57. Dromowe.
    57 *a*. Ngabewe.

CHAPTER II

Material Culture

THE visitor to Rossel has of necessity already become acquainted with the Massim people who inhabit the regions between this island and any port of entry into Papua, whether Port Moresby, Samarai, or, more recently, Misima. To such a one there will be something arresting and strange in the appearance of the Rossel Islander; for while the women, whom he will not see for the first few days, wear the grass or coconut-leaf skirt, *nö* (Pl.VII), universal amongst the Southern Massim, the men wear a dress peculiar to Rossel—a dried leaf of pandanus, *pwona*, drawn tight between the legs, and kept in position by a girdle of nine or ten turns of rope, *padi*, of considerable thickness (Pl. III). While the male attire will serve to distinguish the men at a glance from the Massim, or any other inhabitants of Papua, the women may less readily be differentiated from the Massim women by the custom of wearing the hair short.

Of ornaments, the most commonly worn are armlets, *pyidi*, of plaited cane (Pl. V); leglets, *nipu*, of similar material; arm-shells, *pibwodono* (Pls. IV *a*, XI *b*); nose-sticks, *ni* (Pls. VI, IX *a*); and turtle-shell rings, *kadi*, sometimes with sapi-sapi beads attached, worn on the distended lobe of the ear (Pl. VII *b*).

The arm-shells, made from the same *Conus* shell as those of the Massim,[1] are finished off differently, the shell being cut into two or three portions by cuts in the plane of the axis of the cone. These portions are tied together, and a small arm-shell may thus be made to fit a muscular adult. The nose-sticks, also, though made from the clam, as are those of the Massim, often differ from the latter in shape. The ends of these usually turn up through a right angle and are generally wound round with black thread. According to Bell only chiefs are permitted to wear nose-sticks of more than a certain length.[2] Necklaces, *bö*, of sapi-sapi beads with a small central cowry are also commonly seen (Pl. IV *a*). Combs, *tiemö*,

[1] See C. G. Seligmann, *The Melanesians of British New Guinea*, 1910, Pl. LIX, which figures four arm-shells.
[2] App. I, p. 224.

similar to those of the Massim, are sometimes seen (Pl. V). Tattooing is rare and appears to be a recent importation from Sudest.[1] Depilation is practised. According to Macgregor[2] a small piece of pumice stone is used for this purpose, all hair, except the eyelashes, being removed from the face. Both men and women usually carry small baskets (Pl. X) made from the coco palm or, occasionally, the pandanus leaf. In these may generally be found native money, a lime stick, betel nut, *Piper* root or leaf, trade tobacco (in recent years), and sometimes a sponge for washing the face. Certain baskets, *kwabe*, are made of two layers, so that money can be secreted in the lining (Pl. X *b*, right). Larger and cruder baskets, *pweni*, are made for carrying food, etc. (Pl. X *a*, left). The better baskets have a fine mesh of about 2 or 3 mm. Some of these, called *pende*, are plain. Others, called *teböbe*, are given a design by some of the threads being darkened by being buried in the ground. The patterns are simple geometrical ones, such as are also found amongst the Massim, who have exactly the same technique; although, amongst the Massim, except possibly on Sudest, the baskets are not made in such quantity and in such variety as on Rossel. A very small basket, *pedwong*, is also made in which the threads are not cut off at the basket's base but form streamers a foot or so in length (Pl. X *b*, left). These baskets are held in the hand at dances and are not used for storing articles (Pl. XXIII). I saw no mats, but Rochas apparently saw some mats in a village in 1859.[3]

In connection with exchange, important objects, known as *ndap* and *nkö*, function as money. These are described in Chap. v (Pl. XX). The chief objects of wealth and display are the Massim 'ceremonial' axes,[4] and the more elaborate ornaments of sapi-sapi.[5] The arm-shells and nose-sticks, mentioned above, also come under this head.

The only weapon known to me on Rossel is the spear, *ka* (Pl. III *b*), perfectly plain, and about five to six feet in length.

[1] Macgregor states that the natives are not tattooed (App. I, p. 206), but Bell refers to occasional tattooing on men, consisting of a few straight lines (p. 223).
[2] App. I, p. 208.   [3] App. I, p. 202.
[4] See Seligmann, *The Melanesians of British New Guinea*, Pl. LXI, which figures a 'benam'.
[5] *Id.*, Pl. LX, which figures a 'bagi' and a 'samakupa'.

Macgregor saw one club in 1892, but no other weapon of offence or defence besides the spear.[1] Rochas' party in 1859 was assailed by stones and spears, but apparently the stones were not propelled from slings.[2] Rochas mentions the conch-shell trumpet which appears to have been used by the natives to summon help or convey warnings.[3]

The chief tool is the adze, similar to that of the Massim, but generally fitted with a piece of metal in place of the polished greenstone blade. Some small specimens of this are figured below (Pl. XII *a*). Rochas mentions this stone adze ('petite herminette')[4] which apparently at that time, 1859, had not been replaced by the metal obtained from shipwrecks. Macgregor finds the stone replaced by iron in 1888.[5]

The men frequently carry lime pots, *ko*—gourds with a wooden stopper (Pl. XXII *b*). The lime spatulas, *ja*, are rarely of Rossel manufacture, but generally Massim. The only Rossel spatulas that came to my notice were very crude (Pl. IX *b*). Seligman figures six of these collected by Barton.[6] The betel, according to Murray, is the small kind found in the Gulf of Papua. It is chewed in the usual way with lime and the root or leaf of *Piper methysticum*. It is used excessively and the products are allowed, in the case of chiefs and their wives, to accumulate about the teeth and gums, so that what looks like a false tooth is produced, protruding between the lips. According to Murray, this deposit is called by a special word, derived from the word for 'tooth'.[7]

The tobacco pipe, of Massim type, occurs (Pl. XIV *b*), but is probably of quite recent introduction, for Rochas found the natives ignorant of the use of tobacco in 1859, '...qui ne peut s'explique que par leur séparation complète du genre humain...'.[8] In 1885, Bridge found that one or two of the natives 'knew the words "tobacco" and "pipe", to the use of which most of them were evidently unaccustomed...'.[9] In 1892, Macgregor finds them to have 'taken kindly to tobacco', which is not grown on the island.[10] In 1908, Bell states that the bamboo pipe is used, but is supposed to have been introduced from other islands.[11]

[1] App. I, p. 207 and p. 211. Bell also mentions a wooden club (p. 223).
[2] App. I, p. 193.   [3] App. I, pp. 199 and 202.   [4] App. I, p. 202.
[5] App. I, p. 206.   [6] *Man*, Vol. XVI, 1916. 2.
[7] App. I, p. 220.   [8] App. I, p. 197.   [9] App. I, p. 204.
[10] App. I, p. 212.   [11] App. I, p. 224.

PLATE III

(b) Man sitting.

(a) Young man, full length.

PLATE IV

(b) Old bearded man.

(a) Man with son.

The villages are small, rarely containing more than half-a-dozen houses.[1] They are neatly laid out, with paths connecting the houses, any large stones being piled up artistically or used to surround small gardens of flowers or bananas within the village, which is always plentifully supplied with coconut and banana trees. Some of the villages show a terraced formation, with one or two houses on each terrace. The terraces are formed by cutting into the ground where soft, or by building up with stones in other cases. Frequently there are squatting places in the village of flat stones, with back supports, known as *jagega* (Pl. XVI *a*).[2]

There are, at the present day, three principal kinds of house distinguished by name, *chabaju gmomo*, *yebewede gmomo*, and *gele gmomo*, the last-named, in all probability, introduced from Sudest.

The *chabaju gmomo* (Pl. XIII) is of simple construction and peculiar technique. It is built on the ground, without a floor and without piles to support the ridge-pole, and with no platform for sleeping on. It is, according to tradition, the house the construction of which was taught to the original inhabitants by Wonajö, the chief deity of Rossel. According to the same tradition, Wonajö also insisted that houses on the coast should be roofed with the sago leaf, while houses in the interior were to be roofed with the leaf of another tree, known as *ngwiia*. It is said that this rule is rigidly adhered to, even when inconvenient. Although the raised platform has now been introduced for sleeping on, the custom of sleeping on leaves, or possibly mats, on the earth floor still persists among the few who dislike to depart from the ways of Wonajö. The construction of this type of house is shown in the accompanying diagram. The principal supports consist of three short piles on each side of the house. To these three piles, on each side, is bound a long pole, to which, at intervals of 2 or 3 ft., a piece of thick cane, bent into a semi-oval, is attached, the two ends being driven into the ground. Parallel with these hoops of cane, but at more frequent intervals, are

---

[1] Moreton gave an average of five houses to a village in 1892, only one village containing as many as ten to twelve houses. App. I, p. 217.

[2] Macgregor mentions that these squatting places are often, in the case of coastal villages, on the foreshore, below high-water mark (App. I, p. 207). Murray says that these 'jabbeg', once the scenes of cannibal feasts, were falling into decay in 1911 (p. 229).

placed pairs of poles (only a few being shown in the diagram), to the junction of which is fastened the ridge-pole, which is also attached to each cane hoop. Further longitudinal poles occur at suitable intervals on either side. Resting on the outer bent poles are laths, at frequent intervals, parallel to the

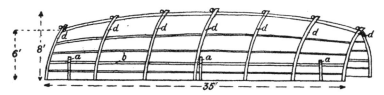

A. Diagrammatic sketch of the framework of the *Chabaju gmomo* viewed from the side.

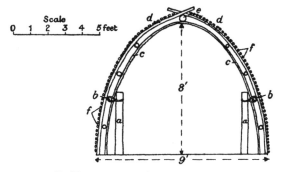

B. Transverse section through centre of *Chabaju gmomo*.

a, a = upright piles; *b, b* = main longitudinal poles; *c* = inner cane hoop; *d, d* = outer bent poles; *e* = ridge pole; *f, f* = longitudinal laths to take thatching.

Diagram I. *Chabaju gmomo*.

ridge-pole. To these are attached the leaves, which form the roof and sides of the house. Although this house is barely mentioned by the earlier observers who attempt to describe only the *yebewede gmomo* and *gele gmomo*, Macgillivray states that the houses observed from the *Rattlesnake* in 1849, appeared to be long and low, resting on the ground, with an opening at each end, and an arched roof thatched with palm leaves,[1] while Macgregor in 1890 says that the houses of the north coast are often very inferior, numbers of these not being built on posts and having only the earth as a floor.[2] The names of the more important parts of the *chabaju gmomo* are as follows: piles = *pworu*, main longitudinal poles = *mbwaibe*, ridge-pole = *weni*, roof = *köbe*.

The *yebewede gmomo* (Pl. XIV *a*) is slightly more elaborate than the *chabaju gmomo*. It occurs in coastal and bush villages, and, according to one informant, was introduced from Sudest. It differs from the *chabaju gmomo* principally in the occurrence of three median forked piles, which support the ridge-pole. It also, usually, contains a raised platform on which the inmates sleep, and is, generally, provided with a door of plaited sago leaf. The roof is generally made of sago leaf, not plaited. Presumably, the *yebewede gmomo* has resulted from the influence of the *gele gmomo* technique on the *chabaju gmomo*.

The *gele gmomo* (Pl. XIV *b*) is a pile dwelling, and of far more elaborate construction than either of the above. It is similar to the 'turtle-back' houses of the South-eastern Massim. It is evidently only houses of this type that have been described by the early writers. Rochas was impressed by the ingenuity and suitability of their construction. He puts their average size at 10 by 3 by 3 metres, and refers to a permanent rudimentary stairway fixed in front of the door. They were ventilated by windows and doors, extremely small, which could be opened and shut. In the middle was a fireplace marked out by stones. Rochas concludes with the remark, 'la construction...est fort bien entendue pour procurer à leurs hideux propriétaires un abri contre les ardeurs du soleil de feu qui les éclaire et qui ferait mieux de les brûler en même temps qu'elle les met à l'abri de l'humi- dité du sol, avantage précieux durant l'hivernage'.[3] Mac- gregor states that the houses are chiefly built on posts about 5 ft. high, being entered by trap-doors through the floor, while cooking is carried out underneath.[4] The construction is shown in the accompanying diagram. The floor is sup ported by six stout piles, three on each side, and three longer

[1] App. I, p. 190. [2] App. I, p. 208.
[3] App. I, p. 202. [4] App. I, p. 206.

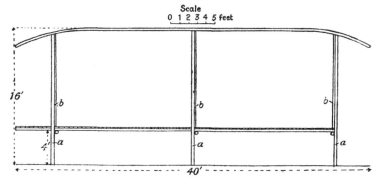

16'

4'

40'

a, a = central piles; *b, b* = transverse partitions of plaited leaves.
Diagram II. *Gele gmomo*. Longitudinal section through ridge pole.

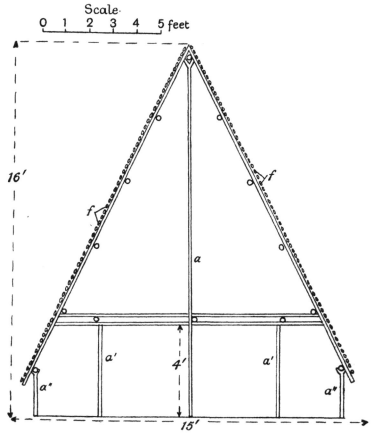

Scale·
0   1   2   3   4   5 feet

16'

4'

15'

a = central pile of roof; *a′, a′* = floor piles; *a″, a″* = side piles of roof;
f, f = longitudinal laths to take thatching.

forked piles, which also support the ridge-pole. Three stout poles are placed transversely across these piles and three longitudinal poles are bound to these. The floor consists of transverse laths bound on to these latter. Six short piles carry two longitudinal poles, from which to the ridge-pole pass a number of poles, which go to form the walls and roof. The house is partitioned at the middle[1] and closed at each end, doors being often provided. There is a platform at one end, over which the roof projects. There seems to be a good deal of variation in the construction of this type of house. Often the floor is raised over 6 ft. from the ground so that the part below the floor can be used as a room, where the cooking is done and where the occupants of the house spend most of their time. In these cases the entrance to the house is usually by means of a trap-door. A trench is dug round the house so as to keep this part as dry as possible, and the earth is beaten flat and kept clean. Sometimes the roof is not carried straight down to the floor, but is supported on short walls, in the Massim style, and the sides below the floor are generally left open, the carrying down of the roof almost to the ground being rather exceptional. The similarity of this type of house to the so-called turtle-back house of the South-eastern Massim suggests that it has been introduced from Sudest. This is confirmed by its widespread occurrence at the west end of Rossel and its absence from the interior of the island, so far as my own observations went. But Rochas observed this type of house only and Macgregor implies that it was the principal type. It cannot, therefore, be a recent effect, due to the opening up of communication with Sudest under European influence. Legend states that it was introduced from Sudest by a Rossel native who had visited the island a long time back.

Every house on Rossel is a family house, and the houses of chiefs do not differ essentially from those of commoners.

Only within recent years have pots been used on Rossel, although they must have been known long before their introduction, owing to contact with Sudest. Cooking in pots (that is, steaming of meat and vegetables) is now beginning to replace cooking by means of hot stones, but this is due to

---

[1] To separate the married from the single, according to Murray (App. I, p. 218).

the introduction of the iron saucepan, rather than the clay pot from Sudest, which is only occasionally seen. If hot stones are used, the indigenous method, they are first heated in a fire and then built up in a mound, together with small packets of food—meat, sago, nuts, etc.—the stones and food being handled with wooden tongs, *pula* (Pl. XV *b*). Pearl-shell is ground down to form the simple tools used in the preparation of foods, such as the *ngwe*, with serrated edge for scraping coconuts, and the *kuma*, sharpened on one side for cutting purposes (Pl. XI *a*). The *ngebi*, a cowry ground down so as to leave a semi-circular cutting edge, is used principally for scraping vegetables, such as taro. Cups are made from the shells of coconuts (Pl. XI *c*).

The main vegetable food is sago, which is very prolific on the island. The palm is cut down, split, and the pith chopped out by the men. A leaf base is erected in an inclined position, overhanging a trough consisting of the base of another leaf (Pl. XV *a*). A sieve of sago fibre is elastically suspended in the inclined trough. Charges of pith are thrown into the trough above the sieve, and squeezed with water against the flexible sieve, so that water with sago in suspension flows through the sieve into the lower trough. This operation is carried out by women. The suspended sago settles in the lower trough, water escaping from the brim. The sago is dried over a fire, and finally cooked in hot stones. Preliminary drying by pressure does not occur, as far as I am aware.

The banana ranks next in importance to the sago. Varieties of both banana and plantain are to be seen in the villages, where they fringe the paths, and in the gardens. The fruit is rarely allowed to ripen, and is generally eaten cooked; for it is not considered nutritious if eaten raw in the ripe state. The coconut is cultivated mainly for the oil, which is squeezed from the ripe nut. The breadfruit tree occurs fairly generally. Gardens are made mainly for the cultivation of taro and banana, but also to a less extent for the cultivation of yams and sweet-potato. The sugar-cane is also fairly common and the pandanus.[1] Tomatoes, cucumbers, pineapples, and oranges, introduced by the Osbornes, are also cultivated sporadically.

---

[1] Macgregor mentions, in addition to the above vegetable foods, via, mangoes, jaica, and arrowroot (App. I, p. 206); also the edible hibiscus and six varieties of sugar-cane (App. I, p. 212).

Horticulture is of the same type as elsewhere in South-East New Guinea. A piece of virgin bush is cleared by the felling of smaller trees and by burning. The clearing is not always fenced; for the domestic pig is usually confined, and wild pigs—that is, domestic pigs that have become wild—are probably not very numerous. After one crop the garden is abandoned, and fresh land is cleared. The main work of preparation is done by the men, but the care of the garden is in the hands of the women. Of wild fruits the paw-paw and many varieties of nuts are of importance.

Domestic pigs and dogs are rather less numerous than further west. Strangely enough, many of the dogs have a well-defined bark; this is rare amongst Papuan dogs, which as a rule emit only a whine. It may be that European breeds have been recently introduced; but such modification of the Papuan strain is less likely to have occurred on Rossel than in districts nearer to Samarai, where the dogs are more uniform in appearance and less like European breeds.

The domestic pig and dog are eaten only at feasts, where complex monetary transactions take place, and which are inter-connected with a series of other social events, such as marriages and deaths. Cannibalism (see Chap. IX) is also ceremonial in the sense that it has a definite place in a wide social context; even less than pig is human flesh merely a variety of diet.

Dogs are used for hunting bush pigs. The leaves of a tree (*unguringu*) are pounded up with water, and pushed up into the dog's nostrils as a necessary preliminary. I was told that the dog attacks the pig, which is then killed by the men with spears. I failed to ascertain whether the pig net common amongst the Massim occurs.[1]

Turtle and dugong are common, and their flesh is highly valued as food. Nets of large mesh known as *dwowo* are used for catching these animals. Smaller nets, *mpwadong*,

---

[1] According to Bell, pitfalls for pigs are made with leaves on top and spears underneath. Sometimes also a rope tied in a slip-knot on the track over which the pigs pass is used. Birds are similarly caught (App. I, p. 225). Murray says that the pig is usually smothered or strangled —which is certainly the case with the domestic pig, as I observed—and that pigeons and seagulls are sometimes smothered in the trees or rocks where they roost, the operation being done so noiselessly that the others are not awakened (p. 219).

are used for fish.[1] According to one account it is only recently that the usual pandanus fibre has been utilised for making these nets, a fibre known as *bureti*, possibly another variety of pandanus, having previously been utilised. The strength of this fibre is supposed to wax and wane with the moon, and therefore it is collected only at the full moon.

A number of taboos attend the making of a net, which recall the procedure elsewhere in Papua. The most important of these is the taboo on sexual intercourse for the two or three months generally required for making a large net. This is considered so important that an almost completed net had been discarded, while I was on the island, owing to the breaking of this taboo by one of the fabricators.

As soon as a net is completed a small feast is held, to which guests are invited. The floats and sinkers are threaded, and temporary decorations (e.g. of sapi-sapi) are placed on the head-float (a larger float at one end of the net). Before the net is used a concoction of certain plants is prepared, with the recital of spells, generally by the fabricator of the net or by someone specially versed in this form of magic. This concoction, wrapped in some coco palm spathe, is tied on to the net. Other 'medicine' is placed in the mouth and spat on to the net to the accompaniment of a muttered spell. The head-float is also specially treated; it is bathed in smoke from coconut shells, and painted with 'medicine', the object of which is to attract fish. None of the first catch of fish is consumed by the fabricators of the net, the whole catch being distributed among the invited guests.

The most important fishing-ground on Rossel is probably the Eastern Lagoon in the neighbourhood of the island of Loa. Fishing in this neighbourhood is subject to special restrictions. Women, for instance, are not allowed on expeditions in this region, and a number of common words are taboo to the crews, who have to substitute special words only to be used in these waters and on the island of Loa (see Chap. XII, pp. 149–150).

Fish spears, *wya*, of several prongs, are used alone, or in conjunction with the nets, but the fish hook appears to be unknown. A fish poison, *pwada*, is frequently used. It is a

[1] They are also probably used for prawns, for Macgregor includes prawns in his list of foods (App. I, p. 206).

root that is probably the same as the 'New Guinea Dynamite', common in the Massim district and elsewhere in New Guinea.

Fishing-grounds are sometimes owned in the same way as garden land, but individual rights on the former seem to be observed only on those occasions when the owner places a taboo on the reef, indicated by a stick placed either on the reef or on shore.[1] Coconuts may also be laid under taboo, or *ngwame*, in this way, particularly on a man's death, when his trees are all placed under *ngwame* for two or three months by the dead man's son. The usual form of *ngwame* is a stick, on which is hung a rough basket of coco palm leaf, containing a preparation that will cause sickness to anyone who breaks the taboo.

Four distinct types of canoe are made on Rossel, three of which differ markedly from the canoes of the Massim, although all are of the same general single-outrigger pattern that we find from Sudest to Orangerie Bay. The simplest type is the small unplanked outrigger canoe, universal, though with local variation in detail, amongst the Massim. This is the *nö* (generic term for canoe), or *pia nö* (female canoe) (Pl. XVI *b*). The other three types are the *ma nö* (male canoe) (Pl. XVII), *lia nö* (sailing canoe) (Pl. XVIII), and *para nö* (*ndap* canoe) (Pl. XIX).[2]

The *nö* or *pia nö* occurs principally at the west end of Rossel, its place being taken by the *ma nö* at the east end. The *pia nö* is also the only canoe which is not taboo to women. It has a foreign appearance beside the other three, and has probably been introduced from Sudest, where a similar canoe is found, which is not taboo to women.[3]

[1] Bell states that the inner reefs are all marked off with sticks and are regarded as the property of certain individuals, the outer reef only being public property (App. I, p. 224).

[2] Rochas gives a brief description which will apply to any of these types. He refers to a sail carried by some of them, and also—which is of particular interest—describes what is apparently a double canoe, one of the dug-outs being smaller than the other—'il en est d'accouplées et alors l'une plus petite que l'autre joue le rôle de balancier' (App. I, p. 196).

Macgillivray, Macgregor, Bell and Murray, who also describe some of the Rossel canoes, make no mention of double canoes, nor did I come across any during my stay on the island. It is possible that the islanders have seen foreign double canoes, for I found an old Mailu prow-board in one of the villages.

[3] Bell states that women are not allowed to go near the reef in canoes nor to enter a *para nö* (App. I, p. 225).

There is a curious custom in connection with these canoes, which I did not fully elucidate. At a village on the north coast, near the east end of Rossel, about district 6, where lies the important *yaba* of Mbasi (see Chap. XII, p. 144), toll is collected from the *pia nö* that come from the west. One small *ndap* coin is demanded from these, but apparently the *ma nö*, and probably *lia nö* and *para nö*, pay no toll. This custom is probably connected with the Mbasi *yaba*, and may be a privilege of its priest or of its owner. (It may even be that the fee is for pilotage through waters in which lurk supernatural dangers, for there are numerous places of this kind on Rossel, the dangers of which may be averted by the actions of certain individuals.) Possibly other canoes may pass this spot in safety, because they have not been profaned by women, or else because they only are part of that culture which is more fully developed at the east end of the island or has suffered less from foreign influences than the west.[1] The construction of the *pia nö* can be judged from the photograph (Pl. XVI *b*) and from accounts of the South-East Massim small canoes.

Two features shared by the three remaining canoes, which I am regarding as the distinctively Rossel canoes, are the decking in of the dug-out for some distance at either end and the building up of the dug-out by one or more planks. A feature of both *lia nö* and the smallest *ma nö*, which thus has the appearance of a very much reduced sailing canoe, is the use of prow-boards, such as we find on the Massim sailing canoes, but with a very different decorative motive. A feature of both *ma nö* and *para nö* is the neat and elaborate binding of thin string round each pair of the sticks that attach the outrigger booms to the float.

The construction of the *ma nö* will be apparent from the diagrams and the photographs (Pl. XVII). It will be noticed that there are two planks on the outrigger side between the prow-boards and only one on the further side. These are tied to the dug-out and prow-boards, and the latter are tied to the dug-out and the narrow plank at either end that

---

[1] I do not, of course, wish to prejudge the question as to whether the peculiarly Rossel culture is earlier or later than the Massim. It is possible that a culture reached Rossel from the east or the north, affecting the earlier Massim culture less in the west than in the east. But if this be so, it is strange that pottery and the drum should have been completely lost.

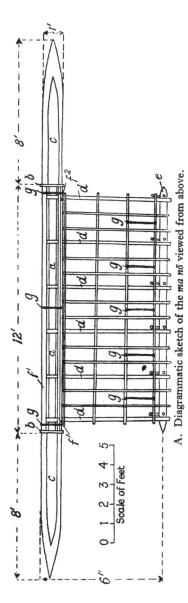

A. Diagrammatic sketch of the *ma nŏ* viewed from above.

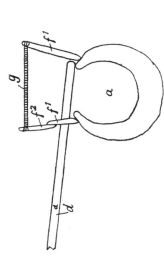

B. Diagrammatic sketch of transverse section of a *ma nŏ* showing arrangements of wash-strakes and cane stay.

a, a = hollow part of the dug-out; *b, b* = prow-boards; *c, c* = deck; *d, d* = the outrigger booms; *e* = the outrigger float; *f¹, f²* = first and second wash-strakes; *g, g* = cane stays.

Diagram IV. *Ma nŏ.*

decks in the remainder of the dug-out. The joins are carefully caulked. These wash-strakes are tied together at three points by stays, formed of split cane. These can be used as seats. The six outrigger booms pass through the lower plank to the opposite side of the dug-out, to which they are attached; the booms thus slant upwards to the float. The cane binding between the wash-strakes is repeated between the two longitudinal poles that are tied to the booms. Two further longitudinal poles are attached to the booms nearer the dug-out; to these are tied several transverse poles which lie freely above the outer longitudinal poles for no apparent reason. Although the carved prow-board is somewhat crude, the only other parts of the canoe that are decorated—the two ends— are treated with a good sense of proportion. The extreme end is called the nose, *tiliwalö*; the slight projection at the base of the solid extremity (white in the photograph, Pl. XVII) is called the eye, *walö*; a few carved lines on the upper surface representing a sting-ray, *yaradö*. The raised lines at the upper edge of the end of the dug-out (white in the photograph, Pl. XVII) represent a bird, *mbu*, flying in a high wind. This canoe is described by Macgregor[1] and also by Bell[2] though the latter's description differs appreciably as regards dimensions and certain other details from that given above.

The *lia nö* (Diags. V–VIII and Pl. XVIII) was described by Macgillivray[3] in some detail, and briefly by Murray.[4] Essentially, it is a larger edition of the *ma nö* with the addition of an arrangement for stepping the mast and a sloping platform which is raised well above the side planks and extends for some distance beyond the opposite side of the canoe from that to which is attached the outrigger. This platform, or balance, enables the float to be heavier or the booms to be longer than would otherwise be possible, crew or passengers sitting in the absence of wind as far as possible from the outrigger, while they move towards the float as it emerges from the water, when sailing with a strong wind. I do not know whether the balance enables this canoe, unlike the Massim sailing canoes, to sail with the outrigger to leeward. The eight outrigger booms pass through the nearer

[1] App. I, p. 213.
[2] App. I, p. 224.
[3] App. I, p. 191.
[4] App. I, pp. 228–229.

wash-strake and are attached to one edge of the dug-out in the same way as in the *ma nö*. The two centre booms support a structure for stepping the mast and supporting the balance.

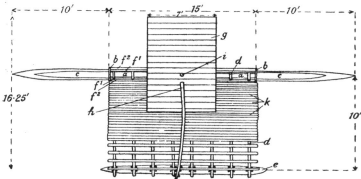

a, a = hollow part of dug-out; *b, b* = prow-boards; *c, c* = deck; *d, d* = outrigger booms; *e* = outrigger float; f^1, f^2 = first and second wash-strakes; *g* = sloping upper deck; *h* = curved boom used for stepping mast; *i* = hole in upper deck for mast.

Diagram V. Diagrammatic sketch of the *lia nö* viewed from above.

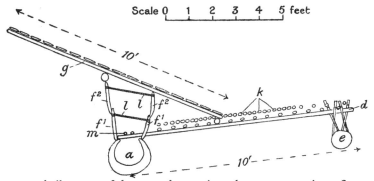

a = hollow part of dug-out; *d* = outrigger boom; *e* = outrigger float; f^1, f^2 = first and second wash-strakes; *g* = upper deck which acts also as a counterpoise; *l, l* = cane stays; *m* = a pair of longitudinal poles used in securing the outrigger booms to the hull.

Diagram VI. Transverse section near the centre of a *lia nö*.

The massive pole that is the immediate support of the mast is bent twice so as to pass over the sides of the body of the canoe through the balance and out to the float to which it is

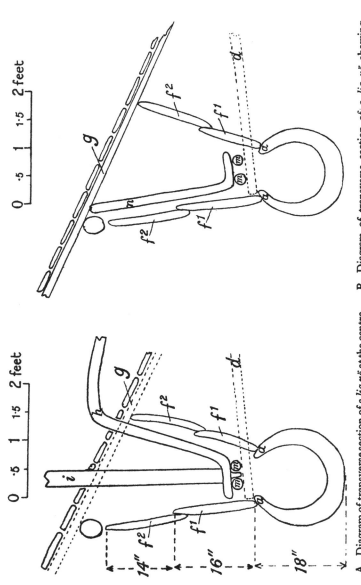

A. Diagram of transverse section of a *lia nö* at the centre, showing method of stepping the mast.
m, m = pair of longitudinal poles under which the boom is fixed; n = one of a pair of knee-shaped vertical poles resting on m, m.

B. Diagram of transverse section of a *lia nö* showing method of attaching outrigger boom to the hull.

Diagram VII. *Lia nö.*

attached by two pairs of rods longer and stouter than those which attach the float to the booms. These attachments in each case consist of two crossed sticks, no string being used. The balance, supported by four bent poles tied to the same two longitudinal poles that take the stepping for the mast, is tied, at the outrigger side, to a longitudinal pole on the outrigger platform. The mat sail is of exactly the same type as that used by the Southern Massim. (Macgillivray also describes this sail.) A steering paddle, about 5 ft.

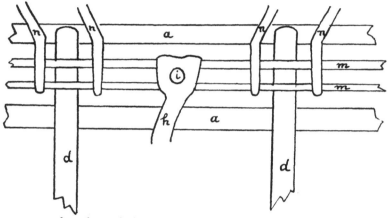

a, a = the edges of the hull; d, d = two of the outrigger booms; h = the curved boom used for stepping the mast; i = the hole into which the base of the mast is fixed; m, m = two longitudinal poles used in securing the booms to the hull; n, n = two pairs of knee-shaped vertical poles used in securing the booms to the hull.

Diagram VIII. Diagrammatic sketch of the central part of a *lia nö* viewed from above with the upper deck removed: showing the method of keeping the outrigger booms secured to the hull. To prevent confusion the wash-strakes are not shown.

long and at its widest 1 ft. across, is kept at each end. The decoration is more elaborate than that of the *ma nö* and contains curves and other elements of the Massim type. One of the prow-boards of the canoe here described, although inferior to the average Massim prow-board, contained the frigate bird spiral; the other was similar to that shown in Pl. XVII *b*. The lozenges on the sides were said to represent a bird called *dö*. The designs are picked out in red, blue and black. The pole that steps the mast is carved into spirals at the end which projects above the float. The carving of each end of the dug-out is the same as that of the *ma nö*. Cowries are hung at various places; and hollow nuts, known as *yuwagun*, are hung along each side of the outrigger platform. These latter are a protection against storms. Other charms that were shown me consisted of a decaying shellfish, *gu*,—protection against big seas; a piece of red wood, *pwe*, and a piece of white wood, *mum*,—protection against sharks. These were said to be the commonest charms. A good deal of magic is used in voyaging and in preparing these and other canoes, which I did not obtain, and which would be of considerable interest. The following are some of the more important terms applied to the parts of the *lia nö* and of the other canoes, in which the parts occur: dug-out = *nöm*, float = *da*, float attachments = *yeme*, outrigger booms = *jen*, prow-board = *dong*, wash-strakes = *kum*, caulking = *kimi*, outrigger platform = *dade*, balance = *iabe*, mast stepping = *doa*, mast = *piuwa*, sail = *lie*, ordinary paddle = *kebe*, steering paddle = *pyi*.

I saw only two sailing canoes at the west end of Rossel and none at the east end. But at the west end I saw a canoe of Sudest or Panaiati type, which had been made on Rossel under the supervision of a visitor from Sudest. This is, apparently, quite a recent introduction.

According to legend, the sailing canoe introduced by the god Mbasi from Sudest was originally of this Massim type (Panaiati), while the sailing canoes of the Massim, or some of the Massim, were of Rossel type. But one day a Rossel man, Dua, visiting Sudest in his sailing canoe, met a Sudest man, Wulawula, in a sailing canoe of a different kind. Each was charmed with the other's canoe, and they decided to exchange.[1] In this same expedition Dua stole from a Sudest woman a yam, which he planted on Rossel, the inhabitants of which were ignorant of yams, or at least of this particular variety.

The third type of canoe, peculiar to Rossel, is the *para nö* (Pl. XIX) which has a number of features of exceptional interest. It is only used for certain purposes and is, therefore, somewhat rare and not often seen in the water; which

---

[1] This same type of legend, in which there is an exhange of canoes, occurs amongst the Massim in another connection.

accounts for its not being mentioned by even so observant a person as Bell. Although the dug-out is decked in for a short distance fore and aft and is fitted with wash-strakes, it is not provided with prow-boards. The wash-strake on the outrigger side is of peculiar form, consisting of a plank bent through an angle of almost 90°. The canoe is exceedingly light for its length, which is considerable; and the float is long and slender, the ends being slightly turned up. The construction may be gathered from the accompanying diagrams and photographs (Pl. XIX). It is built essentially for speed and beauty and would obviously be of little use in

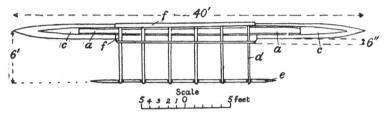

A. Diagrammatic sketch of a *para nö* viewed from above.

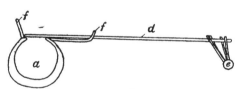

B. Transverse section of *para nö*, showing unusual form of wash-strake.
a, a = hollow part of dug-out; *c, c* = deck; *d, d* = booms for attaching the outrigger; *e* = float of the outrigger; *f, f* = wash-strakes.
Diagram IX. *Para nö.*

rough water. Except for the nose, at either end, which is similar to that of the *ma nö* and *lia nö*, the decoration is quite different from that of the ordinary canoes and consists principally of a series of oval marks, red in the centre, black at the edge, which almost certainly represent *ndap* money or the mussel from which it used to be made. Cowries are placed along the upper edges of the dug-out at each end and a cassowary plume can be seen above the 'eye' in the accompanying photograph.

The *para nö* has no parallel amongst the Massim. It would be convenient to describe it as 'ceremonial,' for I do not fully understand its significance, and some of its uses are mysterious.

Only a chief may own a *para nö*, and, conversely, it seemed to be necessary to own a *para nö* in order to be a chief of any importance, so that it functions as a symbol of high rank. Its alternative name of ' *ndap* canoe ' depends on the fact that it is used on expeditions for the collecting of money required in connection with important feasts. This is probably its principal use. Races between chiefs are also held with these canoes on certain occasions. It may be noted that the canoe is designed principally for speed in calm water, and I imagine that no canoe of the same size in New Guinea could compete with it; but it would probably swamp at once in a moderate sea. Finally, it is connected with songs and dances of a certain type known as *dama*. These are sung by the crews, particularly when racing, and when sung on shore are sometimes accompanied by the beating of paddles on the *para nö*, which thus takes the place of the drum of the Massim. The races are normally held on the day following a night of *dama* dancing. The losers in the race, according to my informant, have to pay the winner a No. 18 *ndap*, which means that the stakes are very high; for a *ndap* of this value constitutes the chief part of the payment for a wife, or a first-class fully fattened pig (see Chap. VII). A certain sacredness seems to attach to these canoes, and women are forbidden even to look upon them.

Mention may here be made of a stone pestle, now in the Cambridge Museum, which was given me by Mr Craig, who had been planting for the Osbornes on Rossel for some years, and had experience of mining. He had collected the pestle, but discarded what may have been the mortar belonging to it. He had not come across any rock on Rossel of similar material. The pestle is figured (Pl. XII *b*), together with a small stone which is used as a rain charm. It is small, and very neatly made, the material being dark. It did not seem to Mr Craig that the natives attached any particular significance to it, in spite of the cult of stones on Rossel.

The stone tools on Rossel, now hardly ever used, were of greenstone, ground and polished throughout, and similar to those used by the Massim, from whom the material, in all probability, and often the completed tools, were obtained, through the medium of Sudest. These stones were mostly hafted to form adzes, known as *ngube* (see above, p. 12). The large ones, *bogubindo*, may have been used as axes.

CHAPTER III

Tribe, Clan, and Family

IT is often assumed by sociologists that the social organisation of a people can be expressed as an organisation of persons in groups, and of groups in larger groups, complexity of social organisation depending on the number and diversity of these groups and their functions. These groups are regarded as having certain formal relations with one another, and as jointly determining the conduct of their members. While the groups as forms persist, membership is constantly changing, and only when a change in culture takes place is there a change in this total social form. For instance, in a given case a tribe is said to be divided, in a certain way, into a number of clans, the clans into a number of unilateral families; the same tribe is also, perhaps, divided into a number of bilateral families, which cut across the clans, into secret societies, and so on.

Some of the groups, on this view, may be groups consisting of only one member, where, for example, we have a monarch or a high priest: and we must also suppose, in order to rise above the particular accidents of the moment, that groups, as parts of the social form, may exist, although without members. Such groups, without members, are mainly required in order to cover all the possible family groups, which might arise without any change of culture. (As will be seen shortly, one of the chief difficulties of this type of analysis is the necessity of distorting the ordinary meaning of the term 'family', in order to express it as a group on a level with other groups, such as household or clan.) The task of the ethnologist, on this view, is to describe the total social form—to describe the groups, their relations, and functions—in other words, to describe everything about the groups which is independent of their particular membership at the moment of observation.[1]

[1] It is not intended by this statement to rule out the study of individual variations of behaviour, for the ethnologist does not study only the culture of the group; he is interested also in those variations of behaviour that are not simple functions of the culture of the groups, for it is these variations that are mainly responsible for cultural change.

The above way of looking at social organisation, more or less explicit in Dr Rivers' last work,[1] ignores an important side of social organisation. In the rough analysis of the main types of social groupings to be found in primitive and advanced societies, Dr Rivers implies that groups such as the clan, occupational group, village, etc., are of the same logical type as the family and other relationship groups.[1] That there is an important difference between these two kinds of groups is shown by the fact that the former are not defined by a relation to some person or persons, whereas the latter can only be so defined. The former are absolute groups, the latter relative. In the former kind of group, the group of every member of the group is one and the same group; for example, the 'village of' every member of a village is the same village. In the latter kind of group, this is usually not the case, the 'family of' each member of the 'family of' a person is usually a different family; e.g. if a person's family consists of the father and mother, wife or husband, and children, then the family of the wife will be a different group from the family of the husband; the family of a son from the families of his grandparents; and so on. In order that these two senses of the term 'group' may not be confused, it is proposed in the following discussion to use the term 'group' for the absolute sense, and 'grouping' for the relative sense.

A peculiarity of groupings is the existence of an order amongst the members of the grouping. Consider, for instance, the family grouping. It is clear that the families of certain members of a person's family will have more members in common with this family than other members—the families of two brothers will contain more members in common than the families of a man and his grandson. If A and B are any two members of a grouping of C, we shall generally find that the same grouping of A will have either more or less members in common with the grouping of C than has the same grouping of B. If the grouping of A has more members in common with the grouping of C than has the grouping of B, then A can be regarded as a 'closer' member of the grouping of C than B. For certain purposes this order within a grouping may be disregarded, but for most purposes the order of the members of a grouping is more important than the boundary

<hr/>

[1] W. H. R. Rivers, *Social Organization*, 1924, Chap. I.

PLATE V

(*a*) Front view of a man.

(*b*) Profile of the same,

PLATE VI

(a) Old man sitting, front view.

(b) Side view of the same.

of the grouping. A grouping is, therefore, best regarded as a 'sequence' of persons, which may or may not have a definite end. A given grouping of A is, therefore, the sequence of persons starting from A, arranged in order of 'closeness' to A.[1]

It is here maintained that a great deal of social organisation can only be expressed in this way in terms of grouping. The attempt to express the total social organisation in terms of groups and their relations and functions, is bound to fail, owing to the neglect of the numerous important relations which establish groupings but not groups.

The objection to the 'group function' formula for the analysis of social organisation may be put in another way. Groups imply discontinuity, a discontinuity which is obvious in the case of certain groups, such as a household, a village, a clan, a secret society, a tribe. The form comprising these groups and their relations can persist unaltered, a succession of persons, *passing through* the persistent form, whose content alone varies. When, however, we come to the families, we find a continuity more or less absent in the above cases. A person's family may gradually change, and its boundary also is an arbitrary one; there is a continuity in the family relation which a person has to a whole series of relatives. It is difficult to see how this sort of social form can be expressed as a persistent group or number of groups of varying content. Moreover, even those groups which are usually discontinuous, such as the tribe, may, in certain cases, lose their discontinuity and be unrecognisable as distinct groups; and in so far as continuity takes the place of this discontinuity in any part of the social organisation, to that extent does it become impossible to express the social organisation in terms of groups and their functions.

It may, of course, be maintained that this element of 'continuity' in social organisation is sufficiently small in certain cultures for an analysis into groups to give a substantially correct picture of the culture analysed. This, possibly, is the

---

[1] A grouping may thus be regarded as a 'sequence' somewhat in the sense used in mathematics. The remoter the term in the sequence, the less does that term have the defining quality of the grouping. To say that a family is a grouping is to say that an indefinite number of persons can be arranged in a sequence relative to a given individual, and that the position in the sequence defines the family distance of that person from the given individual.

case in the more advanced cultures, where groups, such as state, household, school, club, and a host of others, constitute such an important part of the social organisation. That it is not the case in Melanesia is abundantly clear from the paucity of groups which can be separated out in this way, even though the 'institutions', which elsewhere correspond to such groups, are clearly present. The tribe, for instance, is rare in Melanesia, and absent from South-East New Guinea but it is obvious that those social relations are present which elsewhere generate a definite group, which we call a tribe. This is because in this part of the world we have tribal grouping only, and not tribal groups. For every person there is a tribal grouping, but for no two persons is this tribal grouping exactly the same. The social relations which determine this grouping may, however, be just as complex as those which give the tribal characteristic to a definite well-organised group, found elsewhere as a tribe. In the same way, the family grouping, whether in a narrow or a very wide sense, is a grouping of fundamental importance in Melanesia, but families as groups depending on relationship, and not of purely arbitrary extension, are not to be found.

It will now be possible to give some account of tribal grouping on Rossel, although tribes, as ordinarily understood, are absent. Rivers[1] describes a tribe as ' . . . a social group of a simple kind, the members of which speak a common dialect, have a single government, and act together for such common purposes as warfare '.

An obvious objection to this description is that it also describes groups that are clearly not tribes, such as households and villages. If we remedy this defect by substituting for 'a social group' 'the largest social group in a sufficiently wide area', the definition may be of use for some parts of the world, but not for South-East New Guinea; for here dialect changes continuously; and 'being under one government' and 'acting together for certain purposes' are equally matters of degree.

By a suitable modification, Rivers' definition may be used for 'tribal grouping' as distinct from tribe; the tribe of a person may then be defined as a sequence of individuals

[1] Rivers, *Social Organization*, p. 32.

ordered with respect to similarity of dialect, singleness of government, and tendency to co-operation.

This implies, of course, that these three factors are given a certain relative weight; otherwise, the definition is utterly vague. If, however, tribe is to *mean* relations so diverse as 'similarity of dialect' and 'singleness of government', it loses all value; for it should surely be a fundamental principle in the framing of such concepts that they mean some definite social relation. We must not, therefore, include in the meaning of tribe 'speaking a similar dialect', nor can we include in its meaning 'occupying a given territory', which Perry wishes to substitute for the latter part of Rivers' definition.[1] I would suggest that the tribal relation be described as the relation of solidarity, so that the tribal grouping of a person is the sequence of persons towards whom he experiences solidarity—the remoter the member of his tribe, the slighter the solidarity with that person. This solidarity is, however, itself the expression of a complex of relations, political, economic, legal, etc., which it is the object of the sociologist to discover. The nature of the tribal grouping in the case of any particular people, consequently, emerges only after a more or less complete study of their culture. Only a rough estimate of the tribal grouping on Rossel will, therefore, be attempted here.

The 'tribal distance'—to adopt a convenient way, already explained, of describing a grouping—between any two persons on Rossel depends principally on the following relations between those persons—spatial separation, family distance (distance in the relationship sense from persons with whom genealogical connection can be traced), clan distance (distance from persons of the same clan with whom it may be impossible to trace any genealogical connection), and, if the phrase be allowed for the moment, classificatory distance (distance from members of other clans, with whom it may be impossible to trace any genealogical connection). To a certain extent, tribal distance also depends on the degree of 'singleness of government', for there are chiefs whose sway, in a degree roughly proportional to distance, may extend over a number of villages, which thus tend to become tribally united apart from the operation of proximity and

[1] Rivers, *Social Organization*, p. 32.

relationship. These different factors are, of course, cumu-
lative. The tribal nearness of A in village α, to B in village β,
is, thus, partly dependent upon the spatial separation of α
and β; it is increased by the family nearness of A and B,
and by the sum total of ways in which A is near to B in a
classificatory sense; the tribal nearness of A and B is also
greater if both α and β owe allegiance to the same
chief.

A more complete account of this tribal grouping would
exhibit the relative influences of these different factors, e.g.
the relative influence of spatial and family distance. There
is little doubt that close family relationship produces the
closest tribal tie, even though close relatives are separated
by a considerable distance in space. Father, mother, brother,
sister, children, wife, mother's brothers and sisters, constitute
the closest tribal relations,—roughly in the above order.
Such relatives will be tribally nearer to an individual than
comparatively unrelated members of his own village, even
though the former be resident on the most distant part of
the island. As we pass to more remote relatives in the
genealogical sense, this is no longer the case, so that a person
who is distant in the family grouping—a cousin several times
removed, let us say, and of a different clan—will yet be
tribally nearer, if in the same village, than a father's sister's
child in a village several miles away.[1]

---

[1] This may be diagrammatically expressed (see Diag. X) as follows:
$A B C D E F$ is the village of the individual X, A' B' C' D' E' F'
represents the villages which are within a short distance of $A B C D E F$,
and A'' B'' C'' D'' E'' F'' the more remote villages.

$A A' A''$ are near members of the clan and family of X, $B B' B''$ near
members of the family but not the clan of X, $C C' C''$ more distant
members of the clan and family of X, $D D' D''$ more distant members
of the family but not the clan of X, $E E' E''$ members of the clan but not
the family of X (i.e. non-genealogical relationship), and $F F' F''$ members
neither of clan nor family of X. The tribal grouping would be roughly
expressed by the sequence $A B A' B' A'' B'' C D E C' E' F D' C'' E''$
$F' D'' F''$.

It must be remembered that A, B, A', etc., are themselves sequences
of persons and that each distant village would have to be taken separately
in any complete representation of the tribal grouping.

The diagram also expresses the fact that only in some of the
nearer villages are there likely to be close members of a person's family,
while there are likely to be members of his clan in most of the near
villages. The proportion of a segment, left unblacked, expresses the
proportion of villages in which the given class of relatives is likely to

The clan grouping is more easily defined than the tribal grouping, though the usual definition of a clan as an exogamous division of a tribe must be discarded, since there are

occur. In the case of distant villages, in only a small proportion are there likely to be near relatives.

A further concreteness may be given to this scheme by considering the actual distribution of villages on the island. By questioning some half-dozen informants from different parts of the island the names and positions of about 150 districts were obtained. The majority of these districts were said to contain at least one village, and a certain number contained several. The total number of villages on the island according to the 1920 census-returns is 145 (App. I, p. 230). With a population of about 1450, this makes an average of 10 persons per village. Assuming an area of about 100 square miles, and taking into account the irregular shape of the island, this gives an average separation between the villages of about two to three miles, so that a village in the central part of the island is likely to have some half-dozen villages within two or three miles of it, perhaps a dozen within three or four.

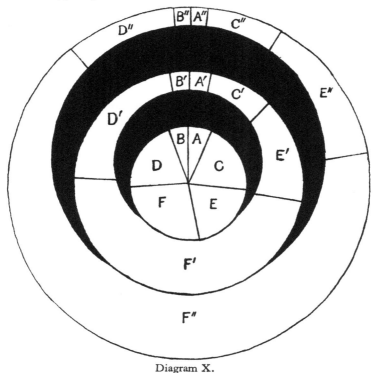

Diagram X.

no tribes on Rossel. Rossel Island does, however, form practically an endogamous group, and, though there have been a few marriages with Sudest in recent years, these must have been rare in earlier days, before the Papuan government had brought peace to these islands.

The clans on Rossel may, therefore, be regarded without appreciable error as exogamous divisions.[1] There are about 15, or possibly a few more, clans on the island, some of which are widely dispersed. Descent is matrilineal. Each clan is characterised by three linked totems, plant, bird, and fish, of which the plant is the principal. The Southern Massim have four linked totems, bird, plant, fish, and snake, of which the bird is the principal. Although the usual questions as to totems only elicit in Rossel three totems, further enquiry shows that there is a fourth totem of a different order, and this is a snake, the fourth totem of Southern Massim clans. In the case of the latter this snake is merely a species of snake, which is not rigidly avoided. The snake totem of a Rossel clan, on the other hand, may be described as a god—it is sometimes regarded as an individual, sometimes as a species. Moreover, those snakes that function as totems are avoided and feared equally by all clans, irrespective of their totems. The three primary linked totems, on the other hand, do not seem to be the subject of avoidance or respect by any of the clans, though it is possible that a person would not kill or eat the bird totem of his father's clan.[2] Avoidance of the father's bird totem, and to a certain extent of all his totems, is usual amongst the Southern Massim and even more pronounced than avoidance of their own totem. The

[1] If we define the clan as a relative grouping, the clan quality is best regarded as a sentiment of blood relationship, which carries with it a sentiment which leads to exogamy. The clan of a person is the sequence of persons towards whom this sentiment holds. The nearer members of a clan are found to be those with whom matrilineal relationship can be traced, the more distant members those who are believed to be related matrilineally, though the relationship cannot be traced. This way of regarding the clan would be necessary if any of the Rossel clans connected up with any of the Sudest clans; for amongst the Southern Massim there is a continuity of clans, which prevents us from regarding them as closed groups. I did not, however, discover on Sudest any clans continuous with any Rossel clans; though my information was insufficient to establish this definitely.

[2] Murray states that the snake is absent from the linked totems of Rossel and that the totem bird is not eaten (App. 1, p. 229).

primary totems of the Rossel clans are frequently food plants. One important clan has the sago as totem, and I came across no individuals for whom sago was taboo—I have seen sago men eating sago and it seems most unlikely that the most important food on the island would be taboo to any one clan.

The plant totems of 14 clans were as follows: *widi* (sago), *ka* (taro), *kmyi* (coconut), *kwuda, wobo, lia, miala, yomo, gwuna, gwia, gwalö, pweme, mbwo, ndua.* The snake totems, or gods, linked with some of these, were discovered, e.g. *ka* with 'Nönö', the snake god of the taro *yaba* (Chap. XII, p. 143), *kmyi* with 'Luwe' (Chap. XII, p. 154), *kwuda* and *wobo* with 'Wonajö' (Chap. XI), *lia* with 'Gadiu' (Chap. XII, p. 168), *yomo* with 'Pere' (Chap. XII, p. 147) and *ndua* with 'Mbasi' (Chap. XI). The bird and fish totems associated with *ka* were *kwe* (bird) and *tubyi* (fish); with *yomo, lango* (bird) and *dara* (fish). It was clear that every other clan had bird and fish totems in addition to its plant totem, but I cannot say for certain whether every clan has the totemic relation to a snake god as well, although this is highly probable. The nature of the snake totems is further discussed under 'Religion' (Chap. XI).

The family is, pre-eminently, the element in social organisation which it is necessary to treat as a grouping and not as a group. The family relation may be described as a relation of solidarity of a peculiarly intimate kind, the expression of a complex of relations, principally economic rather than political or legal. The relation is one that implies an emotional attitude of love and respect, and a realisation of rights and duties, which are not necessarily reciprocal. Although the full meaning of the family grouping is easier to arrive at than that of the tribal grouping, which largely depends on the former, its particular character for any one people emerges only when the culture is fully understood. There is, however, no doubt that the family grouping on Rossel is directly dependent on relationship, including adopted relationships, and that genealogical relationship secures a closer family relation than non-genealogical. The members of a person's family, who are his non-genealogical relatives, may even for practical purposes be ignored, so that we may describe the family of a person as the grouping of his genealogical relatives.[1] There is, of course, no real break of continuity. Beyond a person's family there are his 'classificatory relatives', as we shall see presently; and beyond these there are persons whose 'classificatory relationship' has not been worked out by himself or any one with whom he is acquainted. The tribal relation is sufficient to cover this important relation to persons outside the family. With regard to persons outside the family, but within the clan, it is convenient to talk of a clan relation, which is different from both family and tribal relation; for peculiarities of the clan, such as food taboos, obligations of mutual aid, and particularly the taboo on murder within the clan, make the relation between two members of a clan, however distant their classificatory relationship, a peculiar one, for it can neither be described as a weak family one, nor a strong tribal one.

Although the family grouping depends on genealogical relationship, we cannot say that family distance is proportional to genealogical distance, for close relations by marriage other than wife or husband are somewhat late in the family sequence, and—as would be expected with matrilineal descent—matrilineal relatives are, on the whole, nearer in the sequence than other relatives who are genealogically equidistant: for example, a cousin, who is the mother's sister's child, is a closer member of a person's family than the father's brother's child, even though both are called by the

[1] It is interesting to find that on Eddystone Island in the Solomon Islands, according to Rivers, there is a native term for a grouping almost identical with the family grouping, namely, 'taviti' (*vide* Rivers, *Social Organization*, p. 42). Rivers seems to have attached undue significance to this, and to have imagined this to be an unusual kind of social organisation: this was, no doubt, due to his supposition that the 'taviti' was a 'group', instead of a 'grouping', which it cannot be from his own definition of the 'taviti'. The grouping 'taviti', although without name, is fairly well recognised on Rossel and elsewhere in South-East New Guinea. The family grouping, as defined above, is somewhat wider than the 'taviti', since it includes certain relatives by marriage. It is useful to distinguish both bilateral and unilateral family groupings from the wider family grouping on Rossel, as elsewhere in Melanesia, because, for certain purposes, a man and his close relatives in his bilateral family grouping have important rights and duties in relation to his wife's close relatives, who are, however, also members of his family in the above sense. The 'taviti' appears to be simply a name for the bilateral family grouping, which elsewhere in Melanesia has no name.

same relationship term. Nevertheless, the father is as close a member of the family as the mother, even though of another clan. The near members of a person's family on Rossel are as follows in approximate order: father, mother, brothers and sisters, children, wife or husband, mother's brothers and sisters, sister's children, mother's sister's children, father's brothers and sisters, brother's children, father's brother's children, mother's brother's children, father's sister's children. These, of course, are only a few of the large number of genealogical relatives recognised by the Rossel Islander.

The large number of family relationships of which the Rossel Islander is conscious are denoted by a comparatively small number of relationship terms. The relationship system is, therefore, classificatory in the sense in which any relationship system is, in practice, bound to be classificatory. It is, however, classificatory in a more important sense of the term, for certain of the family relationship terms are used to denote relationships beyond the family—i.e. to denote relationships not recognised as genealogical. In other words, the system is a 'classificatory system' in the usual sense of the term. The term for brother is not only used to denote the relationship between a man and his mother's sons, his mother's mother's daughter's sons, and still more remote parallel cousins, but also to denote the relationship between a man and certain other members of his clan (and even of other clans) with whom he cannot trace genealogical relationship, and even with whom no one in the community may be able to trace genealogical relationship.

This system of relationship is fundamental in the Rossel social organisation, for, by what is largely an automatic functioning of the system, the family and tribal groupings are established. In fact the varieties of behaviour of persons towards one another are mainly dependent upon the relationships, classificatory or otherwise, in which they lie to one another; and these, apart from those established by the choice of a mate, are entirely involuntary ones.

In order to make clear the nature of this classificatory system on Rossel, a theoretical note is appended on the classificatory system (App. III), where it is maintained that Rivers' view of the classificatory system is, in certain respects, untenable, and a somewhat different interpretation of the non-genealogical use of relationship terms is given. If this view, which is supported by the Rossel Island evidence, is correct, the working of the system on Rossel, as well as in other places where the classificatory system holds, becomes intelligible. The actual system of relationships on Rossel is given in the next chapter, which throws further light on the nature of the family grouping, and also, therefore, the clan and tribal groupings.

CHAPTER IV

The Relationship System

ASSUMING the interpretation of the Classificatory System of Relationships given in App. III, Rossel is found to have a 'classificatory system', as distinct from a 'class system'. Although the relationship system is, as a whole, classificatory, there are a few relationship terms used only in a genealogical sense, and there are other relationship terms, which may be said to be only partially classificatory in a way which will be presently described.

The information that follows was obtained principally by means of a pedigree, containing 163 persons, and such that some of the members were separated by six generations in the line of direct male or female descent. The genealogical method, as elaborated by Rivers, was adopted, i.e. terms used between members of the pedigree were listed, together with avoidances and so forth between such persons, and relationships said to exist between persons, these in general being the same 'terms' as the 'terms of address'. About 300 instances were recorded. In addition, a certain amount of information was obtained by direct questioning as to the meaning of relationships, but this was unfortunately very inadequate. The important enquiries as to the relationships equivalent to the products of two or more relationships were insufficient, as well as other matters. Moreover, the relationship system was only partially worked out at the time, so that there are a number of omissions.

As a matter of fact, the pedigree was defective with regard to the large majority of marriages recorded, relations through the father or mother of one of the married pair not being recorded in most cases. However, the extensiveness of the pedigree was sufficient to ensure that, if marriages between close relatives occurred comparatively seldom, one or two such marriages would have appeared in the pedigree. Moreover, direct questioning of the natives on the point revealed the existence of no injunctions to marry close relatives.

Among 40 marriages recorded in the pedigree no instances

of marriage within the clan appeared, although there were four instances of marriage into the father's clan. Statements confirmed the existence of strict clan exogamy and the absence of any other marriage injunction or marriage taboo dependent merely on the clan organisation.

There was evidently no grouping of clans for purposes of marriage,—either into endogamous or exogamous groups of clans—and, therefore no dual organisation (which is a special case of such grouping). This was shown by direct statements, and by the facts revealed by the pedigree.

Thirteen clans are represented in the 40 marriages recorded in the pedigree. Calling these clans $A-M$, we find that the males marry the following females:

> 9 A males marry 1 B, 1 C, 1 D, 2 E, 3 F, 1 G females
> 2 B males marry 1 C, 1 H females
> 2 C males marry 1 D, 1 I females
> 11 D males marry 4 A, 3 B, 1 F, 2 G, 1 H females
> 1 E male marries 1 G female
> 2 F males marry 1 H, 1 M females
> 6 G males marry 1 A, 2 B, 1 C, 1 D, 1 E females
> 1 H male marries 2 F females
> 1 I male marries 1 C female
> 1 $\mathcal{J}$ male marries 1 A female
> 2 K males marry 1 G, 1 I females
> 1 L male marries 1 A female

This is, of course, inconsistent with a dual organisation, because, for example, A must belong to a different moiety from B owing to the A male marriages, and also to the same moiety owing to the D male marriages. And, more generally, the above table shows that there are no endogamous groupings of clans and probably no significant exogamous groupings, though the latter still remain a possibility.

The relationship terminology of address is given below. The native terms at the head of the list are terms used in a classificatory sense—these are followed by terms used in a limited classificatory sense (which will be described)—and finally three terms occur at the end of the list which are not used in a classificatory sense. The terms are given with the possessive suffix for the first person. Mother, father, son, daughter, brother, sister, husband, wife, are to be understood as denoting the direct relations, which are for practical

purposes those of maternal consanguinity and the marriage
relation or the simplest products of these, i.e. brother is
$M\check{M}$ (where M is the relation of maternal consanguinity
and $\check{M}$ its converse), son of a man is $W\check{M}$ (where W is the
marriage relation).[1] The above terms, mother, etc., in heavy
type (**mother,** etc.) (see also App. III, p. 245) indicate the
relationship between a woman and the person denoted by
the term, mother, etc., in its ordinary use as a term indicating an individual or a class rather than a relation—while the
same terms, mother, etc., in ordinary type (mother, etc.)
denote the corresponding relationship between a man and
the person denoted. Where the term is a classificatory one,
it is used in a classificatory sense, in the way indicated in
App. III. This classificatory use will be considered more
fully at a later stage.

(a) *Fully classificatory terms.*

ambo   = brother, **sister.**

adödö   = **brother,** sister.

$\left. \begin{array}{l} ania \\ apia \end{array} \right\}$ = mother, **mother.**

         apia appears not to be used for own mother
         or own **mother.**

aghö   = father, **father,** father's father, **father's** father,
         mother's **father, mother's father.**

         The term is not used for own father or own
         father, and rarely for the other own relatives
         above, and only occasionally for classificatory
         father.

aghöbia   = father's sister, **father's** sister, father's mother,
         father's mother, mother's **mother, mother's**
         mother, father's father's sister, **father's** father's
         sister, mother's **father's** sister, **mother's fa-**
         ther's sister.

         The term is not generally used for the 'own'
         relation above.

         Also father's sister's **daughter** and father's
         sister's **daughter.**

---

[1] The relation M is better regarded not as that of maternal consanguinity but that of matrilineal descent sociologically defined by reference
to a complex of beliefs to be found in the group. See Malinowski, *The
Family among the Australian Aborigines*, 1913, ch. VI.

abje ⎫
awa ⎬   = son, daughter.

Also used for son, daughter, but not, as a rule in the classificatory sense, in the case of these two relationships: also for mother's brother's son, mother's brother's daughter. *awa* is frequently used for the latter relationship, though *abje* is given as an alternative and as equivalent. *awa* is less frequently used instead of *abje* in other cases.

The term *ajemoro* is sometimes used for mother's brother's son and possibly mother's brother's daughter.

agea = reciprocal of *aghö* and *aghöbia*. The only reciprocal 'own' relations for which it is not used are those of son, daughter.

(Note that the mother's brother's son and mother's brother's daughter are therefore included.)

amejö = father's sister's son, father's sister's son.
aghönö = mother's brother, mother's brother.
ajina = reciprocal of *aghönö*.
angwö = wife's brother, sister's husband, and reciprocals.
anö = husband's mother, husband's father, and reciprocals.
ambwia = wife's father, wife's mother and reciprocals.
ambwiabia is sometimes used for wife's mother.
ambweugma = husband's mother's brother and reciprocal.

agaideka This relationship was not obtained by use of the pedigree, but was given by an informant for certain relationships between a man or woman and wife's or husband's brothers or sisters, e.g. by a man to the brother's wife. But the same informant described the *angwö* relationship in a way inconsistent with the many instances revealed by the pedigree. The relationship *agaideka* may, however, be the relationship between a man and his brother's wife, which would not be revealed by the pedigree, because in address the brother's wife is always referred to as the *bodyim* of the husband, addressed by his proper name.

The Relationship System 47

(b) *Partially classificatory terms.*

aghönöwö = mother's brother, mother's brother, only used for close mother's brothers (and mother's brothers) of the same clan. It is the classificatory term *aghönö* limited by the suffix *wö*.

amama = father's sister, only used for close father's sister, but even own father's sister may be referred to as *aghöbia* or *kauwöbia*.

amböbö = reciprocal of *amama*.

amaga is a reciprocal term used between persons three generations apart.

(c) *Non-classificatory terms.*

ama = father.

kauw = direct ancestors of male sex of second generation.

kauwöbia = direct ancestors of female sex of second generation.

All the above terms are used as terms of address, although in many cases the proper name could be used alternatively. Also, though the statement is made with less certainty, all the terms, except *kauw* and *kauwöbia* could be used to express the relationship, e.g. *A* referring to *B*, the brother of *C*, could refer to him as *C wömbo*, the prefix *wö* (= his) replacing the prefix *a* = my.

It will be noted that the term *agea* is the reciprocal of the terms *aghö* and *aghöbia*, and *aghö* is a term used towards males only and *aghöbia* towards females only. Evidently *aghöbia* is merely *aghö* modified by a sex-determining suffix. The terms *kauw* and *kauwöbia* are related in the same way, and *ambwia* and *ambwiabia*. *Bia* is a substantive meaning woman.

We still have to determine what is meant by the classifactory use of most of the terms tabulated. The discussion of App. III makes this task a comparatively easy one, and a few of the facts revealed by the pedigree and more especially by general statements is sufficient to establish, on broad lines, what this means. Taking the relationship *ambo*, we find that this term is employed between brothers and between sisters, between sons of sisters or daughters of sisters, between sons of daughters of sisters or daughters of daughters of sisters.

We find this is also the case between sons of brothers and daughters of brothers and sons of sons of brothers and daughters of sons of brothers, or of course between sons of daughters of brothers or daughters of daughters of brothers. Some 20 or 30 such cases occur in the pedigree. In one case a man calls another brother who is in the relation of father's father's father's father's brother's son's son's son's son. What really happens, as far as I could make out in these cases, is that sons or daughters of persons who are in the relation *mbo* (1st pers. *ambo*) are regarded as in the relation *mbo*; there is, however, one important case where persons are in this relation *mbo* for another reason, namely, because they are the sons or the daughters of one person, and this latter is the most extreme form of the relationship. The use of the *mbo* relationship in this way establishes this relationship between an indefinite number of persons between whom no genealogical relationship can be traced.

The relationship *dödö* holds between persons of opposite sex for the same reason, i.e. because the persons related are children of the same parent or the children of persons who are *mbo* to one another. The other relationships can be regarded as owing their classificatory nature to the fact that a person's *mbo* can be substituted for himself in any relation, so that in the above list of classificatory terms we can always add to the relationship which is used for the definition 'or his or her *mbo*'. But the classificatory nature of some at least of the other terms can be derived directly without reference to this *mbo* relationship, e.g. the term *gea* is the relationship between a man and his sister's son, between the son of a man and the son of his sister's son, i.e. children of *gea*, are *gea* in one direction and *ghö* or *ghöbia* in the other. If children of *gea* are *gea* then an indefinite number of persons are necessarily *gea*, even though no genealogical connection between them can be discovered. The relationship *gea* is like the relationship *mbo*, in that *gea* of *gea* is *gea*, just as *mbo* of *mbo* is *mbo*. Similarly, with the relationship *ghö* and *ghöbia*. These relationships *mbo* and *dödö*, on the one hand, and *gea*, *ghö*, *ghöbia* on the other hand are, thus, in a peculiar position. Both, independently, generate relationship beyond genealogical memory, and, owing to the fact that marriage on Rossel is inconsistent with a class system and that there is no

PLATE VII

(*a*) Group of women and children.

(*b*) Group of women and children.

PLATE VIII

(*a*) Front view of a woman.

(*b*) Profile of the same.

exogamous or endogamous grouping of clans, everyone on Rossel is almost certainly related to everyone else by either the relationship *mbo* or *dödö* and also independently by either the relationship *gea* or the relationship *ghö* or *ghöbia*: by 'independently,' in this case, is meant—without assuming that brother or sister can be replaced by *mbo* in the definition of the *gea, ghö, ghöbia* relationship.

Since it is also given that son or daughter of the *mbo* of a man is *gea* (if not *bje*) as well as other equivalences, it follows that the classificatory nature of *mbo* or *dödö* can be derived from *gea, ghö, ghöbia* or, alternatively, the classificatory nature of the latter can be derived from the former. This point is of some importance in understanding the classificatory system on Rossel. The elevation of particular relationships into 'classifiers' should be avoided, though it is probably the case that the relationship *mbo* is the chief 'classifier' on Rossel—the *mbo* relationship is used for determining relationship rather more often than other relationships that seem to be as close, and this is especially the case when persons who are *mbo* to one another are members of the same clan. For this reason, it is sufficient, with regard to the other classificatory relationships on Rossel, to say that they are the relationships as defined, where ' *mbo* of' can be inserted in the definition wherever it will fit grammatically, e.g. *ghönö* = 'mother's brother' and therefore *ghönö* = '*mbo* of mother's *mbo* of brother', and so on.

We have already discussed in general terms the reasons why one classificatory relationship is said to hold between two persons rather than any of the remaining classificatory relationships (all of which are likely to hold in the case of Rossel, none being eliminated by exogamy or endogamy, brothers and sisters tending to occur in every clan); for instance, quite accidental circumstances of individual memory, of friendship, of death, of locality, and so on, play an important part. Discounting for these factors, we have left the factors, such as genealogical nearness, etc., which we have only partially investigated. We have seen that there is an important sense in which we can talk of intensity of relationship. If a value could be given to this intensity on the ground of the route by which the relationship is said to hold, the question would be completely answered, for every relationship in which two persons stand would have a certain intensity, thus placing all the relationships in an order, and the relationship could also be compared, as regards intensity, to this same relationship holding between all other pairs of individuals in the group, giving a second type of order, that is, the order of intensity of any given relationship with respect to all pairs of persons (of the right sex relation). Unfortunately, this problem was not perceived at the time and only a few tentative statements can be made.

Other things being equal, the *mbo* relationship between members of the same clan is more intense than that relationship between members of different clans; other things being equal, the *mbo* relationship between members of the same clan derived from relationships holding between members of the same clan is more intense than when derived from relationships holding between members of other clans; other things being equal, genealogical relationship is more intense than non-genealogical; the *mbo* derived from relationships, whose intensities add up to x, is more intense than any other relationship, derived from relationships, whose intensities add up to x. A number of other such statements could be made, but there are so many variables, that a total statement in the above form would be too complex to be of any use. With fuller data no doubt, an equation could be constructed to express the facts, but it is useless to attempt that here, with insufficient material, and it is doubtful whether it is of more than formal importance or interest. It would, however, have been interesting if cases had been investigated in which by definite routes a man was, for example, in the relation both of *mbo* and *gea* to another and to have found the reasons why one relationship was selected rather than the other. Of course, numerous instances occurred in the pedigree of multiple relationship by definite genealogical routes, and the question is partially answered by the fact that one of these was selected in each particular case. The natives should have been questioned in all these cases as to their reasons; and the 'collective ideas'[1] responsible for the

---

[1] By 'collective ideas', I mean, ideas common to all, roughly speaking. A more adequate definition would weight the ideas common to most and to the few; and of course, the definition of 'ideas' in this connection offers considerable difficulties.

working of the system should have been obtained by a more direct process.

The relationships in the above table have been defined so as to reduce redundancy to a minimum; though insufficient data were collected for a definition in the way corresponding most closely to the collective ideas, though this has been done as far as possible.

The relationship terms used between cross-cousins are somewhat surprising, though not to those acquainted with the Melanesian systems, and it might be thought, as a result of the arguments I have put forward, that the terms obtained for these relatives are the terms dependent on the other relationships, which, owing to the classificatory principle, necessarily hold. This possibility may be discounted for the following reasons. In the first place, the same terminology, *ghöbia*, *gea*, and *amejö*, *awa*, was obtained by direct question as to the relationship, no actual persons being referred to. In the second place, the genealogical relationship occurs in several parts of the pedigree, and in every case the same terms were used; this was the case with own mother's brother, with mother's brother not 'own' but of the same clan, and with mother's brother of a different clan. Unfortunately, it is not perfectly clear whether the relationships are the same whether the mother's brother be the elder or the younger brother, though one instance in the genealogy occurs where this relationship holds and the mother's brother is the mother's elder brother and one instance where he is the younger brother; but the possibility of a mistake here cannot be excluded. I am inclined to think that the distinction of elder and younger brother (and sister) is not of importance on Rossel, as regards the determination of relationship, though it is of importance among the neighbouring Massim.

Distinctions of age between children of the same parents are of some importance, since they are reflected in terminology. The eldest child is called *abjeka* and the youngest *abjetu*, however many children there may be; if there are three children, the second is called *abjekaliwini*; but if there are more than three children the second is called *abjekabe* and the remainder *abjekaliwini*. The same suffixes may be added to the terms *mbo* and *dödö* used between the children themselves, so that if there are three brothers, the middle brother will be called *ambokaliwini* both by his elder and his younger brother. This seems to confirm the fact that the relative distinction of elder and younger is not of importance, but only the absolute order of birth.

It will be noticed that certain close relatives do not appear in the list of terms directly or by implication. The chief of these are wife and husband. This relationship is expressed by the non-classificatory term *gwam* for wife and *mo* for husband, but apparently these terms are rarely used either in address or for reference. The husband is sometimes referred to as 'the man of', the wife frequently as 'the woman of'. A man often addresses his wife by name, or as *köbiubo*; a woman generally addresses her husband by name, or as *köbini*. There are evidently other terms, meaning husband or wife, which are only used in certain contexts, i.e. *wöbajim* (see below) means 'his wife' and *wöbiagng* (see below) means 'her husband'.

The brother's wife and the **sister's husband** do not appear in the above relationship system (though the term *gaideka*, tentatively given, may express this relationship). In address, a relationship term is, apparently, never used between these relatives, and the name is also rigidly avoided. A peculiar method is adopted in address, and also in reference. The brother's wife is addressed as '"Name of brother" *wöbajim*' and the **sister's husband** is addressed as '"Name of sister" *wöbiagng*', *bajim* being a term for husband, and *biagng* a term for wife.[1] Numerous instances of the above relationship occurred in the pedigree, and the relationship was always expressed in the above form, whether close or distant brothers of sisters of the same or different clans. There were also one or two instances to prove that the relationship, and the avoidances associated with it, were independent of the relationship elder or younger brother or sister.

There is a curious asymmetry in the terminology connected with relations-in-law of the same generation (i.e. relations-in-law defined by the use of the terms 'wife', 'husband', *mbo* and *dödö*), a true relationship term, one that can be used with the first person possessive prefix, being used in only one class of these relationships. The terminology of address

---

[1] Bell refers to this avoidance, App. I, p. 225.

for these cases, where the persons are of the same sex, is as
follows:

between males   *angwa*

(in all cases, whether the persons are married or not);

between females   *kömeri*

awyilö

(in all cases, whether the persons are married or not).

Kömeri is the more usual term and is evidently a term
of address merely, and cannot be used referentially as a
relationship. Possibly the first part of this word, *kö*, is a
prefix meaning 'that'. *Awyilö* is possibly a relationship, but
only two or three instances of its use as an alternative to
kömeri were recorded.

The terminology of address for relations-in-law of the same
generation, where the persons are of different sex, is as follows:

(*a*) If the person addressed is married, the methods of
address and reference are as given above for brother's wife
and sister's husband, 'Name *wöbajim*' and 'Name *wöbiagng*'.

(*b*) If the person addressed, male or female, is not married,
but the person addressing is married, the term *köwyili* is
used (or *möwyili* in some cases; note that *kö* and *mö* are
demonstrative prefixes in other contexts and presumably the
same in this context).

(*c*) If both persons are unmarried, the name is generally
used.

Allied to the terminology of address for 'brother's wife'
and 'sister's **husband**' is that for mother's **brother's** wife,
who is addressed as '"Name of mother's **brother**" *wöbajim*' or as *aghönö wöbajim*. But reciprocally the **husband's**
sister's **son** is addressed as '"Name of **husband's** sister's
husband" *odejimagng*', whether he be married or not. The
husband's sister's **daughter** is referred to by name, and
reciprocally, the name may be used or the phrase *aghönö
wögwam* (i.e. 'my mother's **brother's** wife').

Avoidance is practised between those persons who address
one another by the terms *kömeri* (and *awyilö*) or *köwyili*
(*möwyili*) or by the phrases, 'Name *wöbajim*' and *aghönö
wöbajim*, or 'Name *wöbiagng*': in these cases the name must
not be used.

But men, in the relationship *ngwa*, however close, may use, alternatively, the name, though women in the equivalent relationship (*kömeri*) may not.

Persons in the relationship 'brother's wife' and '**sister's husband**' and those who use the terminology of address used by these relatives, may not use the ordinary terms for certain parts of the body and certain possessions of the other person, whether in address or reference. The alternative words are given below:

	Usual term	Substitute
mouth	*komwapu*	*ukwadada*
eye	*ngwolö*	*wiche*
nose	*nu*	*okwada*
hair	*mbada*	*winje*
ear	*ngwene*	*obenia*
hand	*ko*	*okebe*
leg	*kwale*	*opebe*
foot	*yi*	*opebe*
belly	*yoda*	*ombwane*
teeth	*nyodi*	*okwoma*
basket	*pe*	*wongwe*

This terminology is used for moderately close relatives. Where the *mbo* or *dödö* concerned is of a different totem, the avoidance of the use of the ordinary term holds, provided the relationship is close.

The avoidance of the use of these terms occurred also, so it was stated, between those in a close *ngwö* relationship, although the name could be used between these relatives, and also between persons in the relationship *dödö*, if sufficiently close, whether they are of the same or different clans.

With regard to the other relationships that have been tabulated, those that carry definite avoidance of the use of the personal name are *kauw*, *kauwöbia*, *ma*, *mama*, and *ghönöwö*, and also 'own' mother. This taboo on the use of the personal name is accompanied by an attitude of respect rather than avoidance in these cases, quite unlike the avoidance between a man and his brother's wife, his **wife's sister**, or mother's **brother's** wife; these relatives will not pass in front of one another, and avoid conversation as far as possible, even employing a small boy or girl to convey answers to questions; commands, such as 'Come' between these relatives are conveyed in the 2nd person plural, *abuiengyina* instead of *abuie*, an avoidance form which we also find among the Massim. The avoidance between brother and sister is much less extreme than this.

There is one relationship, that of *binda*, of considerable importance which has not yet been mentioned. It is a relationship established by naming and therefore of a different order from those we have been considering. It affects the whole relationship system, however, for those in the relationship *binda* are regarded as being in the relationship *mbo*. Extensive classifications, therefore, result from every *binda* relationship contracted between persons who previously were less *mbo* to one another than some other relationship. As a rule the *binda* relationship is contracted between a man and one of his close mother's **brothers** and also, therefore, with one of his close sister's **sons**. A woman generally contracts it with a close **sister's daughter.** Unfortunately, I discovered this relationship only towards the end of my stay on the island and my information is, therefore, very defective. Apparently the parents establish the relationship by naming the child; but this can, I believe, happen some years after the first name is given (which occurs soon after birth) or, on the other hand, the relationship can be established at the first name-giving. Those in the relationship *binda* use the terms *abinda* or *ambo* indifferently and behave as close brothers (or sisters) to one another. The close relatives of a *binda* are often addressed by the terms appropriate to relatives of a *mbo*. There appears to be an important economic relation between persons who are in the relation of *binda*, which will be discussed in a later chapter.

As Dr Rivers has shown for other parts of Melanesia, the peculiar terminology for cross-cousins whereby they are classed with the generation above or below, may be regarded as dependent on marriage with the mother's **brother's** wife. (If on Rossel a man marries his mother's **brother's** wife, then the mother's **brother's** son and daughter will naturally be *bje*, the term for son and daughter, and reciprocally the father's sister's **son**, or, **father's** sister's **son**, will be *ma* or *ghö*. As a matter of fact, the reciprocal, namely *mejö*, is a term used for no other relationship. Since the mother's **brother's** son or daughter is the son or daughter by this argument, the **brother's** mother's **brother's** son or

daughter, i.e. **mother's brother's** son or daughter, will be
the **brother's** son or daughter, and therefore *mböbö* or *gea*,
and we find that the latter term is always used. Reciprocally,
the father's sister's **daughter** or **father's** sister's **daughter**
is in the relation *ghöbia*.) In the case of Rossel, this marriage
is prohibited and there is strong avoidance between a man
and the wife of his mother's **brother**, which suggests the
former occurrence of this marriage, on the ground that
strong avoidance is the result of a revolution in marriage
custom. We find, however, on Rossel the same avoidance
between a man and his brother's wife, suggesting former
group marriage or else accessory sexual rights, such as are
sometimes associated with the levirate and sororate. Owing to
the *binda* relationship, whereby a man may class his mother's
brother with his brother, the avoidance of the mother's
brother's wife may be dependent on the avoidance of the
brother's wife, and may not indicate a former condition of
marriage with the mother's **brother's** wife. The terminology
for cross-cousins may then be regarded as dependent on the
binda relationship and the meaning of avoidance of the
mother's brother's wife or of the brother's wife need not be
considered in this connection.[1]

As against this explanation, it might be contended that
marriage with the mother's **brother's** wife could have been
more systematic than classification of the mother's **brother**
with the brother. As a matter of fact, in this respect, there
is little to choose between the two modes of explanation,
for a man apparently has only one *binda* in the generation
above and equally it is to be supposed that he would marry
only one mother's **brother's** wife. There still remains, on
either view, the lack of any adequate explanation why the
alternate generation terms should become universal for cross-
cousins and why the terms for cross-cousins should be
dropped—why classification through this one route should
over-ride classification through the other routes. I would
suggest, tentatively, that this can be understood if we regard
the introduction of marriage with the mother's **brother's** wife

[1] Conversely, we may suppose that marriage with the mother's
brother's wife has disappeared and has been replaced by avoidance
which owing to the classification produced by the *binda* relationship has
led to avoidance of the brother's wife. This is unlikely, because avoidance
of the brother's wife seems to be the most marked.

or the classification of certain men with the mother's **brother** as causing or coinciding with a breakdown of a class system. The problem should then be regarded as the problem of why certain relationships continue to be recognised and referred to by certain terms in spite of the fact that they coincide with any other relationships we like to choose, i.e. instead of our problem being put in the form 'why are cross-cousins classed with alternate generations?' it takes the form 'why are mother's **brothers** not classed with brothers, with uncles and so on?' With the class system breaking down, it still remains of importance to distinguish close relatives such as the mother's **brother** from other close relatives. He is in a certain position of authority, which differs from that of the father and the father's brother, and so on; similarly, with close relations-in-law, for whom we find definite terms. If at the time of the breakdown of the class system it were not important to distinguish close cross-cousins, then it is not surprising that since by easy relationship routes they tend to be both son and mother's **brother's** son, to take one example, this relationship should be denoted by the one term. In the case of Rossel, we do also find the term *wa* in use, and, in all probability, this is the term for mother's **brother's** son or daughter, which is disappearing. The reciprocal *mejö* has survived as the only term, and this no doubt was the term for father's sister's **son** or **father's** sister's **son**.

With regard to the hypothesis of a former class system, it is clear that the breakdown of terminology is too great for there to be any appreciable evidence of such a system. The only evidence of any importance is the classing of mother's **sister's children** with father's brother's **children**, which is more easily explained on this hypothesis than on any other. The reciprocal term *maga* suggests a class system in which persons three generations apart are classed together. The fact that the widely classificatory terms *ghö, ghöbia, gea*, which are used principally between different generations are not reciprocal places a difficulty in the way of supposing that there has once been a closed class system, if we are to suppose that they have survived from a class system.

Apart from this, there are no classifications that suggest a survival of any part of the terminology from any of the simpler closed or open class systems, which are discussed in App. III.[1] Since, however, there is avoidance of the mother's **brother's** wife, combined with a terminology for cross-cousins consistent with marriage with the mother's **brother's** wife, the Rossel system must be regarded as a later stage of the breakdown of a class system than is the case in those parts of Melanesia (Banks Islands) where marriage with the mother's **brother's** wife or widow occurs at the present day. But even in these parts of Melanesia there is insufficient evidence in the relationship terminology of any particular kind of former class system, and therefore still less is such evidence to be expected in the case of Rossel. We do, however, find in Pentecost, where we have the cross-cousin terminology of the Banks and Rossel, classifications which point to a former closed class system. That the breakdown of the classificatory system is of a greater degree on Rossel than we find to be the case in Southern Melanesia is also shown by the fact that a number of the relationship terms are not classificatory or only incompletely so.

[1] The reciprocal term *maga* might be interpreted as a survival of one of the class terms in a 12-class dual organisation (or 18-class 3-phratry organisation, etc.).

CHAPTER V

The Monetary System

I N most of the features of social organisation that have yet to be described, an important economic element enters in the shape of monetary payments. Payments of money are, perhaps, the most important constituents of marriage rites, mortuary rites, and many other ceremonial activities. I use the term 'money' advisedly, for the objects about to be described are used primarily as media of exchange and standards of value; they are systematically interrelated as regards value; and any commodity or service may be more or less directly priced in terms of them.

The money[1] is of two kinds (Pl. XX). The one, known as *ndap*,[2] consists of single pieces of *Spondylus* shell, ground down and polished. The species of *Spondylus* is probably not that from which the well-known sapi-sapi beads are made; for these do not show the yellow tinge which characterises most of the *ndap* money. It is possible that the numerous values of *ndap* are from more than one species of *Spondylus*. The other kind of money, known as *nkö*, consists of sets of ten discs of shell, perforated and strung together, very roughly shaped, and made probably from a Giant Clam.

The pieces of *ndap* money vary somewhat in size, having an area never less than about 2 sq. cm., or more than about 20 sq. cm., with a thickness of a few millimetres. They are generally roughly triangular in shape, with rounded corners, and are perforated near one of the corners. The colour of the polished surface varies from white to red, through shades of orange and yellow; and is generally uneven. As far as could be ascertained, the value of a piece of *ndap* money is indicated primarily by its colour.

The pieces of *nkö* money, sets of ten discs, vary only in size, the value increasing with increase in diameter of the discs. The variation in diameter is from about $1\frac{1}{2}$ to 3 cm., the thickness varying from about $\frac{1}{3}$ to $\frac{2}{3}$ cm., the highest values

---

[1] A slightly different spelling of some of the native terms is adopted here from that adopted by the present writer in earlier articles, referred to in App. III, p. 231.

[2] Briefly described by Bell, App. I, p. 225.

being those of the greatest size. The ten discs composing any one piece of money are of approximately the same size.

Tradition states that the bulk of this money was made by the gods before man appeared on Rossel, or at the time of his first appearance (before the gods had retired to their present humbler position). The *ndap* money was made by Wonajö from a mollusc he found in Yongga Bay at the western end of the island. The part of the bay from which the shell was taken by Wonajö became a *yaba* (see Chap. xii, p. 160), the *yaba* of *ndap* money, presided over by a snake god called Mbyung, who still punishes any infringement of the taboo laid upon this spot. A song which is the possession of certain chiefs at the present day is the song which Wonajö composed and sang while he made the *ndap* from the Yongga shell. It runs somewhat as follows: 'I steal the *ndap* (i.e. the shell). I a bushman "Mongwe". I polish the *ndap*, I polish it. "Mongwe", I make the hole, I make the hole'. 'The rain comes down and falls on me. I polish the *ndap*, I polish it on Ngwö'. Each of these phrases is repeated several times, with variations. Ngwö is Mt Rossel, the home of Wonajö.

Wonajö is said to have used up most of the *ndap* shell on Rossel, and the appropriate material for the higher values is not now to be found anywhere. It is in fact believed that most of the *ndap* on Rossel at the present day, including all the higher values, is the original *ndap* made by Wonajö. I was told, however, that the lowest three or four values are sometimes made on Rossel with Rossel shell, and that the three or four values above these are sometimes made from shell imported from Sudest. But these later additions to the general stock of *ndap* appear to be regarded in a different way—as imitations, so to speak, of the true *ndap*. I was told that on certain occasions the *para nö* (or *ndap* canoes— so called because they are used for carrying *ndap* money). are used for collecting the *Spondylus* shell, which is to be converted into money. The *para nö* are owned only by chiefs; ın fact the owning of a *para nö* is the most important attribute of chieftainship. It may be that the importance of chieftainship on Rossel rests primarily on the privilege of making *ndap* money. I was, however, also told that no *ndap* money is now made on the island, and that the *para nö* are only used for carrying money from place to place, and not for

The Monetary System 61

collecting the raw shell. Perhaps the art of making *ndap* money is disappearing, and this may account for my failure to get any definite information; or it may be that the natives were afraid of revealing information that might be used to their disadvantage.

According to one tradition, the making of *nkö* money also is attributed to Wonajö. The shell is said to have been found in Wolunga Bay, at a spot which is now a *yaba* (see Chap. XII, p. 167), and which only *para nö* may approach. (This taboo on all canoes but *para nö* probably applies to the *ndap yaba* in Yongga Bay also.) The *yaba* is presided over by two 'gods'—a shark called 'Bamwili', and a crocodile called 'Kömwana'. The shell was taken from here by Wonajö, and converted into the *nkö* money. According to another account, Wonajö made the *nkö*, strung it together so as to make one long rope, and placed it in the ground. From here it was subsequently removed by a man who knew the requisite formula for approaching the forbidden neighbourhood.

Whatever may be the meaning of the contradictory information about the manufacture of *ndap* at the present day, there seems to be less doubt that the art of making *nkö* has been lost, and the natives believe, as far as I could tell, that every piece of *nkö* is of great antiquity.

The two kinds of money, *ndap* and *nkö*, form two more or less independent but parallel systems. The *nkö* system may be regarded, in a sense, as an incomplete duplicate of the *ndap* system. This relationship will be explained later. To take the *ndap* money first, there are 22 main values of this, each having separate names; but the names are not etymologically descriptive of the values. These are as follows:

1. Dwondwo	12. Tangwolondo
2. Gamö	13. Kwarunundo
3. Kejim	14. Pimba
4. Pwomondap	15. Yananindo
5. Kwaia	16. Gumindo
6. Uabe	17. Bwelejumgwanagu
7. Tebuda	18. Työmundi
8. Tebudongwo	19. Tejema
9. Tiama	20. Gemida
10. Yelengwindo	21. Pwojuma
11. Yelengwinjinindo	22. Kwojuma

Of these values *dwondwo* is the lowest, and *kwojuma* the highest. In the following account they will be referred to simply by the numbers given in the above list—a device which will not only avoid the needless repetition of clumsy words, but give, in addition, an indication of the value. Some of the intermediate values, about *tebuda* to *pimba*, are subdivided—the subdivisions having value names derived from that of the principal value. These subdivisions did not appear to be of any importance, and the names were not collected. It was found that individual coins of the higher values (if the term 'coins' can be appropriately applied to the single pieces of money) possessed individual names. This was said to be the case for all coins of values 12 to 22, the total number of coins of these values being at least 150. It was stated that some of the coins of values 8 to 11 also had individual names. Since the coins of values 12 to 22 are individually named, we are not forced to suppose that there is some property (e.g. colour) which characterises each set. The shells are sufficiently irregular in marking or shape for every individual coin to be recognised; and so it is possible that the classes of coins having the higher values are merely classes formed by enumeration of their members. It is possible that this is the case even with the lower values where individual names seem to be unknown. It is at least certain that there is no serial change of any definite property to be noted as we pass from the lower to the higher values; certainly, neither shape nor colour shows any such change. Fortunately, however, another interpretation is possible. That all the coins of No. 4 that came my way were of a deep red, the few that I saw of No. 2 white, and No. 7 and No. 8 yellowish, are facts that suggest that there is some combination of characters, of which one is colour, which uniquely characterises each of the lower values, if not also the higher.

Enquiries as to the number of coins of different values on the island elicited the information that there are: 7 of No. 22, 10 of No. 21, 10 of No. 20, 10 of No. 19, 20 of No. 18, 7 of No. 17, 7 of No. 16, 10 of No. 15, 30 of No. 14, 30 to 40 of No. 13.

Naturally it was difficult to get an estimate of the number of lower value coins, but it is probable that the numbers increase more or less rapidly as we approach No. 1, though, no doubt, unevenly. No. 4 was by far the commonest coin on the island, in spite of its having a higher value than Nos. 1 to 3. There must be at least 200 of No. 4 on the island. On this supposition there would probably be less than a thousand *ndap* coins altogether, which would mean about two for every three persons on the island—rather a low figure. It may seem strange that the numbers do not steadily increase from No. 22 to No. 1; but, as will be explained later, value does not depend on scarcity, but on custom, and the economic play of the law of supply and demand has very little effect. Moreover, owing to the peculiar nature of the system, some values are more in demand than others, either above or below. For example, although there are 20 of No. 18 as compared with 7 of No. 17 and 10 of No. 19, the coins of No. 18 have to 'work' much harder than those of either of these adjacent values; but this does not affect the value relationships, which are rigidly determined by custom.

The above 22 values are related in a peculiar way, which makes the Rossel system one of exceptional interest. The values are not regarded as simple multiples of some unit of value—the usual principle in most monetary systems.

The relationship of any value to any other in this series may be expressed by the formula:

$$\text{Value of No. } n = \text{value of No. } m \, (1 + k)^{n-m},$$

where m and n are the two integers representing the number of the value in the above series, and k is a constant.

One way in which the No. m value is related to the No. n value is by the length of time a No. m coin would have to be let out on loan in order that a No. n be repayable. Now this time interval is dependent on the value interval $(n - m)$, to which it is roughly proportional. Thus, if any coin in No. n be lent for a certain short interval of time, the recipient of the loan will have to repay the loan by a No. $(n + 1)$. If the coin lent be No. 4, then No. 5 must be repaid, or if the coin lent be a No. 16, then No. 17 must be repaid. For a rather longer interval of time the loan of a No. 4 requires the return of No. 6 to cancel the debt, and similarly No. 16 requires No. 18; and so on. This clearly means that interest is being charged for the loan, and if we regard the rate of interest as constant, then the relation of every value to every other value can be expressed by the formula given above, which is also the expression for capital No. m at compound interest k for $(n - m)$ units of time.

Any value can thus be regarded as any lower value *plus* compound interest for the number of time units equal to the number of values by which the two are separated, so that No. 22, for example, is No. 1 *plus* compound interest for 21 units of time. If k be evaluated, then every value can be expressed in terms of every other value. If the interest for unit time be taken as 5 per cent., then in terms of No. 1, No. 2 is No. $1 + \frac{1}{20}$ No. 1, No. 3 is No. $1 + \frac{1}{10}$ No. $1 + \frac{1}{400}$ No. 1, and so on, in the compound interest series. An even higher rate of interest seems to be required, for No. 1 has little value, and No. 22 has a very high value. If we assume the impossible, and take No. 1 to be about 6d., and No. 22 about £10, the rate of interest would work out at over 30 per cent. for the short unit of time of a few weeks.

If we do not evaluate k, and thus do not assume a certain rate of interest, we can still speak of all the values being systematically related through the time element, namely, the time required for a loan to increase through the value series, so that every value can be expressed in terms of No. 1 and time, and all the values are equally spaced—No. 2 is No. 1 after a week or two, No. 22 is No. 1 after a few years. The price of any commodity or service could then be put in terms of 'time', and the lowest value unit in the series; e.g. a wife could be said to cost a year, a basket of taro a week, and so on. This does, I believe, come nearer to the native point of view than the supposition of a more or less definitely evaluated rate of interest.

The system in practice is not quite so systematic as the above account suggests. The analysis given above is, rather, the simplest and most pleasing solution of the majority of the facts. Some of the concrete facts on which the analysis is based will now be set forth.

There is a constant demand on the island for coins of particular values to meet various situations; for to only a limited extent can different values be substituted for one another. A man may have to borrow, even though he has money of higher value in his possession than he requires at

PLATE IX

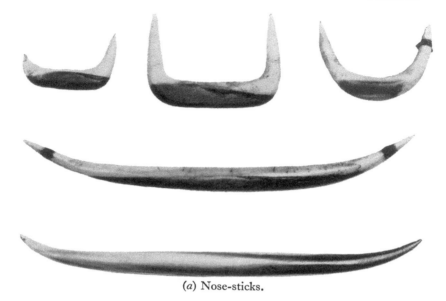

(*a*) Nose-sticks.

(*b*) Lime-spatula.

PLATE X

(*a*) Baskets.

(*b*) Baskets.

the moment. He may have Nos. 11 and 13, but not No. 12 which he requires at the moment. He cannot get change as a rule, for No. 13 is not a simple product of any lower value. He therefore borrows the required value, and if possible he takes the opportunity of lending what he has. No doubt there are occasions when a simple exchange of values takes place, especially between friends and relatives, just as there are frequently gifts in such cases, with an expectation of only a roughly equivalent return, if any; but this does not affect the general processes of lending and borrowing here described. The loan of a No. n and its cancellation in a short time by the return of a No. $(n + 1)$ appears to be the commonest type of loan, and the principle is clearly recognised. There is a term *ma* which is used to describe the relation of a value to the value below, and the natives clearly recognise the principle that a given value may be acquired by lending its *ma* for a short period of time. There does not seem to be any exactness about this period, which seems to vary from a few days to a few weeks. With regard to loans for longer periods, my informants gave me examples of a No. n becoming a No. $(n + 2)$, a No. $(n + 3)$, and so on, in sufficient number to confirm adequately the generalisation I have made above. It was, however, clear that there was no conception of a definite unit of time within which a value passes into the next above it in the series. In the case of long-period loans, the No. $(n + x)$ which the original loan of No. n has become, is generally less than one would expect from the rate of increase for short-period loans. But this vagueness in the measurement of time does not appreciably affect the truth of the above general description.

As we have already seen, the necessity for continual loans is largely the result of the peculiar nature of the system. The same 'amount' of money, where the values are simply related and 'change' can always be given, could perform the same amount of real service (i.e. effect the same number of purchases) with, perhaps, a tenth or less of the amount of lending necessitated by the Rossel system.

Since there are probably less than two *ndap* coins per head of the population, the chances are always against a person having the coin he requires for any particular transaction, and exchanges are, therefore, very much complicated.

ARI 5

This fact makes possible the existence of a profession very much like that of a London bill-broker, working with different material. The members of this profession on Rossel render an important service by transferring the possession of coins, i.e. by borrowing from one who does not want a particular coin, and lending to another who does. Their profit is made by increasing the time unit for their debtors and decreasing it for their creditors, and by keeping their capital on loan as far as possible; in other words, by borrowing at a lower rate of interest and discounting at a higher. In practice, a form of magic is employed, by means of which these brokers, and others who are not members of this profession, claim to act on the minds of their debtors, making them repay within the customary time, while the minds of their creditors are affected in the reverse way. These brokers are known by a special term, *ndeb*. Apparently, anyone who tends to specialise in money operations, determined by inclination and other accidents, is known as a *ndeb*, of which there are, therefore, many degrees. It was said that sometimes a *ndeb* will give up all other occupations, such as horticulture, and devote himself exclusively to money operations. Such a person may become a chief by acquiring much wealth.

It is clear, since the series of values is finite, that the general principle by which interest is automatically charged on loans must be accompanied by some other principle in the case of the highest values. As a matter of fact, a peculiarity enters as soon as we reach No. 18, which is not, as a rule, repaid by a coin of higher value. It occasionally happens that an individual who has started by borrowing a coin of low value contracts an alarming debt in quite a short time by bad management. He repays, let us say, the No. n which he has borrowed by a No. $(n + 1)$ which he also borrows. Asked to repay this he borrows a No. $(n + 2)$, until in quite a short time he is faced by the necessity of borrowing a No. 18. Now, Nos. 18 to 22 are regarded as property peculiar to chiefs, though continually lent by the latter to their subjects. This, of course, cannot be strictly true, as we shall see, but there is a natural tendency for these higher values to be in the hands of the older men, and principally those of high rank. The young man, who has involved himself in debt to the extent of a No. 18, approaches the owner of one of these, and, if successful in his application, is only required to return this same value after a short interval of time, instead of the value above. By continued borrowing of a No. 18 it is thus possible for an individual to avoid increasing his debt. In the meantime, the debtor is acquiring money of lower value by services, etc., and eventually finds himself in a position to request the loan of a No. 18 for a longer period of time—for, perhaps, two or three years. This is done by offering 'security', which is generally a *ndap* of higher value than the one for which it acts as security (or occasionally of lower value, if the loan be a short-period one) and by making payment of low value *ndap* which may be regarded as interest on the loan. Occasionally some other object may function as security, and that which is most usual, if not universal, for *nkö* is a stone axe of the kind used as money on Sudest, and 'ceremonially' in the 'Soi' of the Southern Massim. The amount of this 'interest' depends on the anticipated period of the loan, and for one of several years there are sometimes two or three payments at appropriate intervals. At the end of the period the No. 18 is repaid, instead of a higher value, and the 'security' is recovered.

No doubt the above case is unusual, but was definitely given me by my informant as an example, when I pressed him to follow up the consequences of an initial minor debt. The important instances of this type of loan are those contracted in order to purchase a wife or a pig. Exactly similar types of loan of other high values occur, one of the biggest loans for the longest period being that of a No. 20, when required for compensation of the relatives of a person who is eaten at the mortuary feast of a chief. It is probable that coins of lower value than No. 18 are occasionally loaned on this principle.

There is a form of loan that differs from the kinds described, but one that is probably of little importance. A series of low value coins is sometimes borrowed and repaid a few days later, by a single higher value coin; for example, I was told that No. 1 + No. 2 would become No. 4, No. 3 + No. 4 would become No. 6, Nos. 1 + 2 + 3 + 4 would become No. 8, Nos. 1 + 2 + 3 + 4 + 5 would become

No. 10, and 2 of No. 1 + 4 of No. 2 + 1 of No. 3 + 1 of
No. 4 + 1 of No. 5 + 2 of No. 6 + 1 of No. 7 + 1 of No. 8
would become No. 12.

Nos. 18 to 22 seem to be in a somewhat different position
from the lower values, and one would imagine that they are
not related to each other and the lower values in the precise
manner set out in generalised form above. My informants
did, however, state that the same principles operate with
these; that a No. 17 becomes a No. 18, a No. 18 a No. 19,
and so on—in just the same way as with the lower values.
Yet, as we have seen in the example given above, a No. 18
can be borrowed for a short time without the debt increasing.

A rather anomalous feature of these higher values is their
occasional use as security for loans of lower values. A coin
of high value *ndap*, given as security, is known as *tyindap*,
meaning *ndap* used as security, *tyi*. No. 19 is sometimes
used as security for No. 18, and No. 21 or 22 for No. 20.
It is possible that this is a recent degeneration, resulting from
the decrease in use of the higher values, consequent on the
prohibition of ritual murder by the Government. No. 18 is
the only high value in great demand at the present day, and
my chief informant made the statement on one occasion
that 'all *ndap* above No. 18 are at the present time stationary
—they remain in the baskets of important *limi*—but in olden
days all the *ndap* up to No. 21 were in movement.'

Nos. 18 to 22 are peculiar in one other respect. They have
a certain sacred character. No. 18, as it passes from person
to person, is handled with great apparent reverence, and a
crouching attitude is maintained. Nos. 19 to 22 are proportionately more sacred, are almost always kept enclosed,
and are not supposed to see the light of day, and particularly
the sun. Probably Nos. 17 and below have a sacredness and
prestige proportional to their position in the series, but I am
inclined to think that there may be a real gap, in this respect,
between Nos. 17 and 18. The coins of value No. 22 seem to
have quite lost, if they ever had, the power of circulation.
They are said to be inherited in the male line, and to be
owned by the most powerful chiefs on the island.

So far I have said little about the second variety of
money, *nkö*, which I referred to as a monetary system,
parallel to the *ndap* system. Almost all that has been said

above of the *ndap* money applies equally to the *nkö* money, with a few minor differences. There is a fiction that *nkö* is woman's property, as contrasted with *ndap* which is essentially man's property. As far as I could gather, this meant little more than that it is the duty of women to string the *nkö* on those occasions when this operation is demanded, and to count it, although there seems to be no prohibition on the performance of this operation by men. Women would also frequently keep in their own baskets their own or their husband's *nkö*, and I was told by one informant that it is the task of women to manage and find the *nkö* required at feasts, while the men have only to deal with the *ndap*. According to one tradition, the *nkö* money was made by Wonajö expressly for women, as an afterthought, the *ndap* money having been previously made for the male population only. There may be, however, in this distinction some deeper significance than I succeeded in discovering.

There are only 16 values of *nkö*, as compared with the 22 values of *ndap*. The names of these are the *ndap* names followed by the term *kagnö*. The lowest value *nkö* is called *tebuda kagnö*, *tebuda* being the name of No. 7 of the *ndap* series. The remaining 15 values of *nkö* are denoted by means of the names of the remaining 15 higher values of *ndap*; *kwojuma kagnö* is, then, the name of the highest value *nkö*, *kwojuma* being the name of the highest value *ndap*. For purposes of reference the *nkö* values will be referred to by the numbers 7 to 22, the numbers which denote the parallel— that is, similarly named—*ndap* values. Although this is a convenient terminology for our purpose, it should be pointed out that the *nkö* series is regarded as starting from the highest value and working down, in contrast to the *ndap* series. This idea is reflected in the mode of procedure on certain occasions.

The *nkö* values, as we have seen, are dependent on the size of the discs, ten of which form a coin—the larger the discs the higher the coin. The native names any coin that comes his way by making an estimate of size, and does not, as a rule, recognise the individual coin, for none of these, as far as I could discover, have individual names. This, indeed, would be unlikely, because any coin is liable to change its appearance, owing to the ritual of stringing, whereby the discs of large numbers of coins are separated on certain occasions, and re-strung to form large ropes of money several feet in length, and containing, perhaps, 50 coins or 500 discs (Pl. 22 *a*). As a result of this operation the coins, when restored, are likely to have their discs differently arranged, and may even be replaced by others of the same size. A certain carelessness in these operations is indicated by the fact that a coin which came into my possession had 11 discs. It seems unlikely, in view of this, that coins could be individually known with anything like the same ease with which the *ndap* coins could be known.

The highest values of *nkö* seem to be as mobile as the lower values of *ndap*, and do not suffer from any reverential attitude adopted towards them, or from any taboo on exposure to the light of day. Nos. 18 to 22 are, however, considered to be of very great value, though this may be less than the values of the corresponding *ndap*. The lowest values of *nkö* are probably of greater value than the equivalent *ndap*. I had much greater difficulty in acquiring a few specimens of *nkö* than equivalent specimens of *ndap*, the lowest values of which, such as No. 4, were quite easy to obtain. One coin of low value *nkö*, for which I paid over £1 in money and trade, was sold to me with much trepidation by a native, who evidently feared the wrath of the older men, and implored me not to reveal the sale. This dislike of allowing any *nkö* to leave the island is probably due to a realisation of the fact that there is a dwindling amount, which cannot be replaced. I was told on Sudest by a native of that island, that he knew of only one case of a Sudest native acquiring any of the *nkö*, and that was a generation back, though several moderately high values of *ndap* were known to exist on the island. I did not succeed in discovering the amount of *nkö* on Rossel, or of any particular values of it, by means of direct questions; but on the occasion of an important pig feast I saw a number of ropes of this money, making a total length of at least 40 feet, which would mean over 200 coins (or 2000 discs). It would, however, be quite possible, at a conjecture, for this to represent a fourth of the *nkö* money on the island, in which case the total of *nkö* coins on the island would be less than the total of *ndap*.

The operations of borrowing and lending *nkö* are, on the whole, exactly the same as the equivalent operations with *ndap.* There is, however, one difference in the case of loans of high value *nkö*, which are made by the second of the two processes that have been described for *ndap* loans. The payment of interest in such cases is not only in the form of lower value *nkö*, but also, in general, of lower value *ndap*; whereas interest on the loan by this method of high value *ndap* takes the form, in general, of low value *ndap* only.

The term *dogo* is used for interest payments of the second kind, in which coins of small value are handed over for the privilege of borrowing a high value coin. *Dogo* is picturesquely rendered in pidgin English by 'sentence'; for on the rare occasions on which Rossel has been visited by the Government it has generally been to 'sentence' some of the natives for murder, and the 'sentence' has generally been a period in gaol, this constituting 'payment' for the murder. A *dogo* is for the purpose of paying interest on a loan, which often runs for several years. The coin 'does time,' and the expression 'Työmundi (No. 18) sentence' is a common one to express this most important *dogo*. A *dogo* is generally the occasion of a distribution of food, and there may be guests and dancing. Such a feast is called a *dogo momo*.

A *dogo* may occur soon after or at the time of making of a loan. A feast of 'pig,' and to a greater extent a feast of 'long pig', leaves a train of *dogo* in its wake. Some of these may be made at the feast which is their cause, but others occur subsequently. Moreover, in the case of the longer period loans there may be more than one *dogo* implied by the one loan, though, unfortunately, no actual or hypothetical cases of repeated *dogo* were worked out. The security for a loan is generally given at the first *dogo*, whether or not the loan has already been made. One or two examples revealed that the value of the security is dependent on the period of the loan. In an example given below of a number of *dogo* on No. 18, it was stated that for a two or three months' loan the security—that is, *tyindap*—would be No. 17, for one year No. 19, for two years No. 20, for three years No. 21. The *tyindap* for the usually long-period loans of No. 19 is *tebedundwo*, and for the very long-period loans of Nos. 20 and 21 *pwegayina*. I do not know what *tebedundwo* and *pwegayina* are—perhaps they are not *ndap* in the ordinary sense, or else *ndap* which have completely dropped out from the upper end of the *ndap* series, unlike No. 22, which has nearly ceased to function as a member of the series, but is still regarded as belonging to it.

There are certain technical terms used by the natives in connection with the *dogo*, the elucidation of which will help in making clear the principles on which the payments are made. The term *döndap* is used for those *ndap* values having a certain relationship to a given *ndap*. We can therefore only talk of the '*döndap* of' a given value *ndap*. Roughly speaking, the '*döndap* of' a No. *n* are all the *ndap* values from about No. $(n - 6)$ downwards to No. 1. We can thus speak of the *döndap* of a given value *ndap* in an absolute sense, without referring to any particular loan, but I do not think the interval is strictly six values; in one example given me the interval was ten values, a fact which would accord better with the native feeling for the number 10.

When the *döndap* of a value are referred to in connection with a specific loan for a specific time, the *döndap* is a term for all the *ndap* used for the interest payment. In general, this consists of larger or smaller quantities of coins of those values that are called the *döndap* of the particular value No. *n* in a more absolute sense; but occasionally one or two coins of higher value than the usual *döndap* may be included if the 'sentence' be a long one. It is possible that there is even less rigidity in the notion of *döndap* than I have suggested. The term *dönkö* is used for lower values of *nkö* in relation to a given value of *nkö*, in just the same way as *döndap* is used in the *ndap* system.

The term *ma*, which is used in a relative sense for the value immediately below a given value, is also used more generally for all those values of *ndap* or *nkö* that lie between a given value and the *döndap* or *dönkö* of that value. In connection with the examples given below it was stated that for the three years' *dogo* on No. 18 the *ma* of No. 18 is No. 14; for the two years, No. 13; for the one year, No. 12; and that for the *dogo* on No. 20 the *ma* of No. 20 is No. 19. Evidently, the meaning of the term *ma* has not been completely elucidated. It was also stated, in the same connection, that No. 12 is the highest *döndap* for No. 18, and No. 15 for No. 21, while No. 18 is the highest *döndap* for No. 20, though elsewhere No. 15 is given as the highest *döndap* for this value. I was also told in another connection that No. 8 is now regarded as the highest *döndap* for No. 18, implying that this was a recent change of opinion. Even if we suppose that the system was once mathematically perfect, it is almost inevitable that circumstances should have arisen to cast a blemish on the system, so that these irregularities may not be irregularities of observation, but irregularities in fact.

The following examples of 'sentences' will illustrate the above points, and show the somewhat irregular working of interest. They are, however, all constructed examples, obtained by questioning one or two informants, and not observations of actual payments:

(The numbers in this list are *ndap* values, the number of coins, where there are more than one of the value represented by the adjacent number, being shown within brackets.)

Työmundi (No. 18) dogo.

For 3 weeks:
    Nos. 1, 2, 3, 4, 5, 6, 7, 8, 9, 10 ...   Total 10 *döndap*
For 1 month:
    Nos. 1, 2, 3, 4 (2), 5 (2), 6 (3), 7 (4),
        8 (3), 9 (3), 10 ...   .   Total 20 *döndap*
For 2 or 3 months:
    Nos. 1 (2), 2 (2), 3 (2 or 3), 4 (2 or
        3), 5 (3 or 4), 6 (3 or 4), 7 (5 or
        6), 8 (1), 9 (2), 10 (1) ...   ...   Total 25 *döndap* (about)
For 1 year:
    Nos. 1 (10), 2 (10), 3 (10), 4 (10),
        5 (10), 6 (9 or 10), 7 (9), 8 (3),
        10 (1) ...   .   Total 80 *döndap* (about)
For 2 years:
    Nos. 1 (10), etc.
For 3 years:
    Nos. 1 (10), ... 8 (6, 7), 9 (5, 6), 10 (5, 6), 11 (1)

Yananindo (No. 15) dogo.

Roughly thought out answers gave:

For 3 weeks	...	...	10	*döndap*
1 month	...	...	20	,,
2 months	...	...	40	,,
1 year	...	...	100	,,

Gemida (No. 20) **dogo.**

For 8 to 10 years the *döndap* would be:

Nos. 1 (40 or 50), 3 (10 or 20), ... 12 (2 or 3), 13 (1), 14 (1), 15 (1).

In a *dogo momo* witnessed at a small inland village, but not properly understood at the time, interest was paid on a *nkö* of high value, and security given. The *nkö* had been borrowed some weeks previously for the second highest *nkö* payment in the buying of a pig. A certain amount of food had been prepared for the guests, of whom the principal was the individual who had lent the *nkö*. The interest, consisting of small value *ndap* and small value *nkö*, was strung together in order of value, the highest value *nkö* at one end, the highest value *ndap* at the other end, the junction of *nkö* and *ndap* occurring, therefore, at the lowest values of each (Pl. 21 *a*). At a certain stage in the proceedings a number of individuals grouped themselves in a circle facing inwards, known as a *dong*, an essential feature of the *dogo* ritual. A good deal of discussion and handling of money took place in this circle, and apparently the final bringing together of the interest and decision as to its amount occurred here. Both outside and inside the *dong* money continually passed from person to person, and those ingenious baskets (see Chap. 11), specially designed so that money may be concealed between the walls of the basket, were in evidence. In all probability most of these movements constituted ratifications of loans connected or unconnected with the central feature of the ceremony. Whenever a debt is contracted or cancelled, whether of large or small amount, the money which changes hands is inspected and touched by any persons who happen to be available. A *dogo momo* or any other feast is a suitable occasion for such operations, and at the last feast on the island at which I was present, I must have touched several dozens of coins in this way. The touching of the coins is evidently a witnessing of the transaction. Besides the interest collected and paid at this feast, security for the loan was also provided in the shape of a 'ceremonial' stone axe of Massim type, mounted in its characteristic Massim handle (Pl. 21 *a*). The completion of these money operations was followed by a display of singing and dancing by three male dancers, dressed in grass petticoats, and provided with small dance baskets. This is the usual termination of a *dogo momo*.

The actual values *nkö* and *ndap* involved in the above interest payment were not determined, but I was afterwards told that they formed a series of only four or five values of *nkö* from No. 7, the lowest, and of, perhaps, ten *ndap* values from No. 1. I was told that it is only at *dogo momo* that *nkö* and *ndap* are strung to form one rope; and it is probable that this happens only in the case of a *dogo* for *nkö*, a *dogo* for *ndap* consisting of *döndap* only; but I cannot be certain about this. The fact that the coins belong to a series of values from the lowest up to a given point should be remembered; for this is probably always the case, and we shall see presently that this economic form is a dominant one. It would seem as if a value tends to carry with it a series of lower values.

It is clear that my information about the *dogo* operations is somewhat superficial, and that the institution is more complicated than my account suggests. There is certainly an interweaving of elements throughout this and other parts of the economic system, which would make it impossible adequately to unravel the system without months, if not years, of study.

Passing to the monetary side of pig and other feasts, which appear to belong to one economic pattern, it becomes still more difficult to extract any general principles out of the web of concrete facts observed and interpretations received. Only one feast of importance, a feast of pig, was observed, and I was bewildered by its complexity. A more or less intelligible scheme was, however, finally constructed to fit the facts, though I feel that the validity of this economic form (which is described in the next chapter) is more open to doubt than that of the general working of the monetary system already given, which is at least accurate in essentials.

CHAPTER VI

Monetary Ceremonial

THE Rossel Islander claims our sympathy for his sense of mathematical fitness, and our indulgence for his inability to play properly a pretty, intricate, and useless game, regulated by ingenious rules. The money values in the game are related in a perfectly ordered though unconventional way, but laxities in the following of the rules mar the symmetry of the system, as we have already seen. The coins of *nkö* are—appropriately enough, on a decimal system—sets of 10 discs. Any other number in the neighbourhood of this would have been ridiculous. But the *ndap* series of values need not have terminated at the number 22, when simple multiples of 10 are available, and the payment of interest on high values by means of *döndap* might, with advantage, be determined in accordance with a more systematic rule. It is, however, clear that with little distortion of the actual system and its mode of operation, it could be expressed in a comparatively simple mathematical form. The unit of interest, k, might be an exact constant, and the *döndap* or *dönkö* for interest on high values might be expressed simply as a function of the period of a loan and its value. One is tempted to frame the hypothesis that the system once had a balance and symmetry of this kind (for it approaches very closely such a hypothetical system) and that it has become distorted by accidents of the environment or shortcomings on the part of the performers. This hypothesis is strengthened by the fact that the monetary procedure on the occasion of feasts of various kinds shows further ingenuities indicative of the same kind of imagination on the part of the inventor or inventors of the system. If this original ideal regularity had not become somewhat distorted, I should not, armed as I was with a general knowledge of the nature of the monetary system, have found so much difficulty in understanding the nature of the procedure at feasts.

One fact soon emerged from a study of this procedure, namely, that the number 10 had a peculiar significance. It also became obvious that an amount of counting was done, which did not seem consistent with the view that the native could only count up to 50, as I had been told. An investigation of this latter point showed that the native had no difficulty in counting up to 10,000, or even further. The system is a decimal one, and has few of the crudities of the Massim notations, in which, although the systems are either decimal or based on 5 as a unit, 20 is denoted by 'one man' or 'one man dead', and counting beyond 20 is usually somewhat laborious. The Rossel system is as follows:

1. mö	90. (yili yalapari)
2. miö	⋮
3. pyili	100. yönö ya
4. pari	101. yönö ya ma mö ngwa
5. limi	⋮
6. wini	110. yönö ya ma ya
7. pidi	⋮
8. wale	
9. tya	120. yönö ya ma yulemiö
10. ya	⋮
11. mö ngwa	200. miö yönö ya
12. ma miö	⋮
13. ma pyili	300. pyalö yönö ya
⋮	⋮
20. ma ya, or yulemiö	400. parö yönö ya
21. yulemiö ngwa	⋮
22. yulemiö miö	500. limö yönö ya
23. yulemiö pyili	
⋮	600. wönö yönö ya
30. yulemiö ya, or yipyili	⋮
31. yipyili mö ngwa	700. pidö yönö ya
32. yipyili ma miö	⋮
33. yipyili ma pyili	
⋮	800. walö yönö ya
40. yipyili ma ya, or yalapari	⋮
⋮	900. toa yönö ya
50. yalapari ma ya, or yili	⋮
⋮	1,000. yönö yönö ya
60. (yili ya)	⋮
⋮	2,000. miö yönö yönö ya
70. (yili yulemiö)	⋮
⋮	10,000. yönö yönö yönö ya, or mai yönö yönö yönö ya
80. (yili yipyili)	
⋮	

The thousands may also be counted as follows:

1,000.	yili	6,000.	mwadwong
2,000.	dwong	7,000.	mwateme
3,000.	teme	8,000.	mwadab
4,000.	dab	9,000.	mwadi
5,000.	mwayili	10,000.	mwadi mwadab

In the above system the terms for 60, 70, 80, and 90 are rather a blemish on a notation which is otherwise systematically decimal. In actual counting the fifties are taken separately; that is, having reached 50 the word *yili* is said with emphasis, and counting commences again from 1, not from 51. Having reached 50 again, the two fifties are put together to make 100 *yönö ya*. The term *yili* is an end-term, which can be used for other numbers that may be subsequently added. It is the word ordinarily used for many, and it occurs again as the first of the set of terms for the thousands. Possibly, the tens from 20 to 100 could also be expressed by the terms *miö ya*, *pyalö ya*, etc., since 100 is expressed by *yönö ya*, and *yönö* belongs to the series of terms *miö*, *pyalö*, ...*yönö*. Evidently the terms *miö*, *pyalö*, ...*yönö* have the meaning 'twice,' 'three times'...'ten times' in the above notation, and therefore counting beyond 10,000 presents no real difficulty. Although the series *yili*, *dwong*, ...*mwadi mwadab* is given for the thousands, it was said that it might also be used for the hundreds or the tens of thousands.

A curious feature of this last series of terms, the combination of the terms for 8000 and 9000 to express 10,000, is explained in the legend, which attributes the invention of counting to Wonajö, who wished to count the *nkö* that he had made. Having counted up to 9000 he grew weary, and, unable to think of a fresh word for 10,000 adopted the novel, if unmathematical, device of using in juxtaposition the words for the last two thousands.

The frequent ceremonial of stringing *nkö* together, so as to make long ropes of money, in which the boundaries between the coins disappear, is the reason for the Rossel Islander's proficiency in counting, for counting up to thousands would hardly be required in any other department of life. There are said to be two customary ways of counting the *nkö* on these long ropes; one is in tens, the more difficult but quicker method; the other in pairs.

The series of terms *wö* (1), *miömo* (*miö*) (2), *pyalö* (3), *parö* (*padö*) (4), *limö* (5), *wönö* (6), *pi* (*pidö*) (7), *walö* (8), *toa* (9), *yönö* (10), which, excepting *wö*, appear above as multiplicatives, twice, thrice, four times, etc., are used in pig and man feasts to denote the *ndap* values connected with different parts of the pig or man, and indirectly to denote the pig parts and the *nkö* values which are also associated with them. The meaning of the terms, as used in these cases, would be rendered best by first, second, etc., or No. 1, No. 2, etc.

This division into ten always occurs, and there is a *ndap* value corresponding to each of the ten numbers, and these values form a series of adjacent values from No. *n* corresponding to *wö*, up to the value corresponding to *yönö*, which is therefore No. (*n* + 10). *n*, however, varies according to circumstances, and is, of course, higher for a man feast than for a pig feast. Normally the *ndap* corresponding to *yönö* is a No. 18 for a pig feast, and a No. 20 for a man feast, and therefore the *ndap* corresponding to *wö* are No. 9 and No. 11 respectively.

Corresponding to these ten numbers, which seem to have a special reference to *ndap*, are four terms for *nkö*—*kago*, *mobwo*, *knabwo* and *kagno*—meaning, apparently, the lowest *nkö*, the middle *nkö*, the highest *nkö* but one, and the highest *nkö*, respectively. This series corresponds to that running from *pyalö* (3) to *yönö* (10), so that the 'correspondences' for *padö* to *walö* (Nos. 4 to 8) are *mobwo* in each case. These terms indicate a series of adjacent *nkö* values which are generally of higher numbers (using my number terminology) than the corresponding *ndap* values, but which depend for their range (e.g. the number of the value of any given position) on the particular feast. Sometimes the five *mobwo* are differentiated further, the highest being called *kwagno ibo* and the lowest two *murobwa*.

An example of these 'correspondences' (what the correspondences mean will be discussed later) at a pig feast is tabulated below.

The *nkö* series in this example does not fit into the preceding statement very well. This may be because my informants became muddled in their attempts to explain the system, or because my simplifying hypothesis is wrong. But apart from this uncertainty about the *nkö*, there is no doubt

			1. *Wö*	No. 9	*Ndap*
			2. *Miamö*	No. 10	,,
No. 7 *Nkö*		*Kago*	3. *Pyalö*	No. 11	,,
No. 8, or 9, or 10, or 11?		*Mobwo*	4. *Padö*	No. 12	,,
No. 11, or 12, or 13, or 14?		*Mobwo*	5. *Limö*	No. 13	,,
No. 14, or 15, or 16, or 17?		*Mobwo*	6. *Wönö*	No. 14	,,
No. 18		*Mobwo*	7. *Pi*	No. 15	,,
No. 19		*Mobwo*	8. *Walö*	No. 16	,,
No. 20		*Knabwo*	9. *Toa*	No. 17	,,
No. 21		*Kagno*	10. *Yönö*	No. 18	*Työmundi*

that if we substitute in the above diagram n $(n + 1)...(n + 10)$ for the *ndap* series, and $m ... m + x$, where x is possibly 8, for the *nkö* series, we have a 'form', which applies to most feasts, in which an object, a pig or a man, a house or a canoe, is paid for. It certainly applies to feasts of man, pig, and even dog, opossum, and dugong, though the *nkö* side tends to vanish in these latter cases, and n becomes very small; and it is not essentially different if a feast be the occasion of the buying of a canoe; for we find the same series *yönö* to *wö*, which may be regarded as indicating parts of the canoe, and the series of corresponding *ndap* and *nkö*.

The next stage of the enquiry gives much more indefinite results, if due attention is given to the observed facts and the information provided by the natives. The scheme given below must therefore be received with caution, for there may be serious errors.

A feast (let us say of pig) results from a man A agreeing to buy from B a pig fattened for the occasion. The feast takes place in the village of B, where the pig is killed and cut up in a ritual way, so that it is divided into ten portions, which form a series, the first member of which is the most valuable, the last member the least. These portions may be referred to by the ten terms *wö, miamö, ...yönö*, the term *yönö* referring to the most valuable and important portion.

Each of these portions is paid for by one *ndap*, and the better portions are paid for in addition by means of a number of *nkö*. The *ndap* values for the ten portions belong to a series of adjacent values, and so, more or less, do the *nkö* values, but each *nkö* carries with it the series, more or less complete, of lower *nkö* values. The *yönö* portion of pig is thus paid for by one high value *ndap*, generally No. 18, and a rope of *nkö*, at one end of which is a high value *nkö*, which

PLATE XI

(*a*) Pearl-shell knives and scrapers.

(*b*) *Conus* armshell.

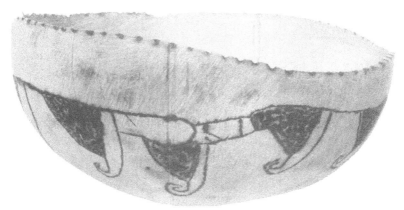

(*c*) Coconut cup.

PLATE XII

(*a*) Adze blades.

(*b*) Rain-stone and Pestle.

may even be a No. 21, and at the other end of which is a low value, possibly No. 7, the lowest, the intermediate coins on the rope forming a series. The less valuable portions are paid for by the appropriate *ndap*, and ropes of *nkö* of smaller length, and headed by a *nkö* of less value. The least valuable portions are paid for by means of *ndap* only. The terms *kagno*, *mobwo*, etc., apply to the ropes of *nkö*, the terms *yönö*, *toa*, etc., either to the pig portion or the 'corresponding' *ndap*, and even to the *nkö* as well.

A, who buys the pig, does not, however, find all this money, nor does *B*, who sells the pig, receive it all. *A* does find the *yönö ndap*, however, and it is by virtue of this fact that he is regarded as the buyer of the pig; he also finds the *kagno*, and probably some of the other *nkö* and *ndap*. Owing to this fact the *yönö* portion of pig is *A*'s in a special sense, and this portion he distributes to his relatives and friends. These persons are those who have helped *A* in acquiring *ndap* and *nkö*, and they find those lower values of the *kagno* rope which is paid to *B*. Other persons who are probably related to *A* in certain ways provide the other *ndap* and *nkö*, and receive the other portions, *A* being responsible for the arrangements necessary for this, and the medium through whom the transaction is conducted. The principal actors, *A* and those who provide the remaining higher *ndap* and *nkö*, do not consume any of the corresponding portion, but only attend to its distribution and the money operations. They can, however, eat of those portions for which they have not provided the principal *ndap*.

B, who receives these payments, has a complicated distribution of this money to make, which is according to definite rules. The highest values are his own, but the greater part of the money goes to definite relations, and to persons who have fed the pig, and so on. *A* and his close relations and others who have been closely concerned with the pig, are not allowed to eat any of it; these individuals, in fact, conduct a sort of mourning for the pig.

The above might be regarded as nothing more than a method by which a number of persons collectively buy a pig for purposes of consumption from a collective owner of that pig. It is, however, rather difficult to suppose that numbers of valuable *ndap* and fathoms of closely strung *nkö* are, in

any real sense, the price of a pig, especially when we remember that some of the *ndap* and *nkö* that enter into this
price imply loans for long periods, and payment of interest
on these loans at several *dogo momo*. It is, I think, clear that
the pig should be regarded rather as a pivot for the ceremonial.
There are, for instance, complex social factors determining
who shall have a pig to sell, and who shall be in a position
to buy, and the buying and selling is not a simple economic
occurrence, but a much more significant and complex social
occurrence. We must suppose a complexity of social facts,
which I am not in a position to define, that determine most
of the general relations of a particular pig feast. The feast,
as an actual occurrence, particularises these general relations.
Of the limited number of possible occurrences there are
certain actual happenings; that is, a particular individual
provides a particular *ndap*, and so on. A certain readjustment
of social relations thus results from the holding of the feast.
A social event, such as an important feast, serves to stamp
in or underline these changing relations between members
of the group, which culminate in the relations in which they
find themselves at the feast. A feast is thus an element of
discontinuity, or rather of emphasis, in the general chain of
social causation; the gradually adjusting relations between
persons become definitely adjusted as a consequence of the
feast, which thus becomes a new point of departure for
further adjustments. Now, A, who buys a pig from B at
an exorbitant price, if we like to put it so, acquires a new
orientation in the group. This new relationship to the rest
of the group, an increase of prestige amongst other things,
is crystallised by the ceremonial of the feast. This is also the
case, in varying degrees, with all the other participants in
the ceremonial. As a chemical mixture exposed to heat for
a moment will culminate in certain changes, which are fixed
by subsequent cooling, so the group, with its slowly changing
internal relations, is stimulated for a moment and photo-
graphed; the photograph persists for a while and the group
moves under its influence, but it slowly fades, and the next
photograph is different.

With greater knowledge of the sociology of Rossel, these
generalities could be particularised. The main threads which
lead up to the fact of A arranging to buy a pig from B would

be known. That some person, *C*, in a certain relationship to *A* provides the *ndap* for the *toa* would not be an isolated fact; it would be understood as a consequence of that relationship, or alternatively as a consequence of some other fact in no way connected with the relationship. Very little can be said on these points, though a little may be gathered from the later chapters, which will throw some light on the sociological meaning of the above monetary ceremonial, which is unintelligible if we imagine it to be primarily an economic operation.

Though we abandon the view that the monetary operations at a feast of this nature are to be regarded merely as a collective buying from a collective seller, it still remains that this is a useful way of describing these operations. But by 'collection' in this connection must be understood an ordered group (or 'grouping' to use the terminology of Chap. III), and not a mere class.

Now, in the collective buying of the pig we have a number of persons whom we can arrange in a series, according to the degree of their participation in this operation of buying; it is only a few of these who participate at all strongly, while a large number participate weakly. Exactly the same applies to the collective selling, though here it is probable that the series is less gradual, and presumably the extent to which the pig is collectively sold is the extent to which the pig was collectively owned. The fact that the pig clearly is collectively sold shows how difficult it is to apply the simpler concepts of ownership in such cases, or at least the danger of reading into the term the associations that it has in other connections. For most purposes we can talk of individual ownership on Rossel, and the native appears to refer quite definitely to the individual owner of a pig. But since we cannot postulate such a legal sense of ownership as can simply be applied in a civilised country, we must mean something else in the case of primitive peoples. If we find, as above, that a person receives money for a pig which he owned, but that the greater part of that money passes more or less automatically to other persons, then the sense in which the pig was individually owned is surely quite an unusual and possibly uninteresting one, and it would be more in accordance with ordinary usage to regard the so-called owner of the pig as no more than the first member of a series of persons who own the pig in a degree dependent on their position in the series.

Unfortunately, I do not know whether the ordering of these series—on the one hand the series of buyers, on the other hand the series of sellers—is determined primarily by relationship. There is no doubt that relationship is an important element, but I cannot say more than that. It is of some importance to note that in the case of a man feast, for which the scheme is practically the same, the money values only being increased, the dependence of this order on relationship is more definite. This is certainly the case with the sellers, or rather those who receive compensation for the relative who has been eaten. I was told that the *yönö ndap* goes to the close mother's brother of the eaten boy, *toa* to the father, *walö* to certain of the father's clan, *pi* to certain of the own clan, *wönö* to the father's brother, *limö* to more distant sister's children, *padö, pyalö, miamö*, and *wö* to the own mother. This is not very well confirmed, though the positions of mother's brother and father in the series are probably correct.

Even if the dependence of these series on relationship and other factors were established, there would still remain to be investigated the factors determining who are to be buyers and sellers; and it is very probable, from the few facts collected on this point, that this also is partly dependent on the relationship between buyer and seller, at least in the non-cannibal feasts.

Some further information as to the concrete working of the monetary system at specific feasts and on other specific occasions will be given in the later chapters dealing with these institutions.

CHAPTER VII

Feasts

THE operations of buying and selling may be divided into two classes—those which are direct and involve only the persons concerned in the transaction; and those which involve groups of persons, are conducted according to certain forms, and are accompanied by a certain ceremonial. Practically every feast on Rossel, unless it is an isolated *dogo momo*, is a transaction of the latter kind; that is, the feast is the total ceremonial accompanying the monetary operation. Certain feasts are, however, in a special class, because the object bought in this way is also consumed, e.g. pig and man feasts. The latter are, therefore, pre-eminently feasts; but there is little doubt that the ceremonial accompanying other sufficiently important changes of ownership of commodities is of the same general type, and gives to these occasions, even though there be less or no consumption of meat, a similar social significance. A consideration of the commodities which the Rossel Islander buys and sells will give us, therefore, an indication of the more important feasts. A few words may be said in the first place as to payments which are not of an order to make a feast.

Apparently, in these minor transactions, *ndap* is the usual medium of exchange, though occasionally *nkö* may be substituted; but my data are very scanty. Objects, such as a basket, a lime stick, or a lime pot, cost only a small *ndap*, usually a No. 4, which, as we have already seen, is by far the commonest *ndap* on the island. A European knife or tomahawk costs a No. 11, a saucepan costs a No. 12; but for a No. 12 *ndap* in this case a No. 8 *nkö* could be substituted, showing, as I have already pointed out, that the lower values of *nkö* are really of higher value than the *ndap* similarly named. Sometimes payment is by series of *ndap* and *nkö*. I was told that the service of working ten days in the garden might be paid for by the *ndap* series, 1 of No. 1, 2 of No. 2, 2 of No. 3, 2 of No. 4, 1 of No. 5, 1 of No. 6, and 1 of No. 7, while the same informant suggested that the wages for one month would be a No. 11, for two months a No. 12, and for three months a No. 13. But another informant told me that for these longer periods there would also be a payment of *nkö*—for instance, a short rope, consisting of a coin of each value from No. 7 to No. 12. If no *nkö* were paid, a higher *ndap*—e.g. No. 14 or even No. 15— would be required. Fish, as well as other food, is frequently sold, and there are certain big fish, according to one account, which will fetch a No. 11 *ndap* even from an own brother. Among the smaller payments, those made to *ptyilibi* (see Chap. VIII) for their sexual services form an important class. Where payment for commodities or services is by a series of *ndap* and *nkö* we seem to be on the borderline of transactions carried out according to the form outlined in the previous chapter, where a number of persons is involved and the procedure tends to carry with it the ceremonial of a feast. For instance, a small canoe costs a series of *ndap* from No. 13 to No. 4, with some of the lower values duplicated, and in addition a series of *nkö* from No. 12 to No. 7. But I do not know whether the terms *yönö*, *toa*, etc., would apply to these *ndap* (and *nkö* and parts of the canoe), and whether there is usually a number of persons involved—on the one hand those who combined to make the canoe, and on the other those who (beginning with the one whom we may call the owner) possess in diminishing degree various rights in the use of the canoe. It is possible that this is so, and that the transaction may carry with it something of the ceremonial that would entitle us to bring the transaction under the heading 'feast'. When, however, we come to the more valuable canoes, such as sailing canoes and *ndap* canoes, there is no doubt that the form applies, and that we can call the transaction a 'feast'. I was told definitely that the occasion was one of importance, that numbers of persons collected to take part in or view the proceedings, that the terms *yönö*, *toa*, etc., for the *ndap* and *nkö* were used, and that ropes of *nkö* were made—all in much the same way as at a feast of pig or man: but I did not follow up the enquiry, and therefore cannot state, but only suspect, that these terms *yönö*, *toa*, etc., apply to parts of the canoe, and that there results from the transaction a form of collective ownership, such as I have suggested in the preceding chapter. I cannot, unfortunately, justify the suggestion, and it may be that the buying of a valuable canoe is a comparatively simple economic transaction, which, however, bows to a certain ritual form that dominates such operations, whether they do, or do not, possess the more complex sociological character that is associated, for example, with a pig feast.

The purchasing of the more valuable canoes, of good houses, of village land, of gardens, of big fish nets, of pigs, dogs and men (when bought for eating), are the chief occasions for feasts; for these are the only expensive objects on the island, excepting such recent introductions as cases of tobacco. (These, however, have come to be fitted into the usual scheme, so that a distribution of tobacco is very much like a distribution of pig.) There are two other expensive items which do not appear in the above list—namely the wife, and also the scarcely less expensive *ptyilibi*, or communal wife (Chap. VIII). I cannot say with certainty that a wife is not purchased according to the above form, but from the accounts I received the purchase appears to be of a different type. This might have been expected, when we consider that marriage is one of the few definitely individual affairs, in which there can be no collective buying, even though there be a collective selling. To a less degree the same consideration applies to the buying of a *ptyilibi*, for only three or four men combine in this transaction, as far as I could make out. The ceremonial of marriage, with its associated money operations, and that of buying a *ptyilibi*, will be described, as far as can be, in Chap. VIII. It suffices to point out here that the money operations and the associated feast are probably of a different form from that which we are here considering.

Since the man feasts, which are always mortuary feasts, are considered in a separate chapter (Chap. IX) only the pig feast will be considered here in any detail. But before the description already partially given in the previous chapter is expanded, the relationship, as regards value of payments, to the other feasts of the same type may be briefly mentioned.

I was given the following for the highest value *ndap* in the most important cases (the lower nine *ndap* values and the *nkö* values being thus given by implication):

Village ground ...	...	...	No. 21
Big house	...	...	No. 20
Coconut garden	...	...	,,
Taro garden	...	...	,,
Sago garden	...	...	,,
Sailing canoe	...	...	,,
Ndap canoe	...	...	,,
Man for feast	...	...	,,
Pig for feast	...	...	No. 18
Canoe (intermediate)	...	...	,,
Case of tobacco ...	...	...	,,

There was some variation in the statements of different informants; for instance, I was told by one informant that a No. 18 is the highest *ndap* in the payment for either a sailing canoe or a *ndap* canoe, and No. 19 was given me by others as the price of a big garden.

A pig feast is known as *bwame bwobe* (*bwame* = pig, *bwobe* = buy). It results from a sort of challenge, which reminds one of the competitive aspect of the Massim *soi*, and suggests that there is something in common between the two institutions. It differs from the *soi*, however, in that it is rare for there to be many pigs concerned in a *bwame bwobe*; though the single pig normally involved is generally one of considerable value, which has been fattened up with great care. The challenge starts by one man, *A*, making insulting remarks about the pig of another man, *B*; whereupon *B* retorts by suggesting that *A* buy the pig and make a feast; and *A* probably accepts and states his willingness to pay.[1] My informant emphasised these points, but I do not understand them. The same informant referred to this transaction between *A* and *B* as being connected with the death of *B*'s father. In the pig feast observed, the buyer of the pig was the *binda* of the father of the seller of the pig, and, therefore, probably a cross-cousin of the seller. During this feast, *B*, the seller of the pig, made a payment of tomahawk stones and lengths of sapi-sapi to *A*, the buyer of the pig, a procedure apparently connected with the fact that *B*'s

[1] There seemed to be a tendency for these transactions to be reciprocated. If *A* buys a pig from *B*, *B* will buy a pig from *A* at some other time, or at least will be a chief buyer from *A* (or from some other person closely connected with *A* as regards ownership of the pig).

father had died. It seems probable that this is an adjustment of the claims on property left at death, as between the dead man's son and his sister's son; and the *bwame bwobe* may be directly connected with this. It is not, however, in any sense a mortuary feast, for I was told that this *bwame bwobe* could just as well have been made before the death of *B*'s father. I also gathered at this same feast that the payment by *B* to his father's *binda*, together with the general pig ceremonial, secured his succession to his father's rank. *B*'s elder own brother might have performed the task, but he apparently gave way to his younger and more energetic brother. Although the whole question is very obscure, I suspect that the *bwame bwobe* tends to be a transaction between cross-cousins; that it is connected with the intimate relationship between a man and his son on the one hand, and his sister's son on the other hand; that it regulates in a sense the succession of rank, either after death or in anticipation (for only one man may succeed); and that it also in some way adjusts the relations between cross-cousins, who both have claims to the property of one man, who is the father in the one case and the maternal uncle in the other.

One other clue to the meaning of the pig feast was obtained, but, unfortunately, not followed up. A young man, of the village of the pig, has one of his names given to the pig, the pig thus becoming his *binda*; when the pig is killed he receives about half a fathom of sapi-sapi from the seller, because the pig is the young man's *binda*.

The *ndap* and *nkö* payments, in the pig feast as at other feasts, are made at different times—the *ndap* at the commencement of the ceremonial before the pig is killed, the *nkö* after or during the main distribution of pig. Apparently the *ndap* are placed in a row when all have been collected, and the principal actors discuss the arrangements for the distribution of pig which is to take place on the same or the next day; the *ndap* are then strung together and given to the seller of the pig, who redistributes them, keeping some, but paying out the greater part to relatives, and to persons who have helped in the preparation of the feast, the rearing of the pig, and so on.

The pig, which has been the object of much attention and admiration, is then despatched by a curious method. It is seized and turned on its back by about eight natives; one or two of these grasp the mouth and nostrils in order to close the air-passages as far as possible, while others place a pole, on which they stand, across the wind-pipe. The pig is very quickly suffocated by this method, which proves very efficient when, as is usually the case, the pig is over-fattened (Pl. xxiv). The women of the village who have reared the pig sing a dirge, with tears in their eyes, while this is going on, and the persons who kill the pig are usually of a different village. The pig is singed and then cut up by one of the expert pig cutters, who is paid in *ndap* for the task. The segments of pig corresponding to the sequence *yönö* to *wö*, as far as I could determine, are as follows:

Middle of back	... ...	*yönö*
Head	... ...	*toa*
Region of chest	... ...	*walö*
Rump	... ...	*pi*
Front leg	... ...	*wönö*
Front leg	... ...	*limö*
Hind leg	... ...	*padö*
Hind leg	... ...	*pyalö*
Lower shoulder	... ...	*miamö*
Lower shoulder	... ...	*wö*

These portions are cut up into smaller portions and cooked in hot stones, piles of which have been prepared. Steaming is sometimes used now, as saucepans have become fairly common. A certain amount of the pig is taken away by visitors to their own villages, but the greater part seems to be eaten in the village of the feast a few hours after the pig has been killed. It should be noted that the seller of the pig and those connected with him, including probably most of the members of the village, do not eat any of the pig, and the same applies to the buyer and possibly a few others.

Early in the proceedings, before the final stringing of *nkö*, there is dancing, which is a necessary accompaniment of any feast. At the feast witnessed, the dancers, all of whom were men, began to prepare themselves by donning new grass skirts, such as are worn by women but with a flounce, and ornaments, such as Massim *bagi* and arm-shells of Rossel pattern. Leaves of croton, and dried crinkled strips of pandanus were tucked about the body, and, most essential of all, small baskets with long pendant strips of shredded coconut were tied to the shoulders or held in the hands. A band of dried pandanus leaf encircled the heads of some of the dancers, and one or two head ornaments of cockatoo or bird-of-paradise feathers were observed. The bodies were smeared with coconut oil. In the middle of the dancing-ground was stuck a pole, with a ripe coconut at the top, and the dancers arranged themselves about this an hour or two before sunset, when they began to work themselves up into the dancing humour, which always takes several hours in New Guinea. This dance pole, known as *ptyilöwe yi*, is merely a mark put by the seller of the pig. The coconut may be removed and eaten by anyone; there is much laughter when it is removed, and apparently the dancers have to be worked up before anyone has sufficient courage to make himself conspicuous by taking it. There is a similar ceremony at a Massim *soi*: a betel nut is put on a big pig at a certain stage in the proceedings, when there is a crowd collected about the pigs; and this betel nut may be taken by anyone.

The dances were of the class known as *ptyilöwe*, and continued during the whole night until about sunrise, women being excluded from the immediate neighbourhood of the dance, where the majority of the men congregate. This rule probably only applied with rigidity to the *ptyilibi*. I was told that only young married women who had not yet borne children were allowed on the outskirts of the assembly, all others being excluded. The presence of *ptyilibi*, or persons desiring *ptyilibi*, was supposed to be very harmful to the dancers.

The dancers are paid for their services in food; but if any songs belonging to other districts are used a payment of money for the use of the songs has generally to be made.

The dance terminates in a curious way at sunrise by means of songs for the removal of the petticoats. This is done by the men in turns, the men taking off their petticoats on the dancing-ground and then retiring. There is a similar procedure for removal of *bagi*, feather headdresses, and baskets, if these articles are returned to their owners. By the time the last dancer is singing his solitary exit song the dancing-ground is practically deserted, and the dance thus comes to an end by a process of 'cooling off', just as it commenced by a process of 'warming up'.

The feast comes to an end with the stringing of *nkö* into ropes, and the re-distribution of this money to the relatives and others connected with the seller of the pig.

The principal *nkö*, corresponding to any given one of the series of ten parts, seemed generally, but not always, to be provided by the same person as the one who provided the *ndap*, and also to be received eventually by the same person as the one who received the *ndap*. The information as to actual persons providing and receiving money at the feast witnessed was meagre; but I found that *B*, the provider of the pig, received the *yönö* (tenth), and also the *walö* (eighth), though the intermediate *toa* (ninth) passed on to someone else; *pi* (seventh) went to *B*'s mother; *wönö* (sixth) went to *B*'s father's brother's son's son, that is, one in the relation *gea* (a brother's son in the classificatory sense); *limö* (fifth) went to *B*'s only elder brother; *padö* (fourth) to others who had helped to rear the pig; *pyalö* (third) to *B*; *miamö* (second) went to a remote sister's son of *B*; and *wö* (first) to *B*. It is possible that some of these persons received only *ndap* or only *nkö*, and that, therefore, the list is very incomplete. As regards those who paid for the pig, the buyer, or principal buyer, *A*, was the *binda* of *B*'s father, and therefore probably a cross-cousin, the *mejö* (father's sister's son) of *B*; but the second most important buyer, providing the *ndap*, and probably the principal *nkö*, for the *toa* (ninth) was a classificatory brother of *B*, of different totem (father's mother's sister's son's son). The own sister's son (*jina*) of this brother of *B* was probably the person who received the *toa* from *B*, which thus reciprocated the previous payment at an earlier feast of this nephew to his uncle for the *toa* portion of a pig. Little was discovered about the relationships of the other contributors of money at this feast, beyond the fact that some were not closely related to *A*.

The four operations described above, which are essential constituents of the feast, namely, *ndap* payments, dancing, pig distribution, and *nkö* payments, and sometimes one or more *dogo momo*, take generally two or three days for their completion; though there may have been weeks of preparation before the holding of the feast, and weeks of adjustment afterwards, in which money payments are completed and *dogo momo* are held.

CHAPTER VIII

Marriage

THE main elements of the ritual of marriage are the payments of *ndap* and *nkö*, associated with a feast, and very similar in form to other feasts such as we have already considered. The grouping of money into tens, which we have seen to be an important characteristic of feasts, is even carried one stage further, for the groups of tens are themselves grouped into tens; it is, however, quite possible that this further grouping occurs in connection with other feasts. It should be pointed out that none of the marriage ritual was witnessed, though several informants were questioned.

A proposal of marriage is made by the man, who sends another person to the girl of his choice, and she, if she be willing, makes him a present of betel nut. As regards the initiative this rule is probably not universal; for women also undoubtedly make the chief advances in many of their love affairs. I was told that if a man already has one wife, it is usual for a woman who wishes to marry him to take the first step. It is not considered essential for a man to obtain the consent of the girl he wishes to marry; he may arrange matters with the girl's father and other relatives; and since it is etiquette for the bride to display considerable unwillingness in public, whatever her real feelings, a really unwilling bride may be taken without much disturbance of public decency.[1]

The consent of the girl having, when possible, been obtained, the man procures a No. 18 *ndap*, which he brings to her father. This is usually paid to the father at a feast for the buying of a house or canoe, held in the girl's village. The No. 18 *ndap* is not paid directly to the father, but through an intermediary, such as the girl's father's *jina*, who puts the coin in his basket. A direct transaction would be considered 'bad form'. The girl is then, or later, led by her father's

---

[1] Bell states that a girl is purchased from her father, who does not inform her until afterwards, when she cries and runs into the bush for a while (App. I, p. 225).

jina (i.e. *mejö*) to the man who is buying her, while he, the buyer, is led by his mother's brother or some other relation. The two are placed back to back, the girl crying and using abusive language. Arrangements are then made for the *ndapatingo* feast, which is generally held two or three days later.

The principal element of the *ndapatingo* is the payment of *ndap* and *nkö*, made to the girl's relations. Several lines—generally ten, but sometimes less—of 10 *ndap* and 10 *nkö* are laid on the ground, and apparently each line starts from the lower value *ndap*, though this is unconfirmed. Each of the 10 *ndap* and *nkö* are referred to by the terms *yönö*, *toa*, etc., with which we are already familiar in connection with other feasts.

The arrangement of the money is as follows:

wö	*Dwondwo*	• |	*Tebudakagnö*	• |
miamö	*Gamö*	• |	*Tebudongwokagnö*	• |
etc.	etc.	• |	etc.	• |
.	.	• |	.	• |
.	.	• |	.	• | 10 of these or less
.	.	• |	.	• |
.	.	• |	.	• |
.	.	• |	.	• |
yönö	*Tebuda*	• |	about *Tangwolondokagnö*	• |

Half of these rows of money go to the girl's father, and to members of her clan, and half to the girl's mother's brother and to members of his clan. I do not know whether the money in each of these lines is strung together to form a set of ten coins; but that is probably what happens.

At about this time the man takes his wife to his own village, though he may reside for a time in his wife's village. Although by no means definitely patrilocal, matrilocal marriage appears to be rarer than amongst the Massim, although children frequently return to the village of the mother on the death of the father. After cohabitation, there is an exchange of lime pots and lime sticks between husband and wife, and a betel nut is shared; after which 'the girl is no longer ashamed'. This ceremony should therefore be regarded as an essential part of the marriage ritual.

The *ndapatingo* feast does not exhaust the marriage payments which have to be made by the husband. An important feast is held some three or four months after marriage, known as *ngue*. The most important element of this feast is the preparation of a rope of *nkö*, which is given to the wife's mother. The man first obtains a valuable *nkö*, known as *gwenakagnö*, from a chief; or rather he arranges that this chief shall bring this coin to the feast, while he arranges with his own sisters that they shall bring *nkö*. His own sisters will bring the higher values and more distant sisters the lower values. These *nkö* are known by the terms *kagno*, *knabwo*, *mobwo*, etc., the terms used for a *nkö* series in a pig feast. All these *nkö* are strung together to form a long rope, which is given to the wife's mother. It is interesting to note that this money is collected mainly from women and given to a woman, which seems to bear out the native theory that *nkö* is essentially women's money.

After the *nkö* has been disposed of, two or three of the husband's brothers, or other close relations, seat themselves by the husband, while facing them are seated relatives of the wife (relatives of her father on the one hand and relatives of her mother on the other). These are claimants for payment for the marriage, who received no pay at the earlier *ndapatingo*. One man will step forward with a low value *ndap* in his hand and place it on the ground, explaining that he had received no pay at the earlier feast. One of the husband's friends or relatives will then place *ndap*, generally two, of higher value on this one, all these being then removed by the claimant. These *ndap* generally form a series, so that a No. 3 *ndap* will have No. 4 and No. 5 placed on top of it. As soon as these adjustments have been made the purchase of the wife is complete, though there may still be a number of *dogo momo* to be arranged for the payment of interest on the two or three big debts that have been contracted. Earlier travellers to Rossel have reported that it is common for a man to be punished by the killing of the woman who cooks his food (see Chap. IX, p. 108). I could not discover any actual instances of this, but my informant agreed as to its possibility; which shows how complete must be the ownership of the woman if this could be done without necessitating revenge by the girl's clansmen or her father's clansmen or at least a demand for compensation. It should be noted that there are no payments or presents made by relatives of the wife to relatives of the husband, so that the No. 18 *ndap* and the money paid at the two marriage feasts can be regarded as the bride price. It must be remembered, however, that this price is not fixed by the simple operation of economic laws, and is even less an economic price than the price of a pig consumed at a pig feast. It is of interest to contrast this system of marriage by purchase with that of the neighbouring Massim, amongst whom it is difficult to find any bride price; though in place of it there are mutual obligations between a man's relatives and his wife's relatives, which extend over an indefinite number of years. Although the balance of payments in the latter case is undoubtedly in favour of the wife's relatives, it is practically impossible to find any sum which we can regard as a bride price. The purchase of a wife, as one would expect, is more definitely an individual affair than any other economic transaction, yet we find on Rossel that it is very similar in form to other purchases, and it is possible that a good deal of the money provided by the man's relatives is not to be regarded as a loan to the man to enable him to buy himself a wife. This does not, however, mean that a man's brothers or nephews or other relatives have any sexual rights over his wife. On the contrary, there is a very strong avoidance of her in the case of these individuals. This very avoidance, however, suggests an earlier condition, in which sexual relations were possible, as Rivers has demonstrated in other cases. Collective purchase, which would be natural enough in this hypothetical state of affairs, may well have survived the change to individualism in the marriage institution. That there should be a collective seller, who is a series of persons, we should have expected, since all relationship is a question of degree. It would have been interesting to determine how distant the relationship may be to entitle a person to some payment, however small, on the marriage of his or her female relative. But these details, as well as others of even greater importance, could only have been gathered with any confidence if a *ndapatingo* or *ngue* had been actually observed, for this would have given a number of concrete threads to work upon.

If a man cannot afford a wife, or if he cannot afford more

PLATE XIII

(*a*) Ground-house, *chabaju gmomo*.

(*b*) Ground-house, *chabaju gmomo*.

PLATE XIV

(*a*) Ground-house, *yebewede gmomo*.

(*b*) Pile-dwelling, *gele gmomo*.

than one wife[1], he may combine with others to purchase a woman for their collective use. The tie in this case, unlike the marriage tie, is principally a sexual one, and the institution has not that open social recognition which characterises the institution of marriage. Still, it is clearly an institution, a definite part of the social organisation, allowing persons in certain recognised situations to contract such an alliance just as persons in other situations will contract marriage. We may even regard it as an auxiliary form of marriage; in which case we might add Rossel Island to that small list of peoples who practise polyandry. If, however, we regard marriage as primarily an institution for determining the status of children born into a society (Rivers, *Social Organization*, p. 37), the Rossel institution falls outside the definition, for it is considered most unusual for children to result from these alliances.

A woman who forms an alliance in this way with a number of men is known as a *ptyilibi*. There are usually four or five male members of such an alliance, some of whom may be married.[2] Apparently a girl enters on a career of this type by becoming the subject of gossip. She is seduced by some man at a feast, and friends of his subsequently hear of this round the fire, and suggest joining in with him and purchasing the girl collectively. The procedure of purchase appears to be very similar to that for an ordinary marriage, a No. 18 *ndap* being first paid to the girl's father at a feast, after which a special feast is held, called *tiadada*, which is the equivalent of the *ndapatingo* and *ngue* for marriage payment. At the *tiadada* the final payments are made by the group buying the girl to the girl's relatives. At this feast a long rope of *nkö* is prepared, which is given to the girl's mother, and subsequently *ndap* are paid in exactly the same manner as at a *ngue*.

According to the above account the amount of money paid for a *ptyilibi* is less than that paid for a wife, for the series of *ndap* and *nkö* described by the terms *yönö*, *toa*, etc., are not mentioned. It is possible that my information is defective

[1] Chiefs often have several wives. Bell found an old man, a chief, with five wives living (App. I, p. 222).

[2] Bell describes this custom and states that it is common amongst young men who have not reached puberty (App. I, p. 223).

on this point, but I am inclined to think that the price of a *ptyilibi* is less than the price of a wife. The *tiadada* has not the open and public character of the marriage feasts, and I was told that the father shows much shame and reluctance in selling the girl, and keeps very much in the background. There seems to be little doubt that this alliance is considered to be, if not shameful, at least less honourable than the marriage alliance.

The *ptyilibi* is not only a collective mistress, but also a source of profit to her owners; for her services are in much demand at feasts, and are well paid for, usually in *nkö*, though sometimes in *ndap*. The greater part of the money received on such occasions is taken by her owners, but I have no exact data on this point. The *ptyilibi* is thus a harlot by consent of her owners, and this custom, by which her owners encourage and profit by the promiscuity of her sexual relations, makes it even more difficult for us to regard the alliance as a form of marriage in any usual sense of the term. It should be noticed that in theory strict faithfulness is demanded of a wife, and there is a legend ascribing the *ptyilibi* fashion to Wonajö, who instituted the custom to prevent a man having relations with other men's wives. There are very heavy punishments for adultery with a chief's wife. A man suspected of this crime might be smothered at night, or, more usually, have his bones broken in sufficient number to cause his death in a few hours. The ghost of a person so treated was supposed to be unable to reach the land of the dead, and to haunt the bush in the form of a diabolical creature called *mbo*—which name is also given to this peculiar mode of inflicting death.

In spite of the general feeling for marital faithfulness on the part of women, a man will take precautions at a feast by confining his wife to the house at night; and I was told that it was common to construct enclosures, in which the married women were confined on such occasions, so that neither they nor the visitors should be exposed to temptation. This sensitiveness on the part of a married man is not expected of the wife; for the husband may be part owner of a *ptyilibi* (no doubt under the cover of secrecy when possible), and will not refrain from intercourse with the *ptyilibi* of others when opportunity and inclination offer. I feel sure that this civilised attitude is not of recent introduction. The *ptyilibi* are very like their more civilised cousins, decorating themselves in a recognisable way on appropriate occasions. They may be recognised after dark at a feast, when they appear openly in the village when other women have retired, but during the day they carefully avoid the public gaze.

Although very rare, cases were known of *ptyilibi* bearing children. This was not regarded as a calamity by the owners, and could not be regarded as a calamity for the child, who, having several fathers, had a better start in life, and a greater chance of rising to wealth and prestige than his less fortunate friends, provided with only a single father. Unfortunately, I failed to investigate at all adequately the relationships generated by the *ptyilibi* alliance; but in the hypothetical case we are considering I was told that the ordinary relationship terms would be used between the child and its fathers and their brothers, and so on. I was told, moreover, that the *ptyilibi* alliance itself was sufficient reason for the use of some at least of those relationship terms which would result if the alliance were regarded as equivalent to the marriage relation —e.g. a man would address the father of his *ptyilibi* by the term for father-in-law—but I cannot say what is the force and extent of this mode of reckoning relationship.

Although there is no feeling against the bearing of children by *ptyilibi*, precautions are taken against this eventuality, the fluids being carefully washed out, though this is not necessarily done after each act of coitus. A *ptyilibi* will also take precautions of a magical nature, e.g. a certain mollusc is eaten while facing the back of the man with whom she has had connection; conception being thereby assumed to be prevented. If, however, she were to eat the flesh of this same mollusc facing the man the view is that she would be likely to conceive. There are said to be other contraceptives and proceptives. I was told of one curious method of causing abortion. The pregnant woman, having arranged with the man, goes into the bush to collect nuts. The man also goes, obtains a black millipede, and hides. At a suitable moment he unexpectedly thrusts this at her, causing her to start with fright. She then repairs to one of the small bush houses, where she may have a miscarriage. One would imagine that such a method would seldom be effective. There are probably mechanical methods of abortion, but I obtained no definite evidence of such.

It frequently happens that a *ptyilibi* marries one of her owners. The other partners are then compensated by the payment of a No. 18 *ndap* to each, and this payment by the one partner to the others constitutes the marriage, as far as I could gather, the father and mother of the girl not being consulted.

Divorce appears to be uncommon, which we should expect amongst a people who purchase their wives. Only failure to work sufficiently hard is adequate ground for a man divorcing his wife; and only if the marriage were very recent would any of the purchase money be refunded. There seems to be no recognised ground for a woman divorcing her husband. She can punish him for unfaithfulness—e.g. for consorting with *ptyilibi*—by making him uncomfortable by simple domestic expedients; but she has no redress, and her husband can treat her brutally with impunity. It seems clear that the position of women on Rossel is far inferior to their position amongst the Massim. On Rossel a man would frequently throw a stone at his wife in a way that would hurt, in order to attract her attention, and she would not be surprised or excited. I can imagine the flow of language from a Massim woman under similar conditions.

Unlike the Massim, the Rossel Islanders believe that the male is the active agent in the production of children, the female being a more or less passive receptacle. The father makes a sort of egg in the mother, which is enlarged by repeated coitus; and coitus is therefore continued until late in pregnancy. If a man is strong, three or four months will suffice to produce a child, but if weak it may take a year or more. If a *ptyilibi* conceive, the child naturally grows rapidly, and is of the substance of all its fathers—i.e. of all the members of the partnership who have had frequent intercourse with the mother. The spirit *ghö* is also derived from the father or fathers, and not from the mother. It is possible that there are other beliefs as to the derivation of the *ghö*, and the nature of procreation; for on this point I did not obtain much information, although sufficient to show that the Rossel beliefs are totally different from those of the Massim. There can be no doubt that the Massim do not understand in the least the nature of procreation. This has been amply demonstrated by Malinowski,[1] and I can confirm his observations for other parts of the Massim area. At the same time, I did not find the belief in spirit children everywhere, though it probably exists. With these beliefs among their neighbours, it is strange that the Rossel Islanders should err by over-emphasising the contribution of the male, and neglecting that of the female.

It might be thought that the institution of *ptyilibi* acts as a preserver of the chastity of other women. This was the impression I received, but there are one or two facts which seem to contradict this idea. For example, it is believed that the menses do not start until a girl has had connection, and gossip generally fixes the responsibility on some boy. Again, in the case of a married woman, if there is any difficulty in delivery she is urged to mention the name of the man who has had connection with her and helped in the formation of the child, for if this is not done the child may refuse to come out.

For menstruation and the delivery of a child there are houses in the bush a little way from the village, which the men do not go near. A woman stays in the bush house, when bearing child, for some twenty or thirty days, and is attended by one or two others. The umbilical cord of the child is buried under a banana tree, which thereby belongs to the chief attendant who remains with the mother during the whole period of her seclusion. At the end of this period the women who have attended the mother are paid at a small feast in *ndap* and *nkö*; but for the principal attendant a rope of ten or more *nkö* is prepared. A month or two after this the father gives a small feast, called *döbwa*, at which a small perineal string is put on the baby. There are a number of food taboos for some months after birth, which apply particularly to the mother, and to a less degree to the father. The mother must not eat pig fat, crabs, or eggs, although the father may; but neither mother nor father may eat anything cooked in a saucepan, whether European or Massim. There is no elaborate avoidance between mother and father for the

---

[1] Malinowski, 'Baloma; The Spirits of the Dead in the Trobriand Islands', in *Journal of the Royal Anthropological Institute*, vol. XLVI, 1916, p. 403 seq.

first few months, such as occurs in parts of the Massim area, but cohabitation does not take place until the child can talk. Apparently, there are fewer taboos for the father to observe than is the case amongst the Massim, in spite of the fact that there is greater reason, owing to their beliefs about procreation, for believing in a sympathetic connection between father and child.

There is a slight manual pressure of the baby's head, called *gömbameye*, but not, as far as I could tell, such as would lead to any deformation.

I found no ceremonies of Initiation into manhood.

CHAPTER IX

Death and Cannibalism

D EATH is due to the final departure of the *ghö*, or spirit. The *ghö*, identified with the breath, normally resides in the neck, *gado*, but in sickness sinks lower and lower, and eventually leaves the body, in some cases, apparently, by the anus. States of mind, such as happiness, and even modes of thought, are expressed by such phrases as 'his neck is good', and so on. It is the *ghö* which is supposed to wander about in dreams, and also the entity which survives and passes to the land of the dead, whether it be *Yuma* or *Temewe*, or, in the case of the ghosts of persons eaten, *Pchi*. The corpse, if the dead man be a commoner, is kept above ground for a day or two, and is then interred under his house in a sitting position, the body being enclosed in a mat. A chief's body is kept rather longer before interment, for as long as ten days in some cases, and is subjected to a special treatment, possibly to accelerate decomposition. A close female relative, e.g. the mother, if alive, or else a sister, scrapes away the skin and places it in a leaf on a platform, on which subsequently the bones are lodged. A number of women then chew up betel nut with pepper and lime, and spit the red mixture over the flayed corpse, wiping the juice all over it. The corpse is subsequently interred under the house, which is not abandoned,[1] though one informant told me that the corpse of a chief used sometimes to be exposed on a platform. I should add that my association with a Government that insists on interment in the ground outside the village may have interfered considerably with my obtaining adequate information as to the native methods of disposal. The above is merely an account obtained from a good informant, no mortuary rites having been witnessed, so that it is possible that important parts of the ritual may have been omitted.

A month or two after interment the bones are removed from the grave. This should be done by the son's wife. All the bones, except the skull and jaw and the collar-bones, are

[1] Macgregor denies this, App. I, p. 211; also Bell, p. 222 and p. 225.

placed on a platform in the village, or near the village, and no further attention is paid to them. The skull and jaw, and perhaps also the collar-bones, are kept in the house by the widow. The procedure is, I believe, similar both for chiefs and for commoners, both for men and for women.[1]

The principal mourner is the widow or widower. A widow must stay by the corpse until it is interred. For the first few hours she should be on the corpse, pressing nose to nose, and weeping a great deal. This ceremonial should be followed by all the widows, if there are several. The widows, as well as other women present, cut their foreheads to make the blood flow; but apparently men never mutilate them-

---

[1] The disposal of the corpse was frequently observed by earlier writers. In 1888, Macgregor found at least one skull in every village and sometimes as many as three or four placed in a conspicuous spot on a shelf or plate (App. 1, p. 207). In 1890, Macgregor noticed several skulls in one village, which the natives said were skulls of relatives, which they had recently dug up (p. 208). In 1892, Macgregor saw a dead body tied up in a reclining position in a shroud made of the leaves of a species of pan palm, the house being closed up, while at another village he saw the head of a man recently deceased buried in a basket in a dwelling-house (p. 211). The natives stated that their method of disposing of the body was to keep the body until the flesh falls off and disappears; then to keep the bones in or near the house (p. 211). In 1901, Le Hunte found a skull exposed on a rock with a piece of broken pottery beside it (p. 215), and Campbell found in one house the body of a man carefully wrapped up in native mats and dried grass, etc. strung up to the beams supporting the roof, while another corpse was lying in a hole in the ground underneath the house, some dried grass and leaves over the body and a few canoe planks over the hole (p. 216). There was no offensive smell from either of the bodies. Campbell suggests that one of these corpses was that of the man killed to accompany the other, who had died from natural causes, to the land of the dead (p. 216)—an unlikely explanation in view of the beliefs described in the present chapter. The grave of a chief and one of his wives was observed by Bell in 1908. The graves were about 4 ft. long by 2 ft. wide and only 2 ft. 6 in. deep. Flat boards had been placed over the chief's grave, and the house had all its four sides enclosed with sewn sago leaf (p. 222). In 1913, owing to an epidemic of dysentery on Rossel, the Resident Magistrate of the South-Eastern Division investigated the method of disposal of the dead and states that burial is effected under the house, the corpse being placed in a sitting position with the head resting on the knees. The body is left for a period for the flesh to decompose, the hole then being uncovered and the body exhumed. The head is removed from the trunk by the women of the village and the remaining flesh removed by hand. The skull is washed in salt water, allowed to dry and then returned to the village; while a general lament is indulged in. The trunk is wrapped in sago leaves and lashed to the fork of a tree. The bones eventually fall to the ground, where they remain, the spot being avoided by all (p. 230). This account, resting, presumably, on actual observation, may be taken in preference to my own, from which, however, it differs only very slightly.

selves. A small shelter is constructed to accommodate the corpse and the widow. During this period the avoidance of the brothers-in-law is very much strengthened. The widow must not even be seen by the dead man's brothers, who give warning when they approach the corpse, so that the widow may conceal herself behind a large leaf. If she is seen she is fined 10 *ndap*, the money apparently being paid to her brother-in-law. My informant stated that it is the mourning-string[1] worn by the widow round her neck, and known as *yedong*, which it is important that the brothers should not see. The widow should fast by avoiding whatever kind of food she especially prepared for her husband, e.g. taro, banana, or sago. This continues for years, and often for the remainder of the widow's life, the *yedong* being worn until the fasting is brought to an end with a ceremony at which she is fed by a close relative of the dead man. If the widow marries again, the *yedong* is discarded, and the fasting ceases, even if the period has been comparatively short. The new husband has to pay a No. 18 *ndap* to the nearest clan relative of the former husband; but I did not understand that any feasts were held similar to the ordinary marriage feasts, and apparently no payments are made to the woman's relatives.

Apart from the widow, the children and the sister's children appear to figure most in the mortuary rites. The son arranges the mortuary feasts; but if there be no son, the sister's son or the brother will be responsible for the chief arrangements. The sister's sons should dig the grave and bury the man. For this service the son makes them a payment of *ndap*. The corpse is decorated according to certain conventional rules. Most of the dead man's ornaments—such as his arm-shells and nose-bone—are placed on the body in the same way that they were worn by him, and his money is hung up above him, or placed on his chest. It is rare for any of these articles to be buried with the corpse, though a chief, owing to a special request, may be interred with a *ndap* coin tied to his wrist;[2] they are removed from the corpse before burial by the sons and the sister's sons.

---

[1] Bell states that 'for mourning, the men wear a single piece of string tied round the neck, the women rows and rows of thin string tied over each shoulder, and loosely under the opposite armpit' (App. 1, p. 224).

[2] Some property in the form of coconut trees belonging to the deceased is destroyed, according to Macgregor (App. 1, p. 212).

The main distinction, as regards mortuary custom, between commoners and chiefs lies in the cannibalism associated with the death of one of the latter. As soon as a chief dies one or more victims must be found, who are eaten by the relatives of the deceased; and this, as far as I could make out, used to be the only recognised form of cannibalism. Owing to the natural reticence of the islanders about a custom, still no doubt struggling to survive, but severely condemned by the white man's Government, it was difficult to determine precisely how the victim was selected. Apparently, on the death of a chief the first duty of the son, generally the eldest son, is to discover who was responsible for the chief's death, since all death is believed to be the result of magic, unless it comes from the infringement of a taboo. On Rossel, which in this differs from the Massim area, the sorceress is of no great consequence, for no woman has that power of evil magic that is so much dreaded not only in typically Massim districts but even on Sudest. Death has, therefore, been caused by some sorcerer—either one who is already suspected, or one who may be divined by suitable methods. The sorcerer, accused, protests his innocence, but performs the main service that is required of him; he surprises some person wandering alone outside the village, and, probably with the help of a friend, seizes him and spears him and brings him to the village in which the chief has died; or he may visit a friend in some village, entice him into the bush and treacherously kill him. The body is given to the chief's son, and the murderer is paid a high value *ndap*. This mechanism sounds fantastic; but I was told the same story by several independent informants, so that it must contain a solid thread of truth.

There seems never to have been any real warfare on Rossel, and no head-hunting, as practised elsewhere in New Guinea; but murders appear to have been common, and most accounts of the island emphasise the treacherous and cowardly disposition of the natives, who do not fight in the open, but murder secretly and in safety. The spear, their only weapon, is intended, so it would seem, for dispatching victims who have already been caught and grasped in the hands, and not for use in the open against others similarly armed. It is not, therefore, surprising that the victims of cannibalism should be obtained by the unpleasant methods described. I had been told by the Osbornes that a few years ago, when cannibalism was still common on the island, an individual, knowing that he was to be 'sacrificed', would hide in the bush for a while; but it was understood that anyone selected for sacrifice would be unlikely to elude this fate, even if he endeavoured to escape it by leaving the island for a while with the white man's help. From this it might seem that some definite relative of a chief is killed at the time of the chief's death, but I could discover no evidence to support this inference. I was told that the victims were always young boys or girls, and also that persons with powerful relatives, such as might make a serious outcry, would not be chosen. The possible victims being limited in this way, an unpopular member of a village might guess that he would be hunted on the next occasion on which a victim should be required, and would therefore go into temporary hiding. This does not explain why the danger to him should continue indefinitely;[1] for it seems hardly likely that there would be collusion between the relatives of the dead man and those of the prospective victim for the sake of the compensation which the relatives of the latter always receive. On the whole, I am inclined to discount the casual evidence of residents and visitors, while admitting that my own information does not solve the problem satisfactorily.[2]

[1] While plotting the various *yaba* (described in Chap. XII) a case of cannibalism was mentioned to me which, though it upsets the theory that cannibalism is only a mortuary rite, may explain these attempts of individuals to evade 'sacrifice' if they be persons who have broken some *yaba* taboo, rather than victims required for a mortuary rite (see Chap. XII, p. 160).

[2] There is some disagreement, on the part of earlier writers, as to the nature of Rossel cannibalism and mortuary homicide. When repatriating natives in 1887, Douglas found that the relatives, six in number, of certain of the returned 'boys' had been killed and eaten, so that the boys were afraid of landing at their own village (App. I, p. 205); yet in 1892, Macgregor finds no proof whatever that the Rossel Islanders are cannibals (p. 211). Le Hunte states in 1899, that, according to Mr Campbell, 'satisfaction must be got out of somebody for a lost life'. This explained the apprehension of some natives, whom he was returning; for they were afraid of what the relatives of those who had died might do to them (p. 214). Campbell also investigated two murders; the reason for one was that the murdered man had set to work to build a larger and better house than any other in the village; whereupon the village rose and speared him. The other, a woman, was killed by her brother because an old man

Although it is probable that warfare was unusual on Rossel,[1] I was told that a long time ago there was a big fight between certain villages in Yongga Bay and natives from further east, and that in quite recent times the canoes of some Sudest visitors were broken up by a bombardment of stones, though I could not discover what happened to the natives thus stranded on the island. It is probable that the Rossel Islanders have always given an unpleasant reception to strangers, judging by the incident of the shipwreck of the *St Paul*, in the year 1858 on the northern reef. Although it was impossible to reconstruct the facts after so long an interval, it was possible to confirm the essential part of a story already well known,[2] my own version of which is given below.

The ship contained a large number of Chinese coolies, who were being taken to Australia. When the ship struck the officers abandoned them to their fate and made off in all the boats except one or two small dinghies. A few of the Chinamen, having with them one or two guns,

accused her of bewitching him before he died (p. 214). A case of murder in 1901 resulted from the custom of killing a man of another village on the death of a chief. A woman also had been killed, owing to the death of another chief not of her village (p. 215). In a later report, Campbell states that when the head man of a village dies, his relations 'at once start out in search of some one to kill. The first person met with is speared. Thus it often happens that a brother kills his sister (as a matter of fact we arrested one youth, who, when out on one of these expeditions, had speared his own sister whom he met returning from the gardens with food), a father his son, or a son his father' (p. 216). Moreton, the following year, states that 'when the head man of a village dies, his wife has to be killed and eaten, but should he have no wife, then the first small boy belonging to another village that is met by the murdering party is the victim' (p. 217); but later Moreton only commits himself to the statement that 'when the head man of the village dies, some one had to be killed and eaten; there is some law as to who it is that has to suffer. This custom is not as prevalent on the western end of the island as it is on the eastern' (p. 217). According to Murray, a rather unexpected form of homicide is the punishing of a thief by killing the woman who cooks his food (p. 219). Bell states that the wife or the man himself may be killed (p. 226). Bell, in 1908, states that it is 'a native custom on the death of a chief to kill either one of his wives, or some small boy or girl to accompany him to the next world which they believed was a mountain at the south-west end of the island, and there to look after him to cook his food' (p. 221).

[1] In 1888, Macgregor states that 'the different small districts seem to live in a state of hostility with each other' (App. 1, p. 206), but in 1890, finds that 'they evidently live at peace among each other' (pp. 207–208).

[2] Murray, *Papua, or British New Guinea*, pp. 132–3.

pulled to the mainland in the dinghies. Here they were killed by the natives, many of whom were themselves killed in the struggle; and the dinghies were all sunk. The majority of the Chinamen apparently scrambled along the reef—a matter of a few hundred yards—to the little island known as Heron Island, a place of two or three acres in extent, and quite devoid of food, other than birds' eggs and shell-fish. The distance of about a mile which separates this island from the mainland prevented most of the Chinamen from swimming across; though many, driven by hunger, attempted it, and were killed as soon as they reached the shore, except for some few who managed to escape into the bush. Those who, in spite of thirst and hunger, remained on Heron Island, were eventually visited by some of the natives who brought them food and water. Some were induced to return with the natives to the mainland, where they were promptly speared or had their legs broken. It seems probable, though I have little information on this point, that a steadily diminishing group of Chinamen were kept on Heron Island by the natives, who provided them with food, and removed one or two to the mainland whenever they were required for a cannibal feast. This method seems to have been carried out successfully by careful deception of the Chinese, who must have been very gullible; for I could get no accounts of any resistance, except on the part of individuals who reached the mainland. A few, however, who won the fancy of Rossel chiefs, survived; and there is a story that one Chinaman, who had become a great friend of an important chief, was killed by mistake when he was wandering alone in the bush; and that the Rossel Islanders suffered for his death, a Rossel youth being killed in payment—whether as part of the mortuary ritual or as a direct expression of revenge I did not discover.[1]

---

[1] This account, which is derived from native informants and from the Osbornes who had often questioned the natives on this matter, agrees largely with Rochas' account, which I discovered after writing the above. Rochas shows the initial incidents to have been somewhat different, however, and the conduct of the captain less discreditable. See App. I, pp. 192–201, for Rochas' story. A footnote to an account of Rossel in the *Australia Directory* is presumably based on the report of the captain of the *Styx*, which carried Rochas to Rossel (App. I, p. 203). The story is elaborated by Heath (App. I, p. 204); referred to by Macgregor (p. 207), and denied (p. 207); doubted by Le Hunte (p. 215); and confirmed by Murray (p. 229).

If we accept the story that the majority of these Chinamen, of whom there were over 300, were eaten in the space of a few months, it would be difficult to believe that cannibalism is no more than a mortuary rite, and it would evidently be necessary to modify the statement made above to that effect. I was much puzzled with the discrepancy between this and the other accounts of cannibalism I had previously obtained, until I came across the story of a chief, who lived about the time of the wreck of the *St Paul*. This chief, known as Muwo, lived at Praga, near Bamba, on the south coast, towards the western end of the island. He was the son of a chief, one of the most powerful on the island. His unpleasant disposition, apparently, became manifest at an early age; for when quite small he accidentally received some dirt in his eye from a commoner with whom, together with others, he was playing. Although apologies were given, and the offender brought a present of *ndap* and *nkö*, Muwo was not satisfied, and begged his father to kill the boy who had inconvenienced him. The father reluctantly consented to this, and even to the son's request that he should eat some of the flesh. This was the beginning of that craving for human flesh, which obsessed Muwo in later years, and made him a terror to his neighbours. The power which he later acquired seems to have resulted from the acquisition of wealth, which would be a simple matter for anyone inheriting considerable capital and skilfully investing it. However his position was acquired, Muwo is pictured later as having an inordinate number of wives and *ptyilibi, para nö*, and houses. He is said to have acquired ten wives, ten houses, five *para nö*, and ten sailing canoes,[1] not to mention fish nets, money, and other valuables. Many of these were obtained by illegitimate methods, owing to the fear he succeeded in inspiring in others. His later wives, for instance, were girls abducted at feasts or at other times, without consideration of the wishes of either the girl or her relatives; though the correct payments were said to have been made in these cases. Women, whom he attempted to seduce or desired to possess as wives, learnt to adopt the expedient of claiming to be of the same totem; for the taboo on clan incest was sufficient to restrain him, though other customs

[1] This decimal symmetry shows that the story has already begun to be assimilated to legendary matter such as the myths of Wonajö and Ye, in which both are provided with ten nephews. See Chap. XI.

he ignored. Many of his canoes were obtained by virtual theft. If a canoe were left inadvertently close to his own he would claim it, and the owner would be afraid to protest. He would brook no interference with his prestige. It is related that at a race of *para nö* canoes Muwo's *para nö* did not come in first, and the chief who owned the winning *para nö* suffered for his impertinence, for Muwo ate him the same day. Muwo did not kill people by *embo* (breaking of bones at night), or by *ngwivi* (the commonest method of sorcery); for in such cases the victim could not be eaten. His victims were taken and speared and cooked, only the flimsiest excuse being given, and sometimes no excuse at all. If he were badly bitten by mosquitoes, or if his gardens were damaged by a big wind, or rooted by bush pigs, he would send his men out to kill someone as compensation, and in such cases would not pay the relatives. Similarly, if one of his attendants offended him, if he were accidentally splashed in a canoe, he would have the offender killed and eat him. At other times he would simply be hungry for human flesh, and send his men out to secure a victim without giving any reason, and in these cases he would compensate the relatives. Fortunately for the natives, the *St Paul* was wrecked on Rossel early in Muwo's career, and most of his victims were Chinamen. I was told that most of the Chinamen were eaten by Muwo, and perhaps it was partly due to Muwo that they received such exceptional treatment. Perhaps it was the supply of Chinamen which first allowed Muwo to satisfy his passion for human flesh at all adequately, and the eventual using up of this supply which led him to terrorise the island subsequently, and defy convention by eating his own kind on other than the appropriate occasions defined by custom. A curious incident is related as having occurred towards the end of his career. A wife of Muwo brought the unwashed new-born child of his sister to him, with the words—'This boy is dirty now. It is hard work for us to feed him and make him strong. So you had much better eat him now'. Muwo replied, 'You must not talk to me like that'; but apparently he gave up his promiscuous cannibalism, at least for a while. Soon after this, Muwo succumbed to sorcery, which had been directed against him from all sides, and it is said that the relations of his victims gave vent to the emotions they had had to suppress, by destroying his gardens, killing his pigs, raping his widows, and so on. Nevertheless, at the first mortuary feast, arranged by his sister's son—for, strangely enough, he is said to have had no sons—five persons were killed and eaten. Muwo's skull can still be seen in the bush near the village of Praga.

It is evident that a great deal of exaggeration has crept into the story, and no doubt a generation or two more will suffice to convert it into a full-fledged hero myth, with little relation to the historical facts that gave it birth. The events distortedly recorded are, however, at present sufficiently recent to be regarded as historical; and I think we must assume that Muwo was a man of exceptional character, who acted in an exceptional way, over-riding the customs of his fathers, and disorganising the routine life of the island. I do not think the rank of chief could have carried with it the power wielded by Muwo; for I could find no evidence at the present day of such an exceptional position of a chiefly class. It is, however, difficult to understand his eating so many of his countrymen with impunity if cannibalism were strictly confined to the occasions on which a chief has died; and it is also difficult to understand why so many of the Chinamen should have been eaten if cannibalism were restricted in this way, even if we allow that most of the latter were accounted for by Muwo. It remains a possibility, therefore, that there are other legitimate occasions of cannibalism besides that of a chief's death, although this was strongly denied by my informants.

To return to the feast which is held immediately after the death of a chief. This feast, at which one or more human beings are eaten, is known as *kannö*, and is probably the most elaborate and important of all the feasts held on the island. In form it appears to be exactly similar to a pig feast, except that there is no dancing, and the relations between the groups making and receiving payment are strained. Apparently, the mother's brother of the victim, rather than the father, takes the principal part in the demand for payment, and receives the No. 20 *ndap*, the most valuable of the *ndap* paid by the dead man's son, or possibly the dead man's sister's son. The series of 10 *ndap* or of 10 *nkö* are denoted by the usual terms *yönö*, *toa*, etc., and correspond to ten portions of the victim, similar to the ten portions of a pig;

PLATE XV

(*a*) Sago-making.

(*b*) Cooking by hot stones.

PLATE XVI

(*a*) Stone squatting-place.

(*b*) Canoe, *pia nö*.

though it is probable that the head is *yönö*, not *toa*, which is
the head portion in a pig feast. According to my informant
the 10 principal *ndap*, i.e. Nos. 20 to 11 (and possibly this
applies to the corresponding *nkö* also) go to the following
relatives of the victim:

yönö	mother's brother.	*limö*	more distant sisters' sons.
toa	father.	*padö*	
walö	father's clan.	*pyalö*	
pi	own clan[1].	*miamö*	own mother.
wönö	father's brother.	*wö*	

These payments are made early in the feast, before the
victim is eaten, and the persons receiving compensation leave
the village as quickly as possible; for, as it was put to me, it
would be terrible for them to get any of the smell of the
cooking, which is taking place outside the village. Although
the dead chief's son collects the money which has to be paid
in compensation, a large part of this is payment by others
for their shares of the victim. I think the *yönö* and *toa* are
always bought by the dead chief's son and sister's son, but
the portions corresponding to these are distributed by them
to their relatives, and they themselves do not eat of their
own portions, though it is possible that they eat of the portion
bought by another man, as happens in a pig feast. The lower
value *ndap* and *nkö* are provided by various persons who
receive their share of flesh, and are, therefore, paying for this
commodity and not making a loan; but much of this is
conjecture, as information about an extinct institution is
difficult to obtain, especially when the older men are anxious
to revive it and are suspicious of the interfering white man.
Apparently, tomahawk stones, used as money on Sudest, are
involved in these payments, as well as *ndap* and *nkö*; and
other valuables change hands on these occasions, but I do
not know by what rules. The distribution of the flesh,
apparently, takes place after the payments have been completed, since this naturally cannot be done in the presence
of the victim's relatives. I had been told by white informants
that circular groups of stones, similar to the *gahana* of
Fergusson in the D'Entrecasteaux and elsewhere,[2] were

---

[1] Bell, investigating a murder, came across the lending of a *ndap* to
a man who required it for payment to the murdered woman's brother
(App. I, p. 223).
[2] See Seligmann, *Melanesians of British New Guinea*, p. 556.

utilised on these occasions as a squatting-place for those partaking of the feast. My native informants told me that it was usual for the food to be brought to this part of the village, but that these circular places were not reserved for this purpose, being used also as squatting-places at other times, and particularly for *dogo* feasts, when a *ndong* or circle is made. The term *ndong* is also applied to these stone circles, which suggests that they are more particularly associated with money operations than with cannibalism.

Apparently the head of the victim is treated differently from the rest of the body, being cooked in a heap of stones by the side of the dead chief. But my informants could give no special significance to this, and said that the skull of the victim is discarded after the feast, and is not associated with the dead chief in any way. As will be pointed out presently, there is no belief in any connection between the ghost of the victim and the ghost of the dead chief, and the only reason given me for the custom of cannibalism was that it was instituted by Wonajö in the remote past. But I have no doubt that there are beliefs and important elements in the ritual, which I failed to discover, that would make the cannibalism more intelligible as part of a wider context. Almost as important as the payments at the *kannö* and the eating of the human victim or victims are the *dogo* for the high value *ndap* and *nkö* borrowed for the occasion. These are the most important *dogo* to occur on the island, and attract large numbers of people—in fact most of the islanders, I was told. These *dogo*, however, are not necessarily held at the *kannö*, some being held weeks afterwards, according to circumstances.

Following close on the *kannö* or even at the same time, is the *kwagwa*, at which a pig may be eaten, at least in those cases where no *kannö* is held. A month or two later occurs the *wili*, at which the bones of the dead man are removed from the grave and placed on a platform, and the skull (and possibly the collar-bones) cleaned and placed in the house of the widow or widower, or in some cases exposed in the village. The *kwagwa* and the *wili* are made, whatever the rank of the deceased; while the *kannö* is held only for a chief or, in exceptional cases, a chief's wife. Unfortunately, I have no further information about these feasts and their significance.

CHAPTER X

Ghosts

THE *ghö*, which during life is the animating principle of the body, becomes the ghost after death and is pictured as a more or less substantial duplicate of the man before death. The shadow and reflection are known by a different name, *ka*,—a term also used to denote a picture. The *ka* is of no significance and disappears at death. Not only men, but all breathing things have a *ghö*; ants, no doubt, are provided with *ghö*, but shellfish have no *ghö*, since manifestly to the native they do not breathe.

There are differences, however, among ghosts, according to their destinations, which depend in part on the mode of death and treatment of the corpse. The ghosts of persons who have been eaten are in a quite peculiar position, for they become clothed in a new body and are, therefore, to all intents and purposes exactly similar to ordinary human beings. However, with no regard for consistency, these beings are supposed to be normally invisible like ordinary incorporeal ghosts. The home of these corporeal ghosts is *Pchi*, a hill on the south side of Rossel, which is a *yaba* and held in considerable fear by the islanders (see Chap. XII, where the *yaba* are enumerated).[1]

Yuma,[2] which is the destination of most ghosts, is a hill at the western extremity of the island, and, though a *yaba*, may be visited under certain conditions and is not greatly feared.

A land of the dead, which is also the true home of the gods, is *Temewe*, the floor of the lagoons, surrounding Rossel. This is supposed to have been in existence before the island was created and man appeared. It is said that only the good go

---

[1] It was, I believe, this *yaba* which was very nearly the cause of a catastrophe some years ago to the pioneer settler on the island, Mr Frank Osborne, who unwittingly attempted to clear a part of this land. Not realising the danger, he persisted too long against the wishes of the natives, but was forced to agree to abandon the task, after a four days' siege, which almost cost him his life. It is possible that the murders of white men, which have given Rossel such a sinister reputation, have resulted from accidental disregard of the numerous *yaba*, the violation of the taboo of which will cost even a native his life.

[2] Referred to by Murray (App. I, p. 220), and Bell (p. 226).

to Temewe, which means, in practice, only those that die young; for the good are those who do not practise sorcery, commit adultery, or steal. It would seem to be those who are chosen by the gods for their virtue who achieve a pleasant immortality in Temewe. The ghost, on its way to the land of the dead, is supposed to reach a certain place, where the choice between Yuma and Temewe is made. There is a woman guarding each of these roads. The candidates for Temewe are examined by a woman wearing a valuable shell nose-stick, who is always making baskets with a vertical design, while those bound for Yuma are speeded on their way by a woman who has merely a wooden stick through her nose and is permanently making baskets with a horizontal design.

On arrival in Temewe, the ghost is well washed and placed over a fire. The bones 'get tight' again. Finally, the hair is dressed and the body well oiled. On those rare occasions when an old man reaches Temewe, the *ghö* has to receive a prolonged washing to make him a fit associate for the people of Temewe: he thereby regains his youth, and becomes one of the company of irresponsible, frivolous, good-natured beings, who have perpetual youth and perpetual happiness. The life of these beings, who are mostly ghosts, is very similar to the life on earth. They marry and have children, make feasts, and cultivate, with little effort, gardens of amazing fertility. Their dogs are the sharks. A mortal, fishing on the reef, will often hear the laugh of the Temewe people, a sort of rattle. This is especially liable to occur when he catches fish or shellfish, which have first been eaten by Temewe and contain, therefore, no fat or substance. This need, however, cause no alarm. They will sometimes, as a joke, steal from mortals, though often the stolen articles will be returned. My informant insisted that they would not, however, steal from white people; for suspicion would naturally fasten on innocent Rossel Islanders. Sometimes the Temewe people will give warnings of the presence of sorcerers, by means of dreams, and are said to have a great dislike of these as well as of cannibals and of men who rape small girls. Sometimes, at night, they will wander into a village and are sometimes seen by mortals; but if on such an occasion a Temewe spirit is caught, then, at break of day, the spirit becomes an ordinary mortal and may even be received into the village as a dead relative returned. Not only do the inhabitants of Temewe visit the living, but the living may visit Temewe in dreams. A man who has been to Temewe will do no work the next day. A similar excuse for idleness occurs when he dreams of a dead relative or of Yuma. In order to visit Temewe, a man will drink salt water and place a small piece of sago in his penis-covering, before retiring. He may, then, if lucky, dream of Temewe, where he will be welcomed and where he will give the sago, which has swollen to the size of a dozen coconuts, to his hosts. He will soon be offered a girl for the night by one of his hosts, for in Temewe there is a freedom in sexual relations, so one of my informants said, which is characteristic of 'down' (i.e. the Massim) rather than of Rossel, with its tendency to strictness in these matters. The girl's father is paid a black shell, not *ndap*, for the privilege, and the girl may bear a child by her mortal lover, after one or two nights only. This, however, is a privilege of young, unmarried men only. My informant even insisted that as soon as a man was married he lost the power of visiting Temewe.

Just as the bits of rock and seaweed and so on, which we can see at the bottom of the lagoon, are really houses, canoes, gardens, etc., of the Temewe people, so also what appear to mortals to be bare stones and dead logs on Yuma are really the villages of the Yuma people, invisible to the human eye. But life in Yuma is a different matter from life in Temewe, less pleasant even than life on earth.

Both Yuma and Pchi, as lands of the dead, are the result of evil entering the world; in fact the lord or superintendent of Yuma is the ghost of the first male victim of sorcery, and, similarly, the lord of Pchi is the first person on Rossel to have been killed by violence, and in this case, the actual person, not his ghost. *Kaijum*, lord of Yuma, was originally a man living in the Yuma district, before people died and before cannibalism was invented. Unlike the Temewe people, the inhabitants of Yuma smell of blood, have all the vices of human beings and grow old and die. Sometimes, the ghost of a man who has just died is met in Yuma by his enemies, who believe that they died from his sorcery, and speared. The ghost is then taken and burnt, and the man is thus completely extinguished. Every night, so my informant said, the people of Yuma disintegrate, just as a corpse disintegrates, and the fluids and bones of everyone become mixed up on the floors of the houses. At daybreak, however, the bodies are reconstituted and the people go about their daily tasks as usual. It is just possible that this belief is the result of a recent dream of a man who visited his deceased mother in Yuma, the account that he gave to his friends becoming fairly generally accepted. This man reached Yuma by mixing a certain herb, to the accompaniment of a spell, with salt water, which he then drank. According to his account, he saw the people in Yuma repair to their platforms in the houses after dusk and he saw every one fall asleep at one time with a simultaneous snore and he saw a big fire light itself in the middle of the house, in which he was staying. Then all the fluids, black and stinking, ran on the floor in a stream and the bones became inextricably mixed. His mother, who had met and welcomed him, he tried to persuade to return to his village; which she promised to do in a day or two. He was warned by his friends in Yuma to eat none of their food, lest it disagree with him—which is very different from the custom in Temewe. Apparently, the mother did, subsequently, pay her son a visit, appearing in the village as a small bird, which soon flew away back to Yuma. This is the usual way in which ghosts appear to their friends and relatives, and it is usual for one who has just been eaten to appear to friends and relatives in this way as a bird.

Since it is not known, when a person dies, whether he has gone to Yuma or to Temewe, there is said to be a method by which this can be discovered, without an actual visit to either. Salt water is first drunk and then two twigs of a certain tree are prepared in some way and a spell is muttered over them. The twigs visit Yuma and Temewe respectively and indicate, in some way, to which place the ghost has gone. Sometimes, so one informant told me, a man on his way to Yuma would be rescued by friends in Temewe, which could be done if the ghost were taken and washed and dried over the Temewe fire sufficiently quickly. The people of Temewe and Yuma and even of Pchi have a certain amount of communication with one another, exchanging certain foods, e.g. fish for products of the bush, but the Temewe people are fastidious and dislike the smell of the Yuma and Pchi folk, who always smell of blood.

Death takes a peculiar form in Yuma. When a man gets old—and the ghost ages in just the same way as the body—his friends tell him that he smells and that his time has come; they lead him down to the salt water and tell him to walk straight on. As he disappears under the sea he turns into a huge fish (possibly a whale is meant), which sleeps for a few days and then dies, the ghost coming completely to an end.

I was told by one of the Osbornes that the ghosts of virtuous people are immortal in Yuma, but that the sinful become kingfish; if a kingfish be killed the ghost passes on to another kingfish and so on indefinitely. If we substitute Temewe for Yuma, and if the kingfish be the fish (which I had taken to be larger), into which the Yuma people are finally converted, the discrepancy with my own information is very slight.

The beliefs about Pchi are rather more definite and consistent than those about Yuma and Temewe. *Kangö*, the lord of Pchi, was the first person on Rossel to be killed by violence. His death was the result of his stealing sugar-cane from a garden on Wuli Island, which he was visiting. His murderers, after discussing whether to eat him, decided otherwise, since he was a person of rank. They, therefore, took him in a canoe to the mainland and stretched him on the beach. One man and a small boy, named *Pibwa*, from a neighbouring village, remained with the corpse, and while they waited the anus of the dead man grew larger so that the small boy could see inside. Given a kick by the other, the inquisitive youth disappeared through the dead man's anus, whereupon the corpse got up and walked away. Kangö is a man without a soul, for his *ghö* disappeared, and Pibwa takes its place; but Kangö does not realise this or that he is dependent for his life on the whims of the small boy Pibwa within him. Every night Pibwa emerges from Kangö through his anus and leads an independent life, returning the next morning, when Kangö wakes from his apparent sleep.

Kangö has ten *jina* (sisters' sons) who reside on various hills on Rossel. There are two on hills by Yongga Bay, one near Wolunga, one near Yabuwe. One of these *jina* (a sister's daughter in this case) resides on Loa, where she was

sent from Pchi by Kangö. She has a little baby that never
grows any older. It may sometimes be heard crying
'Ababab...' when a visit is paid to Loa. It arouses fear
and is considered an evil omen, generally indicating that
someone has died by violence and therefore requires the
assistance of Kangö. Another *jina* of Kangö has only one leg
and his hill is carefully avoided by anyone who has lost
a limb.

The names of these supernatural beings are useful in cases
of sickness. If a man falls ill and there is danger of the *ghö*
escaping, which would mean the man's death, the names of
these relatives of Kangö, ending up with Kangö himself, are
whispered into the ear or the mouth of the sick man. It is
believed that they help to restrain the *ghö*, which is sinking
lower and lower in the man's body towards the anus, from
leaving him. Finally, if all else is ineffective, the name of
Pibwa, if known, is used; for this by a kind of sympathetic
magic is the most effective talisman on Rossel and one that
is known only to a few natives.[1]

Theoretically, the Pchi people are not ghosts in the same
sense as the Temewe or Yuma people. When a man is
killed and eaten, the *ghö* passes to Pchi, but here it waits to
secure a new body. This is the business of Kangö, who
secures a little of the blood from the spear used for the
murder. Wrapped in a leaf this drop of blood is thrown by
Kangö across the sky to fall in the sea at a spot many miles
from Rossel near the main reef of Sudest, which makes a
wide sweep from its eastern extremity. There is a giant clam
at this spot, a friend, or possibly one of the *jina*, of Kangö.
This clam is really a god, just as Kangö may be regarded as
a god, whose home in some sense, is Temewe, the true home
of all the gods. The drop of blood received is returned in
the same way to Kangö and the process repeated again and
again, while the drop of blood grows into the semblance of
the man from which it was originally derived. This passage
backwards and forwards through the sky of the blood of the
victim of cannibalism is seen by the Rossel Islanders as the

[1] Most of the information about Pchi was given me only a few days
before my departure. My informants were rather scared about imparting
it, for the older men were anxious to keep me in the dark on certain
matters. The name Pibwa was disclosed as an inner secret which might
even be of practical value to me.

rainbow, which is thus a sign to all of a recent murder.[1] Apparently, there were rainbows which had a more natural origin, such as those which lay in the wrong direction, but I could not get clear on this point.

In some way all the *jina* of Kangö are supposed to co-operate in this process, so that possibly the blood is also tossed from hill to hill on Rossel and across to Loa, and would thus explain the rainbows appearing in many different localities. The new body takes days or weeks to form and when complete is entered and animated by the ghost, which has been waiting in Pchi. Though the reconstituted individual in Pchi bears a resemblance to the former self, there are certain differences such as a general yellowness of the body, which smells like blood, and a hole in the head and a tendency to behave like a madman.

Most of the things in Pchi are red, such as the penis-covering, their ornaments, their taro, bananas, and even their fish. Kangö himself is red all over and has huge eyes, like saucers; and the ten *jina* of Kangö have the peculiar habit of making ten combs every day, which they lose or give away. The inhabitants of Pchi are immortal and never grow old; they never look one straight in the face; and they never sleep.[2] They appear to be resentful of their fate and try, if only on their first arrival, to revenge themselves on those responsible for their death by causing stones to enter their bodies,—a form of magic very common amongst the Massim, but, as far as I could make out, not common on Rossel (though certain stones owned by women may be made to enter the body; see Chap. XIII).

Although the living may communicate through dreams with relatives in Temewe or Yuma and the latter may oc-casionally appear to the living in the form of birds, there is an important ritual of invoking ghosts from Pchi, which is, apparently, not adopted in the case of Yuma and Temewe.

[1] My attention was first drawn to Pchi by a remark which a small boy made one day that the rainbow was the blood of people who had been eaten. I enquired about this of an old man, who said that it was ridiculous nonsense, and who was most persistent to get the name of the boy who had misled me in this way, so persistent that it proved that there was some truth in the statement.

[2] Some of these characteristics of Pchi may be exaggerations of my best one or two informants, on whom alone I could rely for any infor-mation about Pchi.

I was unable to find out much about this, but the Osbornes tell me that they have often seen gatherings of people waiting in tense silence for some sign from the other world. I think these were, in all probability, the séances mentioned by my informants. A séance may be held by relatives soon after a boy or girl has been sacrificed at the death of a chief, or merely because the relatives have not dreamt of their eaten relative for a long time. Sometimes a number of Pchi people are invoked. The ceremony takes place at night, and starts with a formula, which is sung out by one of the party:

> *'Pchi mo igale ingu makwa ungo muru*   *kwa moba*
>   (leaf on top)   (root underneath)
>   *kwego*   *dongwana*   *abuie*   *angyadi'*.
> (cuttlefish) (big taro leaf) (come) (get food)

The 'leaf on top, root underneath' appears to be a description of a tree supposed to grow in Pchi, which has leaves in the ground and roots in the air. '*Kwego*' may be a reference to the sacred cephalopod on Loa (see Chap. xii), but probably only refers to a present of cuttlefish and taro, which is to be made to the ghost, who is asked in the above formula to come and eat. A certain flower (*ngwalo*), often worn in the hair, and a cane (*nda*), used for binding, are mentioned in another formula: '*Nda ngwalo kwila, nda ngwalo kwa*'. '*Kwila* and *kwa* are, I believe, interjections— *kwila* is sung on a rising and then falling inflection in a drawn-out manner. I do not know the significance. The name of the person they wish to invoke is then called out, and they wait in silence for a response. The ghost, if he comes, will cry out '*Angönö*' (Where?). The audience then precipitately retires if a present of food is being made, returning later to find the food gone and a smell of blood and putrefying flesh to indicate that the ghost has been there.

Although the ghost, probably invisible, may come and take the food, it can only communicate in the shape of a bird. The ghost is, therefore, addressed, '*Yomo gwada kwila, yomo gwado kwa*' (if you are on a tree, cry out), '*kwili ngoneto, akang abuie*' (wherever you may be, cry out to me, come). If there is a bird and it replies, it is the cry of the ghost, and the relatives are satisfied and commence to weep. Even a rustle in the stillness, which prevails after the long-drawn-out cry to the ghost, may be interpreted as a response. The bird, which the ghost simulates or possibly possesses, is a species known as *dadje*, green in colour, which has a curious note '*tatata...*'. If the *dadje* is really a ghost, it does not eat the food proper to its kind, but taro, bananas, or any food eaten by man, and when it gives its cry it looks towards the village first, or gives its note only in response to a suitable question. It is common for the ghost of one recently eaten to return to the village in this form without invitation, and it is said that this happened the day after the first person was killed and eaten on Rossel; but the victim's mother, who was warned in a dream to be on the look-out for him at a certain time, neglected to do so and the bird sorrowfully returned to Pchi and did not appear again. The same bird, *dadje*, is also an omen bird, but, apparently, only if it be really a ghost, though this was not very clear. If its cry is heard, then either a boat is coming to Rossel or someone is going to die.

Although almost everyone goes to Temewe, Yuma, or Pchi, at death, there are a few exceptions. There is a certain method of inflicting death, known as *embo*, which is only rarely adopted and is the appropriate punishment for adultery with the wife of a chief. *Embo* appeared, from descriptions, to be merely the breaking of most of the offender's bones, but it was not perfectly clear that an actual breaking of the bones was meant rather than an intangible breaking of the bones, of a magical nature, having no immediate physical effect whatever. Comparison with a method of sorcery, known as *ngwivi*, which I had established to be purely magical and to involve no physical operations on the victim whatever, made it probable that *embo* is an actual physical operation even though frequently performed at night and secretly on an individual surprised in his sleep. It is said that a person is sometimes smothered secretly at night,[1] though I could get no definite evidence for this, and it may be that this is a process similar to *embo*. However this may be, the ghost of a person who has died by *embo* is said not to go to Temewe, Yuma or Pchi, but to wander in

[1] See Chap. XIII, p. 170.

the bush, a danger to everyone at night. These ghosts, known as *mbo*, are terrifying objects. They are large and strong, and fireflies surround their heads. They can thus be distinguished though difficult to see. A circle of fireflies with a dark space in the middle means precipitate flight to the sensible man. A *mbo* is always on the look-out for victims. He breaks their bones and sucks their blood until they are dry and shrivel up.

The firefly, which may indicate the presence of a *mbo*, is, on certain other occasions, an omen. A single firefly, circling round the head or alighting on the head, indicates the approach of a sorcerer or else the death of someone or, if neither of these eventuate, the approach of a boat to Rossel.

Frequently *mbo* is spoken of as a single individual, a blood-thirsty giant with broken bones, who lives somewhere in the bush. That *Mbo* (or the species *mbo*) belongs to the world of visions and dreams, the world of Kangö and ghosts, is shown by an experience related to me. A native, named Kadwö, was wandering in the bush hunting wild pig, when, suddenly the scene was transformed 'like a cinematograph picture' to Pchi, and he met Kangö himself and conversed with him. Suddenly the giant Mbo, in a house near by, raised his arm and attracted the attention of Kadwö. Fortunately, at this moment, the vision broke and Kadwö, very frightened, found himself back in his normal environment. It is interesting to find Mbo living in Pchi; and the statement suggests that there is a connection between Mbo and the more common ghosts of Pchi, who are certainly held in greater dread than other ghosts from Yuma or Temewe.

There is a class of supernatural beings which may be mentioned here, since they resemble somewhat the terrifying Mbo, though there is no evidence that they were once human beings. These are the *Pojem*, said to be similar to the *Dagananapa* of Sudest and perhaps to *Taukaikaitau* (eater of men) of other Massim peoples. They are ogres who live in certain of the big creeks, and my informant said that there were six of them in the island. A story is told of one of them, who lives in Pwennegwa creek (Yabuwe district), on the north side of the island. This Pojem was seen by one man to leave his lair and steal some sugar-cane and coconuts. The Pojem on his return smelt the man and talked as follows:

> 'Pi da pi tung   gwa   gwamba iy bwo
> (man not man)   (fern)   (water dripping)
>   pwabada'.
> (water remaining and not falling)

This phrase, the translation of which was unintelligible to me, proved that the Pojem was not a real human being. The Pojem was then seen to throw the food into the water and then dive down into his dwelling, which lay at the bottom of very deep water. The Pojem is described as having peculiar hair and very big temples, or possibly horns. He carries a spear with a hook on the end, which he uses for catching human beings, whom he devours. The Pojem are very dangerous when the moon is full, when they may even catch women and small children in their houses. One should always be careful of sitting down by the side of deep water, and small children should not be let out of sight for fear of these creatures. I could discover no explanation of their existence; Wonajö did not create them, they did not come from Sudest, and they are not ghosts.

CHAPTER XI

Religion

THERE is a hierarchy of gods on Rossel and there is a certain system both in the way these gods are related to one another and in their treatment by the natives, which makes it possible to separate religion from the other institutions on Rossel. I am using the term religion for beliefs about and ritual directly connected with the gods.

In dealing with many peoples, there is no advantage and even a positive disadvantage in defining religion in this arbitrary manner, because many of the institutions we are accustomed to call religious, would be to a large extent excluded. But on Rossel so many beliefs and so much behaviour is directly connected with the gods that it is advantageous to treat this side of native life separately, especially as it serves to mark a further contrast with the Massim culture, which contains little religion in this sense of the term. I do not, of course, wish to beg the question that, in an important sense of the term 'religious,' many of the monetary operations and other activities of the Rossel Islander are religious, just as the Soi, the Kula, and many of the chief institutions of the Massim are largely so; but this question of terminology does not concern us in the present connection.

An interesting feature of Rossel religion is its systematic nature; something of the orderliness of the monetary system has crept in and arranged the gods, instead of leaving them scattered about the universe in that free-and-easy way characteristic of many primitive religions and particularly of the Massim. Rossel Island has, for instance, quite definitely a supreme deity, known as *Wonajö*.[1] He, most appropriately, resides on the top of Mt Rossel, the highest mountain on the island, for the creation of which he is responsible. Curiously enough, he is not the ancestor of the race; for the inhabitants of Rossel are descended from a god, *Mbasi*, whom Wonajö expressly invited from Sudest to be their progenitor. The origin of a number of elements of culture is ascribed to Mbasi rather than to Wonajö. Since there is a

---

[1] First mentioned by Murray (App. I, p. 220).

system in the religion, a great deal can be expressed in general terms, but this task is better undertaken after the more important myths relating to gods and man have been described.

Before Rossel, or indeed any of the islands of the Louisiades, existed, there was only open sea and reef. The reef, which now surrounds Rossel, enclosed a large lagoon, the floor of which was Temewe, where there lived an immortal race, whose chief was Wonajö. After untold generations, Wonajö made the land within the reef and himself repaired to a new home on Mt Rossel, Ngwö (see Chap. XII, p. 143). There he still normally resides at the present day; though the mysterious island of Loa at the eastern end of the reef (where many of the ordinary words of the Rossel language may not be used and which is rigidly taboo to women) is also regarded as the home of Wonajö to a less degree only than Ngwö.

After creating the land, Wonajö made the clouds and the stars, but not the sun and the moon. The clouds that almost perpetually cover Rossel are the ashes of the first fire made by Wonajö, which he threw up into the sky to conceal the island from the older island of Sudest.

Although, originally, in Temewe Wonajö and his people seem to have been human in form, on Rossel he is supposed to take the form of a snake by day and assume his human form only at night. Most of the gods have this double character, alternating between the human form and that of a snake, though there are certain gods that take the shape of other animals and many are normally stones. The gods as snakes are dangerous to man and are supposed to swell to an enormous size and then to swallow any human being who has the temerity to approach the sacred places in which the gods reside.

Man was not created by Wonajö; for the progenitors of the Rossel race are a snake god Mbasi and a girl, *Könjini*,[1] said to be of fair skin, whom Wonajö found on the island and whom he wooed in vain.[2] Mbasi was a friend of Wonajö,

[1] Bell says that some of the natives believe that they originally came from an island to the eastward (App. I, p. 226). There are many features of Rossel culture that suggest an influence from the Solomons, and even from Polynesia.

[2] I could discover no myth to explain the presence of Könjini on the island.

and it was at the latter's request that Mbasi, said to be of dark colour,[1] left Sudest and married Könjini on Rossel. When Wonajö visited Sudest, or sent over one of his snake friends, he paddled over in a wooden dish, having no knowledge of canoes; though there is a myth that ascribes to Wonajö the *para nö*, which can be used only in calm lagoon water and is never sailed.

Mbasi arrived in a sailing canoe (*lia nö*) bringing with him the sun and the moon, the pig, the dog, and the taro. Wonajö placed the pig on the north side of the island, the dog on the south, and the taro he planted in a place, now a *yaba*, presided over by a snake god, whom he appointed to this task. An egg was produced from the union of Mbasi and Könjini and from this egg came the first two human beings. Before the hatching of the egg the sun and the moon had been instructed to hide in the bush at a place called Ngwanamba, now an important *yaba* on the north-east of the island (see Chap. XII, p. 146); while Mbasi and Könjini retired to a beach near by, where they were converted into stones, which remain at the present day as one of the most important *yaba* on the island (see Chap. XII, p. 144). Later the sun and moon went to bathe, the sun choosing the warm salt water, the moon the cold creek water, and then they ascended into the sky. But the sun found the moon too cold, and the moon found the sun too hot. Wonajö, therefore, arranged for them to traverse the sky at different times, the sun by day and the moon by night. Moreover, finding that the moon, the sun, and the sky, were too close to the earth, he raised the whole heavens to their present height with a long pole.[2]

The first two children from the original egg had four children by their intercourse, two boys and two girls. From these four came eight, and from these eight sixteen, until in a few generations there was a substantial population. The clan divisions, with the rule of exogamy, were instituted at this early phase by Wonajö and Mbasi, who gave each clan

[1] That Könjini was fair and Mbasi dark-skinned is not indicated very definitely.

[2] There were some obscurities in the account of the sun and moon, which I was unable to relieve. An explanation of the phases of the moon, for instance, was quite unintelligible. A point of considerable interest was some suggestion in the accounts given me of a connection between the sun and the hatching of the first egg. One informant suggested that the sun had connection with Könjini.

PLATE XVII

(*a*) Canoe, *ma nö*.

(*b*) Canoe, *ma nö*.

PLATE XVIII

(a) Sailing-canoe, *lia nö*.

(b) Sailing-canoe, *lia nö*.

its specific totems. Totemism appears to have been already in existence amongst the gods. The plant totem of Mbasi was *ndua*, a kind of banana. Könjini's totem was *mwado*. The totem of Nönö, the taro-*yaba* snake god (see Chap. XII, p. 143), was *ka* (taro). Wonajö, curiously enough, has two of each of the three linked totems (see Chap. III, p. 39), two plants, two birds, and two fish. This double set of totems of Wonajö falls into line with a general tendency on the part of Wonajö to have two of everything, so an informant suggested—he has, for instance, two homes on Rossel, and he has two *dama* (songs), and he made two kinds of money, *nkö* and *ndap*.

The origin of one of the totems of Wonajö is given in a tale that describes him as wandering in the bush on his way to Ngwö. He discovers a beautiful flower, which is supposed not to exist now. This he puts in his hair and adopts as his totem, composing a song about the flower—a song which exists at the present day as a *dama*. The totems given by Wonajö and Mbasi to the descendants of the latter were the totems of the gods in many cases, if not in all—e.g. the first two girls were given the plant totem *kif* and the first two boys the totem *ka* (taro), the plant totem of the snake god Nönö; the children of one of the girls were given the totem *wobo*, a plant totem of Wonajö. Betel nut, sago, and coconut were the next plant totems to be assigned, and later *ndua*, the totem of Mbasi.

Matrilineal descent was established after all the totems had been distributed. With the plant totem of a god, which was assigned to one of these mortals, the other totems—bird and fish—were associated. A clan has, therefore, its three totems and an intimate relation to a certain god; and when a clan is now asked for its totems, the god is often given as a fourth totem.[1] But the name of the god is given as if it were a species of snake, just as the other totems are given as species and not as individuals. Furthermore, it was stated that snakes of these species were sometimes encountered, and when recognised, were avoided. There is a story of a man

---

[1] A reference to the totems given in Chap. III will show that the totems of 7 clans were proved to be of this pattern, a snake or reptile god being one of the totems of each. It is, therefore, probable, though not proved, that all the totemic clans are of this nature, having a special relation to one of the gods; though the gods are too numerous for each of them to be represented by a clan.

who ate a snake of the Nönö species (Nönö is the guardian of the principal taro *yaba*) and died soon afterwards, when snakes were seen to emerge from his body. This was not the penalty for eating his own totem, as far as I could make out: it was the penalty for injuring a god. Either we may suppose that every snake of the Nönö species partakes of the nature of the individual snake god Nönö, or that there are many Nönö snake gods, and that Nönö, the one snake god, is merely the chief of these. However we regard these snake species that function as totems, it is interesting to note that their inclusion as totems brings Rossel totemism into line with that of the Massim; for the Massim have exactly the same kinds of four linked totems, namely, plant, bird, fish (occasionally sea or land mammal), and snake (occasionally other reptile); though the Massim differ in that there is nothing peculiar about the snake totems and in giving first place, in probably all cases, to the bird totem.

Since every god is associated with a *yaba* and many of the gods are, in a certain sense, the totems of clans, we should expect a division of religious function amongst the clans and an association of clans with particular *yaba*.[1] This, in a general way, is certainly the case, but I was unable to prove that a given *yaba* is always either possessed by or controlled by the appropriate clan, though this may be the case. It was, however, fairly clear that the gods are of equal importance to all the clans, and a given god is neither particularly favourable to nor favoured by the clan totemically associated with his *yaba*.

Some light is thrown on this aspect of the gods, whereby they are classes rather than individuals, by a myth which my informant obtained from one of the older generation and which he thought was not known to many on the island. The myth tells of a fight which took place between the snake gods of various species and a tribe of fish in the heroic age,

---

[1] In connection with a certain accusation of sorcery against a man, I was told that his innocence was rendered probable by the fact that he 'swore by Wonajö' that he had not committed the supposed deed. Further enquiries showed that it was usual for a man to take an oath on the strength of his *yaba* or the *yaba* of his clan, e.g. the expression 'True, Sun and Moon on top, I no steal him' was given me, and also 'Gadiu Mpwaliuwe it is true' (Gadiu is both stone and snake in the thunderstorm *yaba* in Mpwaliuwe; see Chap. XII, p. 168).

before man had appeared on the island. The fight is witnessed by two men, Luwe and Pume, who, however, turn out to be not true men but snake gods, one, if not both, of whom are guardians of *yaba* (see Chap. xII, p. 154). A feast is in progress amongst a number of brightly coloured fish, who, at one time, are supposed to be in the water, at another time, in the bush. Wonajö assembles the snakes, who sit around on stones and in trees, and he tells them that they must fight and kill the fish. Luwe and Pume, in hiding, then hear the song of the snakes, led by Wonajö: '*Dwilu twa lu yile yalo mpwulu mbwago mbwabo dodogwa pamo*', meaning roughly, I was told, 'We do not understand their talk; many men sit down there to-day; to-morrow we will fight them; I am ready, we are ready'. The snakes that fight are Wonajö, Mbasi, Gadiu (Chap. xII, p. 168), Mbyung (Chap. xII, p. 160), and Nongwa (Chap. xII, p. 153). All of these are connected with *yaba* at the present day.

Each of these snake gods is accompanied in the fight by a host of similar snakes (or gods or men,—according as we choose to regard them), so that Wonajö appears as the chief of snakes of the Wonajö kind, Mbasi of snakes of the Mbasi kind, and so on. Each is provided with a peculiar weapon. Wonajö is armed with the man-catcher,[1] Mbasi with tomahawk stones (of the Massim ceremonial kind apparently), Gadiu with bows and arrows, Mbyung with stones (probably thrown from slings), while Nongwa uses his fingers only (striking the nose of his opponent, not with the fist, but with the extended finger, in some mysterious way, which I could not understand). Those associated with Wonajö, i.e. all snakes of the Wonajö kind, also use the man-catcher, while the Mbasi snakes all use tomahawk stones, and similarly for the associates of the other five principals. The snakes win the fight and the fishes are exterminated or flee. After the fight, Wonajö, Mbasi and Mbyung retain their general snake-form, while Gadiu and Nongwa are turned to stone, where they may be seen in the *yaba* of each. It should be noted that the spear, the only weapon on Rossel at the

---

[1] From the description given me there is little doubt that the weapon is the man-catcher which has been reported from East Cape amongst the Massim, but not I believe east of that. Known as *wyeli*, it is said to be used in children's games at the present day. As I, unfortunately, neglected to get one made the nature of the weapon must be left in doubt.

present day, does not figure in the myths. The bow-and-arrow, though it occurs as a toy or medical instrument on Rossel and elsewhere in the east of New Guinea, does not occur as a weapon amongst the Melanesians of Papua. The man-catcher has not been recorded east of East Cape. The sling is common amongst the Massim, but the tomahawk stones, apparently referred to in the myths, are used only for purposes of currency and ceremonial.

One of the few exceptions to the general rule that the gods have the form of snakes, even though they may also appear in human form and in certain cases are stones, is provided by the god *Ye*. There is something evil about this god, which is not characteristic of the other principal gods, however dangerous these may be, and his animal form is a huge fish-hawk, whose *yaba* is the island of Loa, or, at least, part of this island, which appears to be taboo for a number of reasons, one of which is the presence of Ye. To Ye is attributed the origin of sorcery, which, to the mind of the Rossel Islander, as of many other primitive peoples is the most evil thing in the world. In the 'Golden Age', before death had come amongst the descendants of Mbasi, Ye lived with his snakes in the district of Pemewe, at the south-west end of Rossel (see Chap. XII, p. 155). Ye (or his sister—I am not clear which) one day obtained from a sex *yaba* in Yongga a portion of the plant which excites sexual desire. This plant was burnt by the sister when Ye was in the neighbourhood and Ye, as a result, had connection with her. A dog nearby laughed at this incestuous relationship, and Ye, angry at what he had done, converted the dog's speech into an unintelligible bark, so that he would not spread the news of his shame, and he himself killed his sister by the *ngwivi* method of sorcery. She and Kaijum, lord of Yuma, were the first to die by this method. The sister of Ye seems to have been the first for whom a cannibal mortuary feast was made (though, according to the myth, it is Ye who eats the man, sacrificed on account of her death). Ye then fled to Loa, where he still resides as a fish-hawk. A *ghönö* (mother's brother) of Ye's sister, discovering the death, took the head of the corpse, wrapped in a leaf, intending to take it by canoe to Loa. When the mortuary party reached the passage between Tiama Island and the mainland at the eastern extremity of the island, they decided to go no further and the remains were deposited on shore a few yards above the beach. This spot is now a *yaba* of exceptional danger and there is only one man who can go anywhere near it with safety. It is believed that the head is still there, the flesh still putrefying and the leaf, in which it was placed, still green—even the eyes are open and not yet disintegrated. This *yaba* was made under the direction of Wonajö, who laid down a number of pieces of wood as marks to show where the head was to be placed. These pieces of wood are now visible as stones. Associated with this *yaba* is a very bad sickness which tends to break out in times of drought, when the sun makes the head stink. The remaining bones were left behind, and are associated with a *yaba*, connected, I believe, with sorcery.[1]

Ye, the fish-hawk, figures in some curious tales of the heroic age. In these myths, Ye appears to have made his home on Loa, Wonajö residing on Ngwö. Ye and Wonajö are pictured as in continual conflict, which is, however, only half serious. Ye, or rather the ten *jina* (sisters' son) of Ye, first play some trick on Wonajö and his ten *jina*. The latter then retaliates with some similar trick. Ye returns the compliment and so on. The tone is playful rather than serious. In the first incident given me, Wonajö is retaliating for some practical joke by Ye. Wonajö is taught to catch or eat fish—I do not know which—in a ridiculous way, which makes him feel foolish. Wonajö then invites Ye and his *jina* to come and get some trees for food or some such purpose. Wonajö's *jina* demonstrate how to cut down the trees, but in such a way that Ye's *jina* are deceived and they cut themselves badly. Ye, in retaliation, then invites Wonajö to come and catch clams. Ye's *jina* open the clams with stones, without letting Wonajö see; but when Wonajö's *jina* ask how to open their clams, Ye says 'Oh, use your hands', and the *jina* of Wonajö hurt themselves badly. Wonajö then invites Ye to a feast at Ngwö. In the night, when Ye and his *jina* are asleep, Wonajö, by a spell, makes Ngwö rise to the heavens, he himself then descending on his bit of ground

[1] Ye is also the name of two crocodile gods, who are in charge of *yaba* associated with sorcery. It is possible that this similarity of name indicates some connection which I did not discover (see Chap. xii, pp. 155 and 167).

to the normal level. Ye and his *jina* have to prepare a rope from pandanus or some other tree, by which they descend to earth. Ye then invites Wonajö to Loa. Ye provides the canoe and they all sail over to Loa, but when Wonajö and his *jina* are asleep, the others leave in the only canoe, so that Wonajö is stranded. Wonajö, however, merely causes two trees, one on Loa and one on Rossel, to bend over and meet, when they are tied by him, so that he and his *jina* are enabled to walk over safely. Ye, after arriving on Rossel, breaks up the sailing canoe, and parts of it may now be seen under water, converted to stone. The mast-holder—a stone like a mortar—is supposed when interfered with to cause a big wind. This is described as the last incident in the game, after which Wonajö and Ye meet and agree that they have 'squared up'.

Although in the above tale, Wonajö scarcely has the dignity of a supreme chief or a supreme god, he figures in most myths of origin as final arbiter of the process of creation, if not as creator; or, in the case of introduced objects or objects for which no cause is assigned, it is Wonajö who assigns these objects their place in the world of Rossel. Although Ye appears as an equal of Wonajö in the heroic age, Ye is only a subordinate god confined to a *yaba* on Loa at the present day, carrying out an office defined by Wonajö, just as Mbasi, more important as a creator and as an introducer of useful objects than Wonajö, can only affect human destiny through the *yaba*, where he now exists as a piece of rock, and where he is approached by a ritual ordained by Wonajö. Whatever the gods may have done in the heroic age, they are now localised and only interfere in human affairs in a mechanical way through the *yaba*, with which each is connected. Even Wonajö is only directly dangerous or helpful to man through the *yaba* primarily associated with him, on Mt Rossel.

Almost all, if not all, religious procedure on Rossel occurs in connection with the *yaba*. Every *yaba* has its god or gods, and every *yaba* (with perhaps a few exceptions) is connected with some aspect of nature directly affecting man, whether it be food supply, weather, or sickness. The *yaba* are unified by their relation to Wonajö, to whom the institution of most, if not all, of the *yaba* is ascribed. Even at the present day, it is supposed that Wonajö exercises a direct supervision over the *yaba*, visiting them every night to see that all is in order; the nightmare is due to the passing by of Wonajö on one of these nightly visits. The care of the *yaba* is in the hands of man, whose religious duties fall under two heads: one, the proper care of the *yaba*, a constant duty; the other, the performance of certain rites at certain times to ensure the special favour of nature or the gods. The first duty applies to almost every *yaba*, but is the care of certain men only, connected with the *yaba*, whom we may call priests; and it is a general rule that there should be one priest for every *yaba*. The second duty applies only to certain *yaba*, and on those occasions when the ritual is performed, not only the priest of the *yaba*, but others who accompany the priest in a subsidiary capacity, may enter it under the priest's direction.

Every *yaba* is a potential source of danger. If the stone or principal object of the *yaba* is fouled by falling branches of trees or disturbed by some prowling animal, nature reacts in a way generally harmful to man. Every *yaba* has its own peculiar maleficent reaction and the principal duty of the priest is to keep it clean and undisturbed in order to prevent this reaction. Since every *yaba* has its own peculiar reaction, any disturbance of nature may at once be attributed to the appropriate *yaba*, though it may, in some cases, be difficult to decide between a number of *yaba* whose reactions may be similar; for example, rain is the maleficent reaction of many *yaba* and may also be produced by individual magicians, who, however, generally make use of stones, which are similar to the rain-making stones of many of the *yaba*.

Thunderstorms, pre-eminently a sign of anger on the part of Wonajö, may also result from any serious disturbance of the principal *yaba*, and winds of different quality and direction are assigned to most of them. In the case of the Wonajö *yaba*, and possibly the Mbasi and sun-and-moon *yaba*, a serious violation of its sanctity might cause a reaction so terrible that Rossel Island, if not the world, might be destroyed. My most imaginative informant gave me a terrifying picture of what might happen if the gods were angered by any serious negligence or sacrilege on the part of mortals. Not only would the sun and moon retire and plunge the world into a darkness illuminated only by the lightning flashes of the accompanying storm, but all the *yaba* objects—the stones, the snakes, trees, crocodiles, and so on—would prowl around the island devouring every human being they came across, if these were not already destroyed by violent earthquakes and tidal waves.

Where a stone is the principal object of a *yaba*, a shelter is sometimes built over it to guard against the undesirable results of contact with the débris of the bush or of interference by animals. While every *yaba* has a maleficent reaction, which it is the principal object of its priests to prevent taking place, certain of them have a beneficent reaction, which is normally maintained, provided they are not neglected by those whose duty it is to attend to them. The sum of these beneficent reactions of the more important *yaba* may be regarded as that which makes the normal life of the Rossel Islander a possibility. It gives him rain and sun, low tides and fine water for fishing; gives him sago, coconuts, and taro, and in fact all his food; gives him sexual desire and makes him fertile.

The universe is like a machine, with a few exposed parts, which, so long as they are kept clean, ensure the smooth working of the whole. That is the chief religious duty of man; but the machine requires oiling at times, and we find that this is a more positive duty of the priests of certain of the more important of the *yaba* that give a beneficent reaction. Although unable to observe this latter procedure, I was given an account of the annual ceremony that takes place at the sago *yaba*, situated near the important *yaba* of Mbasi and the sun and moon *yaba* (see Chap. xii, pp. 144–5).

A sago palm appeared of itself on Rossel, and Wonajö, having discovered it, ordered two men, Pere and Mbuwa, who are really snake gods, to cut the tree down, so that they could try it as food. They prepared the pith in the usual way, drying it, and baking it, and then cut it into portions for them all to try. One bundle of sago was put aside, and, later, Wonajö returned to take it. When he touched it, however, there was thunder and lightning. Wonajö, therefore, wrapped it in a leaf and hid it in the bush, declaring the place a *yaba*. The sago bundle is now a stone and the maleficent reaction of the *yaba* is violent thunderstorms, while its beneficent reaction is abundance of sago and the calm weather which occurs early in the north-west season.

At the end of the south-east season, the priest of the sago *yaba* repairs to it with a number of others and sits down close to the shelter in which the stone lies. He alone is in possession of a certain verbal formula, which enables him to approach and touch the stone with safety. The remainder of the party make a sort of pudding of sago and coconut and various herbs, and one of them makes a special dish, which is to be eaten by the priest. The food is eaten by the party when the priest gives the signal, it being necessary for all to eat at the same time. The *yaba* is then carefully cleaned, grass and weeds being pulled up, not merely cut down, and a fresh shelter is made for the sago stone. Finally, the stone is covered with red paint by the priest and is placed in its new shelter. Only the priest may handle the stone and tread on the ground in its immediate vicinity: those who accompany him are not allowed beyond a certain mark, as it is believed that the violation of this taboo would arouse the maleficent reaction. Three days later the priest returns alone and recites certain formulae, removes the ashes remaining from the ceremonial cooking, and neatly piles the coconut shells which have been left behind. He brings with him in his basket a small quantity of the scraped coconut, which had been used at the rite of three days before, wrapped in a piece of the spathe of the coco palm, which has been used in preparing the sago. After the necessary incantations have been made at the *yaba*, this little bundle is taken to the seashore, where it is tied to one of the immersed roots of a mangrove. This ends the ceremony, which ensures the period of calm weather at the beginning of the north-west season, the pleasantest period of the whole year in the eyes of the natives. The painting of the stone appears to be more directly connected with the supply of sago; for I was told that if the red paint were washed off by rain, the sago would be uneatable.

In the basket carried by the priest when he visits the *yaba* there is one good *ndap* and one set of *nkö* of large diameter. When Wonajö handed this money to the first priest he said 'This belongs to the *yaba*, not to you, but it is your business to look after it'. Ever since, it has been handed on, always from father to son, so my informant insisted.[1] Although the priest is not paid in money for the service he does the community in ensuring calm water and abundance of sago and in preventing thunderstorms, he receives contributions of fish, which are caught as a result of the fine weather, for which he is largely responsible.

There are probably similar ceremonies connected with other *yaba*. I visited the summit of Mt Rossel, the home of Wonajö, but discovered nothing of interest there; though Mr Osborne tells me that on a previous occasion he had seen a pile of coconut shells at the top; and I was told by one informant that the summit is occasionally visited and that part of the ritual consists in the visitors smearing themselves with coconut oil. It is, therefore, probable that an important ceremony takes place at this *yaba*; for it is held in such awe by the natives that only a few could be persuaded to accompany us, and most of these appeared to be in a condition of terror long before we reached the summit and they could not be persuaded to remain after dusk even at the camp, which was some 500 ft. below the *yaba* itself. A small snake which we found in the camp we did not venture to kill—it might have been a god.

Rites, similar to but less elaborate than the above, occur at other *yaba*, which have only a maleficent reaction, the object being, in these cases, to bring the maleficent reaction to an end. For instance, a plague of mosquitoes or sandflies leads to representations being made to the priests of the *yaba* concerned to repair their neglect in not having properly done their work. In the mosquito *yaba* in Maiuwe (see Chap. XII, p. 164) there is a stone, but no guardian animal. The stone was placed there originally by Wonajö. If there is a plague of mosquitoes, the priest of this *yaba* cleans the stone and pours on it the juice of a lime, incanting the while, uttering the names of various gods and ending up with that of Wonajö, the most important of all. The neglect of the latter would cause the mosquitoes to become even more numerous. The informant, who told me of this *yaba* and outlined the procedure, stated that, in the formulae connected

---

[1] If succession in the priesthood is really definitely patrilineal, this explains why the owner of a *yaba* is rarely its priest, for inheritance of the *yaba* seemed to be matrilineal (see Chap. xv).

with every *yaba*, the name of Wonajö occurs as the most essential part of the spell.

It is clear from what has already been said how great is the importance of the *yaba* in the lives of the Rossel Islanders; yet, in spite of this, a *yaba* scarcely differs in appearance from any other patch of land or reef. Generally, it contains a visible stone, or some other object, such as a tree, which, in some cases at least, does not differ in appearance from other stones or trees.[1] The *yaba*, as a rule, has also a guardian, generally a snake, which is liable to swell up and devour any unauthorised person who approaches.

The guardian of a *yaba* is sometimes seen by the natives, for any animal seen in the vicinity, of the right species, is thought to be the guardian and carefully avoided. Both guardian and stone, either of which may be absent in the case of certain *yaba*, are really gods and are regarded as existing, in some sense, in Temewe, where they are human in form and constitute a society, presided over by Wonajö. The sun and moon, however, are not to be found in Temewe for they are always in the heavens. It is interesting to note that although Mbasi has the human form in Temewe, he wears the Massim girdle, not the peculiar girdle of Rossel, and he frequently visits the Sudest Temewe by canoe. Native thought is very illogical and confused on these metaphysical points, and differing views are given, according to the bias of the informant.

In the next chapter are enumerated most of the *yaba* on Rossel. There are, no doubt, many omissions, but an attempt was made to secure completeness by first ascertaining the names of districts on the island, some hundred in all, and then enquiring for the *yaba* in each district, using, where possible, informants from the neighbourhood. Although the information obtained about each *yaba* is, in most cases, very scanty, it is. sufficient to give some idea of the variety and extent of the natural processes believed to be controlled by this mechanism.

[1] I observed very few of the *yaba*, for it would have been impolitic to attempt this, but I was shown the Mbasi stone from a distance and found it to be nothing but a bit of outcropping volcanic rock, situated below high-water mark. Another *yaba*, which I stumbled upon by accident, contained only a tree in no way peculiar.

CHAPTER XII

Sacred Places

THESE sacred places, or *yaba*,[1] are so numerous that they are best treated geographically. The numbers on the map (p. 8) correspond to districts, whose names I recorded. The positions are relatively correct, but there may be considerable absolute errors, though this was guarded against as far as possible by fixing certain of the districts by known points on the map. The numbers without a suffixed letter denote coastal districts, while a number with a suffixed letter denotes an interior district behind the coastal district of the same number.

1. MILEWE

A *yaba*, known as *Pyaba*, with a stone, *Yanö*, and two crocodile guardians, *Yobo* and *Gobo* occurs in this district. The *yaba* is connected with coconuts. The stone is by the side of a river, in which the crocodiles normally reside. The priest at this *yaba* is supposed to talk to the crocodiles at intervals. A certain red product of a plant is placed by the priest by the side of the stone and this is supposed to lead to an abundance of coconuts. The crocodiles see this offering and wander along the coast at night, producing a beneficial effect on the coconuts. No woman is allowed up this river and canoes are careful to keep to the centre of the stream. If anyone but the priest were to land on the bank near the stone he would be eaten by crocodiles; even if this did not happen at the time he would be taken on some other occasion, even while asleep in the upper part of his house. This idea of the inevitability of punishment for violating the taboo on a *yaba* is very common, in spite of the general belief in the localisation of the gods of the *yaba*.

[1] The pidgin-English expression for these sacred places is 'tabura'. I find on going through my notes, that there is a slight doubt as to whether *yaba* is the correct term. I always used the term 'tabura' in obtaining my information.

It should be noted that some of the names of *yaba* recorded here are descriptive. In each of these cases, the *yaba* has probably also a proper name, which I failed to record.

There is another *yaba* for coconuts at Bamba (district 28), about which I obtained no information, and one in district 51 which is closely associated with Pyaba. The influence on coconuts of the above *yaba* only extends from districts 54 to 6. I obtained a myth of the origin of coconuts, which is similar to the Massim and other myths of the origin of this food, but does not explain the connection of the above *yaba* with coconuts:

Before the time of coconuts, a dugong, called Chima[1], one day sends his *jina* (sister's son) to catch fish. The boy spears a sting-ray, but the latter, shaking itself free, kills and devours him, all but the head. Chima takes a canoe and finds only the head of his nephew. He brings the head back, puts it in a house and ties up the door, telling his two wives on no account to enter. He then departs for Sudest. His wives, their curiosity aroused, do not wait long before they peep inside, when they discover that objects, themselves like heads, have sprouted from the original head—like eggs from a fly, as my informant put it. This strange fruit is tried on Chima's dog, *Pidyi*, who asks for more. Then the women try this food and some of the oil escapes into the sea. The oil meets Chima on his way from Sudest, and he wonders whether the fine water is due to this substance which he sees on the surface and whether his wives have interfered with that which he left in the house. He arrives at Rossel, entering by the Ebaleti passage, and questions his wives, who deny that they have entered the house. He does not believe them, but takes the coconuts and plants them, and when the fruit appears, distributes them to his friends.

A most important *yaba* occurs in district 1, connected with the eye and vision. It lies amongst mangroves and originally a creature—a very large mollusc, as far as I could make out—could always be seen in the vicinity. The *yaba* is known as *Tiuwe* (or possibly this is a district, containing it) and the object is known as *Wada*. The latter, however, is no longer to be found there: it was removed by Wonajö to the edge of the reef because the natives used to see the creature and their eyes became badly inflamed. Sickness of the eyes is attributed to this object at the present day, and the *yaba* is carefully tended by a priest. Thunder and lightning are also associated with it, and a northerly wind known as *Bwago*. The *yaba* appears to be held in great dread.

[1] See also pp. 153 and 165.

2. DYÖDOWAIWE

A little way back from the coast mangroves is a *yaba* known as *Pwembaiu*. A crocodile, called *Nonon*, is connected with it. This crocodile is a friend of the two crocodiles of the coconut *yaba*; but it does not devour people and feeds only on sticks, which it takes for dogs. The nature of this *yaba* is rather obscure.

3. DYINDYÖWE

A *yaba* lies on the edge of the salt water, to the east of the village of Dyindyö. Its maleficent reaction is equally rain and a swelling of the testes, hence the names *Pthyi yaba* (rain *yaba*) and *Wye yaba* (testes *yaba*). The *yaba* object is a tree, called *Yibobo*, and a sting-ray acts as guardian. If the tide leaves some driftwood against this tree, that is sufficient to cause rain and sickness.[1] I was told by one informant that the tree and the sting-ray were not different entities, but that the tree sometimes walked about and turned into a sting-ray. There is said to be a similar tree in the neighbourhood of East Cape (9). The above *yaba* has the wind *Jibe yobo* associated with it, which is the same as that of the Mbasi *yaba*.

[1] One of my police and my cook-boy one moonlight evening drew too close in a dinghy to this *yaba*, of the existence of which they were un-aware, with consequences disastrous to their peace of mind. The dinghy was suddenly violently rocked and almost capsized, according to their account, although there was no visible agency either above the water or below, and the sandy bottom below the shallow water was clearly visible, and the water was perfectly calm before the event. They attributed the phenomenon to supernatural agency and returned to the village in great terror. They were assured by the owner and priest of the *yaba* that they would suffer for the sacrilege and that he had no power to avert the inevitable consequences. He was of opinion that the least hopeful element in the situation was the fact that the policeman had been wearing his uniform. He, himself, although a village policeman, always removed every emblem of his office before performing his priestly duties at this *yaba*. Although I visited the spot, which had nothing peculiar about it, and observed the water in the vicinity at various states of the tide, I could discover no explanation of the incident. It is just possible that the motion of the boat might have been produced by the rapid motion and fast leap of a sting-ray, for the movements of this animal might be, so I understand, sufficiently rapid to elude observation. If this be the correct explanation, the coincidence is certainly remarkable.

3 *a*. YELIUWE

Between the coast and Ngwö there is a stone, on which Wonajö rested on his way to his final home on Mt Rossel. This stone is called *Ngwabe* and is covered with a huge pile of leaves which have been deposited by passers-by for generations.[1] Wonajö had just left the home of Pere, an ophidian friend of Wonajö, near East Cape (9), and there is a similar stone, on which Pere is supposed to have rested, situated near Dyindyö (3); this, also, is covered with leaves. On this stone Pere is supposed to have composed his song '*Kanjeb*', now a *dama*, and Wonajö likewise composed a *dama* while seated on the stone Ngwabe. It was here that the flower, *Wobo* (also given as *Namabwe*), fell on Wonajö and caused him to make it his totem. These stones are not strictly *yaba*, for they are not connected with natural processes, though they are, of course, taboo.

3 *c*. NGWÖWE

Ngwö is the residence of Wonajö, and, with the exception of the Mbasi *yaba*, probably the most important *yaba* on the island. In theory, negligence or sacrilege in connection with this *yaba* might not only bring the guilty to an untimely end but might involve the whole island, if not the world, in a general catastrophe.

4 *a*. TUNUBAWE

A *yaba* for taro, known as *Pwangyelawe*, presided over by a snake called *Nönö*, occurs here. Before Mbasi arrived from Sudest, Wonajö sent his friend Nönö to Sudest in a wooden dish, with a message for Mbasi. Nönö returned first, making the passage through the Sudest reef, which, appropriately enough, is known to Europeans as the Snake Passage. After Mbasi's arrival Wonajö placed Nönö in charge of the taro, which the former had brought with him. Nönö is invoked by the priest of the *yaba* to make the taro crop a good one. Apparently, the priest may be asked to use his influence in

---

[1] I passed this stone on my way to a village in Yeliuwe (3 *a*), and, when no one was looking, pushed my stick through about two feet of leaf and mould without encountering the stone at the base.

favour of the taro of any particular man—he is subsequently given a basket of the root as pay.

There is another *yaba* for taro near Bamba (28), but I do not know whether the snake god Nönö has any connection with it.

6. YABUWE

Here is a *yaba*, ranking, possibly, first in the importance on the island. The locality is known as *Kengwe* and includes a small portion of lagoon as well as of bush. The supposition that I intended to visit this *yaba*, in spite of opposition, was the chief cause of my inability to get any appreciable amount of information on the island during my first month. Apparently, the approach for other than priests to the neighbourhood of the *yaba*, without breaking the taboo, is very difficult, and, moreover, the natives would naturally not expect a white man to take any notice of any such taboo. They were, therefore, fearful of what might happen if I interfered. It was, therefore, necessary for me to state that I had no intention of visiting any *yaba* which they did not wish to show me. The stone Mbasi lies in the salt water, a rock of several tons in weight, to judge by its appearance. The stone *Könjini*, the wife of Mbasi, lies a short distance away above high-water mark and concealed by vegetation. Each stone is primarily connected with generation, which is natural enough in view of the myth of origin of the Rossel race from the union of Mbasi and Könjini. Mbasi is connected with the male organs, and Könjini with the female organs. Part of the maleficent reaction of these stones is sterility and lack of sexual desire. There are, however, a number of other reactions, connected particularly with the Mbasi stone. Normally, the *yaba* is responsible for the gentle north-east wind, known as *Jibe yobo*; but if there be inattention to the *yaba*,—if, for instance, driftwood be driven on to the stone, or someone, other than the priest, approach it,—not only would the sexual organs of all the natives be affected but there would be a disastrous flood. This connection with a flood is as strongly emphasised as the connection with sex, and there seems also to be some relation between Mbasi and the tides. In storms, and possibly at night, the stone is supposed to move about, and I doubt whether anyone

PLATE XIX

(a) Canoe, *para nö*.

(b) Canoe, *para nö*.

PLATE XX

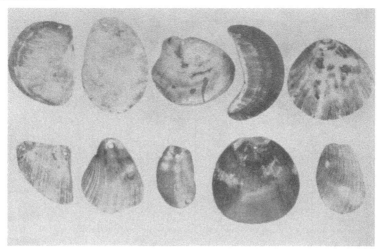

(*a*) Money, *ndap*.

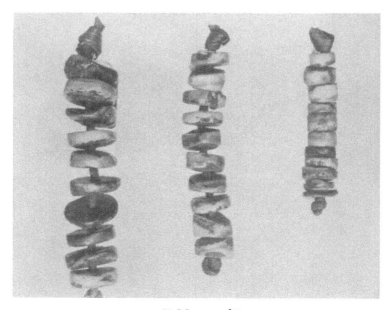

(*b*) Money, *nkö*.

would dare to pass the *yaba* in a canoe at night.[1] The stone often varies in size. No woman is allowed to pass this spot in a canoe, a cause of considerable inconvenience since a wide détour must be made through the bush at the back. Men, in a canoe, lower their voices when passing this *yaba* even at a distance.

Not only is this *yaba* connected with sexual desire and fertility, but also with venereal disease, though it may be that there are two other stones in this neighbourhood, whose maleficent function is the production of venereal disease. I was given the name *Yabawe* for this 'pokus tabura.' The terms *Mwa bobo* and *Pia bobo* for the male and female stones were given me, but I also find *Phyunjwe* as the name of a 'pokus stone'.[2]

A story is told of a man from Piron (off Sudest), who, coming ashore from a schooner, took some water from near this *yaba*. He died shortly after as did many others later, and this is attributed to the influence of the *yaba*.

It is interesting to note that at the present day the Mbasi *yaba* is owned by two brothers of one totem, while the priest, who alone may enter the *yaba*, is a man of another totem.

Not far from the Mbasi *yaba* is the sago *yaba* of almost equal importance to the Rossel Islander, owing to the fact that sago is the chief food and to the fact that this *yaba* is especially connected with the calm weather which intervenes between the south-east and the north-west seasons.

The wind of the *yaba* is a gentle wind from the north-east known as *Mwalo*, but also a stormy wind from about the same quarter known as *Mbwia*. The priest is supposed to be able to make either wind at his discretion.

The *yaba* is known as *Kung* and contains a single stone,—a petrified bundle of sago which is housed and specially treated at certain times, as indicated in the previous chapter. It is interesting to note that this stone is not only regarded as a bundle of sago but also as a snake, while it may appear in Temewe in human form.

[1] There is also a small white snake *Wi*, which is always near the Mbasi stone and is dangerous to man. It does not seem to be an incarnation of Mbasi.

[2] This suggests that venereal disease of some form is of long standing in New Guinea, contrary to the usual opinion. I also found a reference to some disease of the genitals in a legend from the south-east coast of New Guinea. This disease is probably venereal granuloma, for both syphilis and gonorrhoea appear to be recent introductions.

6 *a.* CHALIBAWE

Ngwanamba is the original hiding-place of the sun and the moon, before they mounted into the sky. I could not discover much about this *yaba*, though it appears to be of great importance. No stone or animal of the *yaba* was mentioned, but the priest has important duties. I was told that, in the case of this *yaba* more than any other, was it imperative for the priest not to have anything foreign with him on his visits, not a strip of European calico nor even an object made on Sudest.[1]

The rising of the sun and the moon depends on the correct performance of his duties by the priest, and the failure of the sun to rise would also mean anarchy amongst the *yaba* and wholesale destruction of the Rossel Islanders by the *yaba* objects. Yet there is always only one person who knows the priestly formulae except when that person is an old man, when he imparts the necessary information to a younger man who will succeed him in his office.

In this same district there is a *yaba* for song. There are many of these on the island and they do not seem to be taboo in the ordinary way. A basket is put on the stone, which is to be found in the *yaba*, and the next morning water is placed in the basket and drunk. It makes a high sweet voice 'like a woman crying'; a bass voice, it should be noted, is never cultivated.

7. PEAWE

There is a stone called *Gmweda* which is not taboo and is connected with certain 'fish', called *gmwe*, which are good eating. So long as the stone is kept clean, the fish come inside the reef close to shore and are easily caught; but should a stray leaf or twig fall on the stone, the shoal remains outside.

A similar stone, not far off, in district 8 or 9, is connected with a fish called *mwabö*. This stone appears to be taboo. The priest keeps it clean and scrapes coconut over it at certain times, which causes the fish to have plenty of fat.

---

[1] I was told towards the end of my stay, that I might visit this *yaba*, if I was prepared to strip completely. I could not discover why my clothes should be regarded as more foreign than my body.

9. YILINOWAWE

A *yaba* known as *Kebokwo*, specially connected with the sailing of canoes, occurs here in the mangroves on the edge of the salt water. The snake *Pere* lives here and his function appears to be to wreck at night canoes that are in the neighbourhood of East Cape: the victims of such a wreck are eaten by Pere and Wonajö. The latter put Pere in charge of this *yaba*; and the priest who knows the formula can ensure the safe passage of canoes. I believe Pere is generally invoked in the magic connected with the sailing of canoes. I also found his name next to that of Wonajö in a spell for causing a certain kind of sickness (see Chap. XIII, p. 174).

Connected in some way with the above *yaba* is one known as *Pwalegwing*, on which is a tree that walks about at night and turns into a sting-ray, exactly similar to the one in district 3.

In the same district is a lawyer-cane *yaba*, *Rama yaba*. The object on this is something that appears to be cane, but is really only cane at one end and snake at the other. A stranger, entering this *yaba*, becomes entangled in the cane, which tries to crush him, and is then eaten by the snakes, which are continuations of the cane.

On the beach near East Cape is a *yaba*, *Tomeliu*, with a stone. It is also called *Yobo yaba*, or wind *yaba*. This stone gives the easterly wind from Loa. When a canoe goes to Loa, leaves are intentionally put on the stone, so that a wind will arise, but these are removed if it gets too strong. Either Pere or the snake of the lawyer-cane *yaba* is supposed to be the guardian of this stone.

Somewhere in the neighbourhood of East Cape is a *yaba* known as *Ngama*, with a stone connected with a certain sickness and big seas on a part of the reef. These seas have the peculiarity that they appear quite insignificant until a canoe is nearly on them, when they appear as big as mountains.

In this district also is the *yaba* containing what is supposed to be the head of the first victim of sorcery and connected with Ye, the fish-hawk on Loa (see Chap. XI).

On the reef opposite Yilinoa is a *yaba* in which resides a fish called *Wangö*, which has a mouth as big as a house. What its function is I do not know.

9 *a*. LILEUWE

The *Gono yaba* or taro-grub *yaba* is situated here. A stone, *Iyembo*, was left by Wonajö inside a large clam shell. Before taro was brought to Rossel by Mbasi, this grub used to feed on another plant, but confined itself to taro when that appeared. Wonajö, therefore, made this *yaba* to control the grub's activities. Only if the stone is disturbed by fallen leaves or by animals, etc., do the grubs leave the clam and destroy the taro.

There was a formula, by means of which the grubs can be induced to return to the clam shell. This formula, however, has been lost by the natives; it was in the hands of a woman, who neglected to pass it on before her death. As a result, the Rossel taro is very poor and fears are held that it will be completely destroyed by the grub. I discovered no other instances of the loss of the formulae connected with any *yaba*.

Nönö, the taro snake, is supposed to be connected with this *yaba* as a sort of guardian (see p. 143).

LOA ISLAND

Some ten miles from East Cape across a wide lagoon is the island of Loa,[1] on the edge of the reef. This island was surrounded with taboos until the Osbornes recently cleared most of it and planted coconuts, but even now it is approached with care and misgiving, although most of the taboos have been violated. A Rossel woman, even, has landed on Loa and neither she nor any one else appears to have suffered for this extreme sacrilege.[2]

Ye, the fish-hawk, who figures in the myth, recorded in the last chapter, lives on Loa, although his former home was on Rossel. Although Ye is greatly feared and liable to devour visitors to the island, most of the taboos that have to be observed on Loa and the fishing-ground in its neighbourhood appear to be connected with a cephalopod, known as *Lab*. Lab is the cause of the taboo on the use of the number 7

[1] Some of the beliefs connected with this island are recorded by Murray (App. I, p. 220). Bell refers to the use of different names on Loa (App. I, p. 226).

[2] I was told that some other woman had recently taken advantage of this example and had declared that she would no longer go a mile out of her way to the gardens in order to avoid a certain *yaba*.

on Loa, which must be rendered, if required, by the number 6 spoken twice. If the number 7 were uttered anywhere in the neighbourhood of Loa, Lab would swell to an enormous size and devour the offender and those with him. Although Lab is regarded as female, i.e. she is a woman in Temewe, she allows no woman to approach Loa. Lab is the cause of the south-east trade wind. Every year, at the end of the north-west season, she is rejuvenated and might be seen as a woman in her prime in Temewe; but she grows old as the year approaches its end; and in the north-west season she is a feeble old woman. As Lab grows old her husband grows young; for he is the north-west wind and alternates between youth and age in the same way. He is described as a fish, like a snake, and his *yaba* lies on the reef to the west of Rossel. Although there are not the numerous taboos on this *yaba* that we find on Loa, only those persons (for there appear to be several) acquainted with the necessary formula will go near it, and only the dialect of Western Rossel may be used. On Loa, it is a matter of indifference what dialect is used, but there are certain words which must be replaced by words only to be used on Loa. The use of any of the forbidden words is supposed to arouse the anger of Lab, if not the other gods on Loa. A list of words for which there are substitutes on Loa is given below. I failed to discover any grammatical differences between the Rossel and Loa languages.

	Rossel	Loa
sun	*kwadön*	*mwadö*
moon	*dwon*	*tabamö*
rain	*pchi*	*mbwam*
fire	*due*	*ndung*
water	*mbwa*	*tala*
lime pot	*ko*	*tchimi*
paddle	*yili*	*tenukwa*
(a certain very large fish)	*chedye*	*delo*
snake	*pchilöpö*	*tapa*
fat man	*mawe*	*limue*
stone	*chöbö*	*yeluwa*
tree	*iyi*	*lim*
basket	*pe*	*chimöbe*

	Rossel	Loa
swordfish (?)	*teni*	*mpwo*
blood	*wö*	*uwoda*
banana	*pwebe*	*pwadö*
north-west wind	*ndemi*	*mbwaine*
cook	*jeje*	*dondo*
food tongs	*pela*	*ndanikö*
male organ	*ndwö*	*kwailiguna*
female organ	*mpe (ptyö)*	*jimi*
ndap	*ndap*	*mbono*
työmundi	*työmundi*	*mbonamandö*
tejema	*tejema*	*bonejim*
dwojuma	*dwojuma*	*bonejim*
kwojuma	*kwojuma*	*bonejim*
gemida	*gemida*	*mbonda*
nkö	*nkö*	*uwa*
feast (general?)	*na*	*mwe*
white	*kwaukwau*	*nyibinyibi*
black	*kwodokwodo*	*bwumbwum*
Sudest	*Yam*	*Mwanandyibe*
rope	*yilogwa*	*ylimiti*
rat	*yima*	*loadangwala?*
fowl	*kwe*	*loadangwala?*
dugong	*pwau*	*geluba*
alligator	*pia*	*ngodaba*
kill	*yange*	*mbungi*
sleep	*dwo*	*kwa*
sick	*nibi*	*ginima*
sick (fever?)	*buono*	*ndi*
chief	*limi*	*iye*
sorcerer	*gwivi*	*pweabiu*
witches' stone	*gomibe*	*wuabe*
ghost	*ghö*	*kuwe*
pig	*mbwmö*	*mbwio*
dog	*wa*	*mbwio*
Wonajö	*Wonajö*	*Könö*
European knife	*gölijöba*	*göliwolomina*
European pipe	*dwaiwuna*	*limona*

I was told that the Loa names for the last two objects
were recent inventions. Apparently pidgin English may be
used on Loa and could even be used in place of the Loa
word for an object. It should be noted that the same term
denotes both pig and dog on Loa. Certain objects, which one

would have expected to be denoted by different terms on Loa, were not so treated, according to my informant, e.g. wind, sea, canoe, lime stick, coconut, sand beach, fish net, fish spear.

It may be noted in this connection that there are certain words, which are, at all times, taboo for women. For example, the term *nö* for canoe, which is used by men on Rossel and on Loa, may not be used by women, who use the term *duru*;[1] the sea is called *nchi* by men and *choli* by women; Loa is called *Yiubwa* by women. On Western Rossel there appear to be no separate terms for use by men and women; at least both men and women use the same words for 'canoe' and for 'the sea'.

An expedition to Loa is generally for the purpose of fishing; yet I was told that the various names of species of fish are taboo in the neighbourhood of Loa, only one term *könö* being used for any species, except that called *chedye* on Rossel and *delo* on Loa. A limitation on the fishing on these occasions is the necessity of catching some multiple of ten fish in the case of each canoe; if less than ten are caught before the canoe returns, they must all be thrown away.[2] The fish that are brought back from such an expedition may not be eaten by those who have not, on some occasion or other, visited Loa; women and children, therefore, do not partake.

Besides Lab and Ye, there is a small animal, a 'possum' so my informant said, which was placed on the island by Wonajö in a tree, which has also a supernatural character. My informant told me that not long ago a man who did not know the Loa formulae was left on Loa, while the rest of the party went fishing. He came across this animal and thought he would kill it; but, as soon as he touched it, it increased in size, becoming as big as a dog. He ran away, as the creature swelled to the size of a pig; and when he reached the salt water, he looked back to see a creature as big as a cow. By this time, the fishing party had returned with the priest who knew the formula for this *yaba*, and the

[1] According to Murray the term is *didi* (App. I, p. 220).
[2] Another informant told me that although 10 is the ideal number of fish, a smaller number could be taken, though 9 should be avoided, for this would arouse the anger of Lab. Why 9 rather than 7 I could not make out.

animal was quickly reduced to its normal size. But in order to be on the safe side with the gods, the man who was the cause of the trouble was sacrificed; his bones were broken and he was thrown into the sea.

There is a woman on Loa who takes the form of a bird, and is said to have come originally from Pchi. If this bird is seen on Loa, it is an omen that someone has died or is about to die. She is, I believe, the wife of Ye, though my informant was very confused on this point. Her male children are supposed to have incestuous designs on her, and Ye consequently keeps his children on the mainland and forbids them visiting Loa.

There is a spring of fresh water on Loa, which is supposed to come from Ngwö, the home of Wonajö. The story runs that the only man who knew where this water was situated died without revealing its locality. It is said to be near the salt water and to be hidden and sealed by a leaf.

11. DONGWE

Here is the *yaba* known as *Pimalö*, on which resides a small coloured snake, known as *Kwudi*. I did not discover the function of this *yaba*, but the snake was supposed to have the usual characteristics of swelling to an enormous size and devouring anyone who approached it.

11 *a*. MBOIUWE

In this district we find a *yaba* known as *Penengo*, on which are a number of stones connected with rain and wind. The chief stone is known as *Dödwa*. If the priest of this *yaba* covers up this stone with leaves and incants a certain formula, a violent squall is produced. Another stone, known as *Dodongwaiebo*, may be induced to produce a big wind by a similar procedure. If a woman were to go near these stones a similar but more violent effect would take place. There are also a number of smaller stones, associated with gentler rain and wind. Calm weather is produced by anointing the stones with coconut oil and by appropriate formulae. The priest has to spit on the stones and mutter certain spells to produce the desired result.

12. KÖNAWE

There is a *yaba* on shore, called *Dwomo*, and one on the reef opposite, called *Chima*. Both are connected with a dugong (possibly the dugong referred to on pp. 141 and 166) and a snake. The maleficent reaction of the Dwomo is a swelling of the legs. A canoe that leaves by the passage near the *yaba* on the reef is liable to be wrecked by the dugong, unless there is someone on board who knows the *yaba* formula.

12 *a*. KWABAWE

In a *yaba*, known as *Tölöba*, is an animal, which, if disturbed, causes a fatal sickness, one of the signs of which is a whitening of the skin.

13 *a*. YEBOWE

Pchi, a land of the dead, lies in this district. Although there is no sacred stone or guardian animal on this *yaba*, it is considered highly dangerous and avoided. I do not know whether the district is owned and whether there is a priest (see Chap. x).

Connected with Pchi is the giant clam on the edge of the Sudest reef where it approaches Rossel. It is this object, known as *Töbe*, who plays a game of catch with Kangö of Pchi, in which the ball is at first a clot of blood from a human sacrifice and appears in its flight as the rainbow (see Chap. x). Töbe is a danger to canoes, but Wonajö imparted to the Rossel Islander a formula that would protect any who might be carried on to this part of the reef. The *yaba* is regarded as equally the property of Rossel and Sudest.

14 *a*. MBOMUWE

On the hill at the back of this district there is a snake called *Mungwa* (or *Nongwa*?) put there originally by Wonajö. Only the small area of the *yaba*, not the hill, is avoided. This is probably the god that fought with his hands in the myth of Wonajö's fight with the fishes, though I was told by the narrator of this myth that he became turned into stone (see Chap. XI, p. 131).

20 *a*. NGÖWE

In the myth of Wonajö's fight with the fishes, given in Chap. XI, two men are mentioned as observing the fight in hiding. One of these, *Luwe*, resides as a snake on a hill at the back of this district. He was told to go there by Wonajö, but was given no work to do, and, therefore, is not connected with any natural process, such as is generally characteristic of a *yaba*. Luwe together with Pere and Wonajö is invoked in a certain form of sorcery (see Chap. XIII, p. 174).

22. BOROWE

There are two stones and a tree close together in this district, having special functions. Of the two stones, one, known as *Liö*, is male; the other, known as *Ghu*, female; and a crocodile, *Ra*, is guardian of the *yaba* that contains them. The stones are connected with sexual desire. Betel nut or tobacco is placed on the appropriate stone and then given to the man or woman whom it is wished to stimulate sexually. Probably only the priest can take the betel or tobacco into the *yaba*,—and for this service he is paid—for it is believed that the crocodile would devour any unauthorised person who entered the *yaba*, and a general sickness throughout Rossel would result. This latter maleficent reaction is also supposed to take place if the priest does not keep the *yaba* clean.

Close to the stones, and constituting, probably, a separate *yaba*, known as *Tai yaba*, is a tree, connected with fishing. If a twig from this tree is tied to a fish net, large quantities of fish will be caught.

25. TAMUWE

Three snakes were mentioned to me as occurring in this district,—a large one, *Mbodi*, on a hill, and two small ones, *Yiliwale* and *Sal*, at the foot of this hill. They have no particular function, but are dangerous, and the *yaba* are avoided by all; for, according to my informant, there is no one now in possession of the necessary formula for safely approaching them. Some years ago, a man from Eastern Rossel, residing with his wife in this district, ate one of these snakes (presumably a snake of the same species as the one snake of the *yaba*, if we are to assume that the snake of the *yaba* is strictly an individual and not a class). Shortly after, snakes emerged from his mouth, belly, and elsewhere, and devoured him completely except for his jawbone, which was found the next day.

When a man is devoured by a god in this way, his soul, *ghö*, is also believed to be destroyed and therefore does not go to any of the lands of the dead.

Somewhere in this district is a *yaba* connected with 'possums', which is utilised in some way when the latter are hunted. There is also a stone, associated with a south-westerly wind, known as *Chaiu*.

26. DOOWE

A *yaba* known as the *Gwöjin yaba* is situated here. It contains a stone, connected with the high tides of the north-west season. There is also a guardian snake, *Labmwe*. If there is a very high tide, the priest of the *yaba* with a number of helpers pays it a visit. A mixture of food containing principally coconut oil is first prepared, and this is poured into the salt water, the priest calling upon the tide to recede. The strong-smelling juice from the leaf of a certain tree is then prepared and the stone is painted with this. Both the stone and the snake are addressed in a formula that winds up with the name of Wonajö.

26 *a*. PEMEWE

This is the original home of Ye, the fish-hawk on Loa, originator of certain kinds of sorcery, if not of sorcery in general. There are two stones, *Myi* and *Pweu*, in this *yaba*, connected with the sickness, which can also be produced by certain forms of sorcery. The guardian of these stones is a crocodile, known as *Ye*, who has a brother of the same name on the north side of the island (district 55 *a*). This crocodile, Ye, becomes a snake when he leaves the river and visits these stones. A wide berth is given to the *yaba*, for the crocodile is considered to be particularly dangerous. The connection between this god and the Ye of Loa was obscure; but there clearly is some connection and it is possible that the two may be regarded as identical; for the Rossel gods do not obey the laws of physics or even metaphysics.

On the edge of a river in this district lies the *yaba* known as *Ka*. This consists of two stones, one large and one small, which lie in a cavity in a rock. In the creek by the side of the *yaba* lives a fish, which is like a snake (possibly an eel), known as *Kabia*, and acts as guardian of the *yaba*. The stones are connected with big sores, known as *yumo*, which break out on the body. These sores are treated with the leaf of a certain tree and with an incantation, in which the snake Kabia is addressed.

Near the *yaba* of Ye there is a sacred crab, but I have no information about this *yaba*.

27. NGAGUWE

A crocodile, named *Ched*, lives in a river in this district, and one priest owns the formula by means of which he is controlled. This crocodile is not dangerous and never eats people.

27 a. KWUNEWE

In ancient times a small white snake, *Ngwudi*, came from Sudest and took up his residence in this *yaba*, known as *Wuma*. He built a house and placed in it a number of Massim articles, in particular a very fine Bagi. A native of Rossel once tried to steal this Bagi, but was attacked by Ngwudi. The man's brother who was priest of the *yaba* fortunately arrived in time and made the snake desist, but the house, known as *Jebonom*, was turned into stone. Ngwudi is never seen at the present day, but the house is visible as a huge rock, and close to it is a sacred tree, closely associated with Ngwudi. One priest, but no other person, may visit this spot.

28. BAMBAWE

A *yaba* for coconuts is said to occur in this district, but I obtained no information about it.

29. BUMAWE

In a creek lies a stone, called *Teluma*. Its guardian is a cuttlefish, *Piamgwi*. A bad cough results from any disturbance of the stone.

29 a. PIÖWE

A *yaba* for taro is situated here. Wonajö brought the taro from Eastern Rossel (where it was introduced by Mbasi) to Western Rossel, and instituted this *yaba*, with its small stone, *Chuma*, and guardian snake, *Pwa*. A ceremony, similar to that which takes place at the sago *yaba*, is conducted by the priest at certain times to ensure a good crop of taro. The priest and a number of helpers repair to the *yaba* and cook food which is eaten by all, the priest leading. The stone is painted with a white paint. The maleficent reaction of the *yaba* is a sickness that attacks the knee, due to the snake, Pwa, invisibly eating the tissues within. This sickness would attack any stranger visiting the *yaba* but may be cured by appropriate medicine administered by the priest.

31. CHAJAWE

In this and other districts in the neighbourhood are a number of stones,[1] connected with rain. It is not clear whether they are connected with particular *yaba*, for the owners would sometimes keep them in their houses. There was no evidence that these stones, like most, if not all, of the *yaba* stones, were believed to be men in Temewe (or what I have called gods). These stones are all connected with north-westerly squalls, which are produced by painting the stones with the preparation from some plant, by subsequently covering them with a banana leaf, and finally placing them in the salt water. It is interesting to note that the rain and wind stones, whether of *yaba* or not, of Western Rossel seem to be connected more particularly with westerly winds, while those of Eastern Rossel are mostly connected with easterly winds. The production of the south-east weather and north-west weather as definite seasons we have already seen to be in the hands of two most important *yaba*, situated at the extremes of east and west.

31 *a*. BUBUWE

In this district lies Yuma, one of the lands of the dead. Yuma may be visited by certain persons who know the appropriate formula, but there appears to be no office of priest with definite functions (see Chap. x).

Apparently unconnected with the land of the dead is a huge snake, *Donga*, who lives on the top of Yuma mountain. This snake was one of the first to come from Sudest to visit Wonajö, after the latter had created Rossel. It was he who made the Snake Passage, *Ngomogn*, through the Sudest reef and also that known as *Ta*, near the west end of Rossel, by which the messenger of Wonajö to Mbasi and later Mbasi

[1] Bell refers to rain-making by means of stones (App. I, p. 226).

himself travelled. Wonajö welcomed his friend and made him a mountain, which would be in sight of Ngwö.[1]

Although the passage, Ta, is incomplete and therefore of no practical use, it is believed that a canoe could pass right through at this point, if there be one on board who knows the appropriate formula.[2] I was told that there was a stone connected with the snake on Yuma and that there is a priest who has to keep it free from débris. A portion of reef opposite Yuma is taboo, for it is regarded as the fishing-ground of the Yuma snake. The *yaba* is known as *Gheng*.

33. MANGOWE

In a *yaba* here, known as the *Aghin yaba*, there is a tree or a number of trees yielding a sweet-smelling substance. The trees were planted by Wonajö, though the *yaba* has some connection with a similar *yaba* in district 49, which originates from Sudest. The substance obtained from these trees is a love-potion. If a woman desires a man she gets some of this substance from the *yaba* and gives it surreptitiously to him; he will then be filled with desire for her. It is evidently not a *yaba* in the more usual sense of the term.

Another *yaba*, known as the *Ka yaba*, is connected with taro. It contains no stone or animal, but only a small tree. There is one priest of this *yaba*, who has to make and eat food at certain times and recite certain formulae, in which the tree is asked to ensure a good taro crop. The priest is, apparently, asked to do this whenever a new garden of taro is made in the district. The *yaba* is not harmful to strangers who approach, but if unauthorised persons enter or if the tree is damaged in any way or not kept free of débris, bad taro is the result.

In this or a neighbouring district is a tree, called *Wonijili*, closely associated with another tree called Boijili, which is

[1] Mr Frank Osborne told me that he paid a visit to the top of this mountain with one Rossel native. He *did* find at the top a snake of such size that he did not pause to investigate, and is unable, now, to say what was the cause of this illusion, if it were an illusion. There are pythons of considerable size on the mainland of New Guinea near the eastern extremity, though I do not think they have been recorded from the Louisiades.

[2] Unfortunately I had no time to follow this up. Obviously, the position of a man who claimed to possess this formula would be an impossible one.

connected with sorcery and the two Ye snakes or crocodiles, and lies on the other side of Yongga Bay (district 44). Wonijili and Boijili move about at certain times over the water with a whirling motion and are seen as waterspouts. They are harmless at these times to those who spit towards them and pronounce the necessary formula. If the formula were not known, a canoe in their proximity would probably be upset and the crew devoured.

34. YANIUWE

A *yaba* for the south-west wind and rain, known as the *Chaiu yaba*, is situated in this district. On the *yaba* is a large stone, containing a hole, which is plugged with sticks and leaves by the priest, when rain is desired. The rain ceases when the sticks and leaves are removed. It is not considered dangerous for anyone to approach this stone.

34 *a*. MEDIUWE

A *yaba* connected with hunger occurs here. The sacred object is a tomahawk stone, *Meribiung*, which was brought from Sudest with a similar stone now in district 53. The stone is kept in a shelter, which is renewed with ceremony at certain intervals; it is wrapped up in the spathe of the coconut and tied round with string. If rain or débris reaches the stone, everyone on Rossel is afflicted with a great hunger, which cannot be satisfied. If this happens, the priest visits the *yaba* and burns a certain wood, the smell of which passes to the stone and brings this reaction to an end. The beneficent reaction is the normal healthy fluctuation of appetite. The guardian animal of this *yaba* is the monitor lizard (*Varanus*, or *Goanna* in pidgin English), connected with the other tomahawk stone (see pp. 166–167).

36. BIOWE

A cockatoo *yaba*, known as the *Mkwa yaba*, is situated here. It consists of a stone with no guardian. If the stone is not kept free from foreign bodies, there is a plague of cockatoos. Lime is squeezed over the stone as a corrective on these occasions, to the accompaniment of incantations known to the priest, a procedure exactly similar to that used in the mosquito *yaba* of the adjacent district.

37. TEBEWE

This district contains a mosquito *yaba*, *Gwijama yaba*. A stone was placed here by Wonajö. It reacts when disturbed by causing a plague of mosquitoes. It is soothed by the use of limes, as in the cockatoo *yaba* above, and the mosquito *yaba* of district 47.

39. KWOWE

There is a *yaba* of rather unusual kind in this district to judge from the information given me. The *yaba*, known as *Womedjomugi*, contains a stone, associated with which is a crocodile. Not only will this crocodile devour any person other than the priest, who trespasses on the *yaba*, but will pursue anyone who has committed a theft from a garden, if influenced by the appropriate spell in the hands of the priest. If food has been stolen from a garden, the owner will sometimes consult the priest of this *yaba* and get him to put this mechanism of punishment in action. The discovery of the thief thus depends on the supernatural powers of the crocodile and apparently the priest has not the power to use it in pursuit of his own private ends.

40. MOIUWE

The *ndap yaba*, *Gaija*, lies here in the salt water by the side of the mangroves near the head of Yongga Bay. This is where Wonajö found the material from which he made the original stock of *ndap* money. I was told that no one may on any account go near this *yaba*, though another informant suggested that a *para nö* (*ndap* canoe) could visit it. But most of my informants agreed that there is very little shell which could be used for manufacturing money at this spot now. There is a guardian snake of the *yaba*, known as Mbyung— one of the five deities in the myth of Wonajö's fight with the fishes (see Chap. XI, p. 131). Mbyung is not normally at Gaija for he has his own *yaba* (in district 41 *a*) not far away.

A story was told me of the breaking of this taboo on the *ndap yaba* by a man from further west. Those closely concerned with the *yaba* (probably the priest and the owner and their relatives) demanded and obtained a boy in payment. The boy was killed and eaten. This arouses the suspicion

PLATE XXI

(b) Deformity of hand attributed to magic.

(a) Rope of *ndap* and *nkö* and introduced 'ceremonial' axe.

PLATE XXII

(*a*) Rope of *nkö*.

(*b*) *Dama* dancers.

that there may be another basis for cannibalism. Since a *yaba* is propitiated, in many cases, by the ceremonial preparation and consumption of food, it is possible that an intense maleficent reaction of a *yaba* may be treated by the ceremonial consumption of the most valuable and expensive of all foods. This possibility is borne out by the indications, that have been mentioned, of the cannibal propensities of Wonajö and others of the gods. The natives may well have conspired to deceive me on this point, for fear that I should tamper with the *yaba*, where these sacrifices occurred.

The danger, not only from the gods themselves but from their human agents, of breaking a *yaba* taboo is also shown by an incident while I was on the island. A chief's canoe broke loose and stranded on a certain reef *yaba*. The chief implored me to use my influence to prevent the owner of this *yaba* from practising sorcery on him for his sacrilege.

Not far from the *ndap yaba*—possibly in the next district— is a *yaba*, connected with a peculiar kind of sickness, which causes a man's head to become like a coconut. There is, however, preventive medicine to prevent the disease from developing. The snake which belongs to the *yaba* is called *Mwodebini*, and the *yaba* is ascribed to Wonajö. There is said to be no priest to look after it.

41 *a*. WÖBÖWE

The snake *Mbyung*, who is guardian of the *ndap yaba*, normally lives in a rocky pool in this district. It is never visited now, so my informant said, because, not long ago, a man was eaten there by the snake.

42. LEIUWE

A *yaba*, associated with madness, *Godigodi yaba*, occurs here. There is a small bush in which resides a big black snake, *Olomo*. Anyone entering the *yaba* is liable to be afflicted with a madness that takes the form of loss of memory and ridiculous behaviour. This can be cured by the priest of the *yaba*.

42 *a*. MBAWE

A snake, called *Darada*, was given as his residence the hill, Ti, in this district. He is not dangerous and is not connected with any natural process affecting the Rossel Islander.

44. MBOWE

The chief function of the *yaba* in this district is a certain kind of sickness, which normally results from the practice of sorcery. The object in the *yaba* is a tree, known as *Boijili*, a brother of the tree Wonijili, of the other side of the bay. With him Boijili sometimes dances over the water, the two appearing as waterspouts, which are said to be not uncommon. But the evil reputation of the tree Boijili depends on its connection with that most dreaded form of sorcery practised by a *ngwivi*. A *ngwivi* must obtain a twig from this tree and rub it between his hands. If he then presses it against his victim's ribs, the ribs are broken and the victim sickens and dies. In all probability, a twig of Boijili is only part of the equipment of a successful sorcerer and is not fatal by itself, for there is little doubt that the *ngwivi* method of sorcery is similar to the *tabusima* method of the Massim, which depends on the invisibility of the sorcerer and his weapons and his effects.

Boijili is supposed to have been put here by Wonajö; and he also has a connection, which I was unable to fathom, with the two Ye. Perhaps the connection is through Ye, the fish-hawk, who used Boijili in the magic by means of which he killed his sister. But this is mere conjecture.

This *yaba* belongs to an individual, but anyone could obtain a twig from the owner (or the priest?), for which, so my informant said, he did not pay. At the present day it is not obtained so openly, for fear that the knowledge would reach the Government, through a village policeman or in some other way, and an accusation of sorcery result.[1] When the tree is touched by profane hands in this way, its maleficent reaction occurs, so that the thief suffers from the very sickness he is anxious to induce in some other. This does not happen when the medicine is obtained through the priest.

44 a. TONGOWE

There is a sickness *yaba*, *Mbyi yaba*, in this district. The *yaba* object is a stone, *Myode*, and there is no guardian animal. Its reaction is a feverish headache, which does not,

[1] Needless to say, such perfect circumstantial evidence of attempted sorcery would be lost on most Governments, through lack of the special knowledge on their part necessary to appreciate it.

apparently, depend on the state of cleanliness of the *yaba*; for the *yaba* is not tended by anyone, and it is supposed that the mere act of cleaning the stone would cause an epidemic. A medicine for curing the complaint is known, which is applied to the sufferer and not to the stone.

WULI ISLAND

A *yaba*, of which the chief object is a spring of fresh water, occurs on this island. This water is said to be invisible to any but Wuli men. A priest tends it and it is supposed to be used for drinking purposes only in times of extreme drought. If this water dries up, the priest merely calls on Wonajö to fill up the cavity in which it occurs. There appears to be no particular reaction, maleficent or otherwise, associated with it.

In the salt water near Wuli are two stones, known as *Denobyubadö* (*dö* is a suffix to express duality), a few feet apart, and dangerous to canoes. The stones come together and crush any canoe that passes near; and if a canoe capsizes in deep water—on its way to Sudest, for instance—the stones are believed to rush to the spot and break up the canoe, bringing the crew back to the *yaba*, where they are cooked and eaten, a portion of the catch always being given to Wonajö. There appears to be no owner or priest connected with this *yaba*.

Another stone lies further west of Wuli on the reef that forms the large lagoon on the west of Rossel. This was thrown on the reef by Wonajö from a hill near Ngwö. It appears as a canoe to anyone who comes close to it, so that the unsuspecting will imagine a passage through the reef at that point and smash themselves to pieces on the *yaba*.

On the reef, far to the west of Wuli, lies the north-west monsoon *yaba*, *Pwajele*, in which resides the snake-like fish *Kwe*, the husband of Lab, the cephalopod on Loa. Kwe, in his Temewe manifestation, is an old man, who shuts himself up in his house in the south-east season; but in the north-west season he is a young man of greater power than Lab, who is at the height of her vigour in the south-east season (see p. 148 *seq.*).

46. MAMIAWE

The *yaba* of fish nets occurs here, or *Pwa yaba*. A stone *Dua*, on this *yaba*, is connected with fish generally. The *yaba* does not appear to be owned by an individual but by the local group, and there is no priest. It is unusual in having no definite maleficent reaction. There is no guardian animal; though my informant suggested that fish in general were the equivalent of the guardian animal, whether individual or species, of other *yaba*. When a new fish net is made in a village in the neighbourhood of this *yaba*, the man who is making the net repairs to the *yaba*, cleans the stone and pours coconut oil on it, saying, 'To-morrow I shall complete my net, and I want to catch plenty of fish'. No doubt there is a special formula, known only to certain men of the district. The name of the fish net—every fish net is given a name—must be mentioned in these spells; but, strangely enough, the name of Wonajö must be avoided. If Wonajö's name were mentioned no fish would be caught. This emphasis on Wonajö's impotence in connection with the marine arts has already been mentioned[1] and it is interesting to find this confirmation in a small detail. My informant emphasised the importance of the taboo on sexual intercourse in connection with the making of the fish net and the utilisation of the *yaba*.

47. MAIUWE

Another mosquito *yaba* is situated here. It contains a stone, but no guardian animal. Mosquitoes result from lack of care on the part of the priest in keeping the place clean, and the stone is treated with lime juice in just the same way as the similar stone in district 37. In the formula for this *yaba*, unlike that for the fish net *yaba* above, the name of Wonajö is an essential constituent, without which the incomplete spell would make matters worse by inducing the full maleficent reaction, with rain and wind as well as swarms of the pernicious insect. As I found to be the case with most other *yaba* where a positive statement was made,

---

[1] In the story of the feud between Wonajö and Ye, Wonajö is represented as a thorough 'bushman' (Chap. XI, p. 133), and in another connection he is represented as visiting Sudest in a wooden dish (Chap. XI, p. 128).

the services of the priest were said *not* to be rewarded by any payment of money.

49. KWALEWE

A *yaba*, known as the *Kwalebiuga yaba*, which occurs in this district, consists of a piece of land which is supposed to be one portion of land, the other portion of which is on Nimoa, beyond Sudest,[1] where it has a similar function. The *yaba* is associated in some way with the Aghin *yaba* (in district 33) and it has a similar function, by virtue of a small bush, the leaf of which is used as a love potion. From the account I received, it would seem that this substance only acts on the female sex, while my notes suggest that the similar tree in the Aghin *yaba* may be used to stimulate the male and possibly only the male. A leaf from Kwalebiuga is sold, the price being one small *ndap*, by the owner of the *yaba*. This is the only instance I came across of payments in money for the useful products of a *yaba*, but this may be because the benefits to be derived from a *yaba* are, in nearly all cases, communal ones.

It was stated that no woman could buy a leaf from Kwalebiuga, though leaves were frequently stolen by women, in spite of the fact that the penalty incurred by a woman entering the *yaba* is such a stimulation of desire that continual uninterrupted intercourse would be insufficient to satisfy it.

This *yaba* is connected with two others which owe their origin to Sudest; that in district 34 *a*, which contains a tomahawk stone from Sudest, and that in district 53, which contains a similar object. The 'Goanna', which is the guardian of both these *yaba*, is also believed, so far as I could make out, to visit the Kwalebiuga as well as the Aghin *yaba*.

50. DAWAWE

A *yaba* of low tide, *Ma yaba*, occurs here on the edge of the salt water. It contains a stone, *Akheng*, associated with

---

[1] This bit of ground, seen from the sea, does, as a matter of fact, present quite a different appearance from most Rossel landscape and from that of the immediate neighbourhood, and reminds one irresistibly of the comparatively bare grassy land common on Sudest and the Calvados which makes this region a totally different scenic world from Rossel.

which is a dugong, *Chima*[1]. The stone was put there by Wonajö. In order to produce low tides, the stone is cleaned by the priest and a ceremony is performed at certain times, the preparation and consumption of food being, as usual, the chief item in the ritual.

51. MBULAWE

A coconut *yaba*, *Dimödö*, occurs here, which is associated with the principal coconut *yaba* further east, in district 1. The two crocodiles of the latter occasionally visit the stone, *Konna*, of Dimödö, which is treated in the same way as the stone, Yanö, of the eastern *yaba*. It is, however, both less dangerous and less potent.

52 a. YOMONGOWE

A headache *yaba*, containing a stone, *Noro*, is situated in this district. A priest looks after the stone, which was placed here by Wonajö. There is no guardian animal.

53. PIÖWADAWE

A *yaba*, containing a stone, within which lives a fat white snake, *Yimora*, lies in one part of this district. A story is told that once some food, belonging to the snake, was stolen by a man in the neighbourhood. The result was that Yimora and all the snakes of the same species subsequently destroyed this man's house and killed all the inhabitants. Yimora is associated with taro. He responds to certain spells, which are muttered over the taro, which is being planted. Yimora is called upon in these spells and he visits the garden and causes the taro to grow rapidly. Snakes of this species are often seen in the gardens and are carefully avoided and never killed. This *yaba* is probably local in its effects, unlike the more important and more dangerous *yaba*.

In this district, or possibly somewhat further east (districts 54 and 55) lies an important *yaba*, containing three Sudest tomahawk stones. *Meli* is the name of the *yaba* (or, collectively, of the stones). The stones were brought by a snake from Piron, a small island north of Sudest. The snake was a friend of the Yuma snake, who also came from Sudest.

---

[1] This is evidently the dugong who figures in the legend of origin of coconuts, recorded on p. 141, and possibly the dugong mentioned on p. 153.

The stones are supposed to have disliked the perpetual beating of drums on Piron and to have come for peace and quiet to Rossel, where the drum does not occur.

According to another account, the stones were brought over by a Sudest woman in a Sudest sailing canoe. The stones made themselves a house, which was shattered by the north-west wind (apparently a brother of this woman from Sudest, who thus becomes related to the powerful god Kwe, and to the goddess Lab, the cephalopod of Loa and regulator of the south-east trade). Wonajö then appeared and made the stones a house of sago leaves and instructed the Rossel Islanders to renew it at frequent intervals. Wonajö ordered the 'Goanna', who is also associated with the tomahawk stone *yaba* in district 34 *a*, as well as the sex *yaba* of district 49 and possibly 33, to look after these stones and make a big thunderstorm if they were defiled in any way. This 'Goanna' is supposed to affect the children of any person who comes across it, inducing a general crookedness of the body. The stones, or at least the principal stone, *Benuman*, is connected with dysentery, which is the maleficent reaction of the *yaba* and accounts for its importance to the native.

54. WOLUNGAWE

The *nkö yaba*, *Nkögha*, lies here in the salt water in Wolunga Bay and is the original site from which Wonajö obtained the shell which he converted into the *nkö* money. Only a *para nö* (*ndap* canoe) is allowed to go near this *yaba*. There are two animals associated with it, one a shark, *Bamwili*, the other a crocodile, *Komwana*. Wonajö originally selected a dog for this office, but since the *yaba* lies below water, he threw the dog into the bay where it became converted into a shark.

I was told that there is also a *yaba* associated with rats in this district.

55 a. MPWALIUWE

There appear to be five inter-connected *yaba* in this district. The principal object is *Ye*, the snake or crocodile, brother of the Ye (of district 26 *a*) and somehow connected with or identical with the Ye of Loa. Ye is guardian of the four other objects in Mpwaliuwe, all of which are stones.

The function of three of these is to produce thunderstorms; and of one to produce an illness of the lungs; while Ye is connected with sorcery.

The thunder stones are *Dora*, a small shining stone, *Piawabini*, a red stone, and *Gadiu*, a small shiny green stone. The last-named is the fifth snake who figures in the myth of the fight with the fishes (see Chap. xi, p. 131). All five of these snakes have now appeared as existing entities—gods, as I have called them—in the *yaba*. Some of them appear at the present day as snakes, some as stones. Gadiu was the snake who used the bow-and-arrow, but no mention of this was made when I was told of the Gadiu stone in Mpwaliuwe.

The three stones mentioned above have only the one reaction of thunder and lightning, if they are disturbed in any way. The priest has, therefore, to keep them clean. The fourth stone, *Belo*, lies in a small creek some way from the others. If there is no rain for some time, this water becomes stagnant, and the stone reacts by causing an epidemic of lung trouble.[1] The priest, in that case, has to try to make rain. The stone lies at the bottom of a round basin, and a provisional expedient, in times of drought, to prevent this sickness appearing, is to pour water over the stone.

The function of this Ye is as obscure as that of the Ye in district 26 *a*. The latter Ye is supposed to have been the first to attempt sorcery, after he had committed incest with his sister (though this has already been ascribed to the fish-hawk Ye of Loa), and the Ye of Mpwaliuwe copied his method. How the *yaba* is used by the sorcerer, apart from the use of the name Ye in his spells, I did not discover.

---

[1] It would be interesting to know if complaints of the lungs are more common after a period of dry weather.

CHAPTER XIII

Sorcery

MY information about methods of sorcery is very scanty, but it was clear that sorcery has not the same significance for the Rossel Islander as it has for the Massim. This follows from the nature of the religious system on Rossel. A great deal of sickness results from the maleficent reactions of the *yaba*, and therefore a much smaller proportion of sickness and death needs to be accounted for by sorcery than is the case with the Massim, for whom practically every illness and every death must be explained on this hypothesis. It should be noted that both on Rossel and in the Massim area a 'natural' explanation of sickness and death is entirely absent.

The Massim have a peculiar belief in the power of women to cause sickness and death by the direct action of their souls, which leave the body for this purpose to feed on the victim in a mysterious manner. This belief fits into a wide scheme of beliefs, concerning the activity of these *alawai*, as the women in their disembodied state are called in the Suau district; and the whole social life is strongly coloured by the conception, which rationalises or gives rise to many aspects of Massim conduct. Probably sickness and death are attributed in a greater degree to *alawai* sorcery than to any other type. The absence on Rossel of any similar body of beliefs concerning this peculiar kind of magical power of women marks a most important difference of culture between Rossel and the Massim, and possibly accounts for the very different status of women on the former island. The difference between Rossel and Massim sorcery in other respects is probably not very great, except in so far as the Rossel sorcerer derives his power from some *yaba*. The general metaphysical beliefs of the Rossel Islander, and, in particular, the existence of *yaba* and gods specially connected with sorcery, would lead one to expect all sorcery to be a utilisation of certain *yaba*. I found no evidence of this, apart from the statement of my informant that Ye would probably be mentioned in any spell, the essential technique of sorcery being similar to that of the Massim sorcerers.

The type of sorcery which appears to be a constant source of anxiety to the Rossel Islander is that known as *ngwivi*. In order to become a *ngwivi* a man must fast for ten days (according to my informant, who had a strong bias for the number ten), must drink salt water, and mutter certain spells. By this procedure he is enabled to become invisible, or to take on the appearance of some animal, such as a dog. The *ngwivi* generally works at night and tackles his victim in his sleep, the usual method being to break or disarrange in some way the upper ribs. The victim realises next morning what has happened, and soon dies.[1]

The effect of *ngwivi* sorcery is sometimes very indirect. I was told that if a person on whom this form of sorcery had been practised were to go out fishing, and meet a certain kind of fish, normally harmless, he would be attacked and torn to pieces. This fish, known as *Beme*, is about two feet long, and is supposed to occur in pairs near the various passages through the reef. It may be that they are the guardians of *yaba* at these places, for a rock is mentioned as being connected with the Beme fish at Pwennegwa passage (Yabuwe district). But why *ngwivi* sorcery, and that variety of it in which certain ribs are broken or twisted, should produce the effect above mentioned is very puzzling; probably the information is either false or misleading through its incompleteness.

This is the ordinary *ngwivi* sorcery, but a *ngwivi* may use other methods; for instance, he may place poison on the mouth of the sleeper, or cause a milder illness by merely touching the victim. The *ngwivi* is, I think, the same as the *tabusima* of the South Coast Massim. It is a type of sorcery which can only be believed in and cannot be practised, and is easily confused with real action. A frequent jest of the *tabusima* amongst the Massim is to drive a spear into the victim; this may have no immediate visible effect, for both the spear and the wound are invisible, though none the less real in the eyes of the native. There are, of course, innumer-

---

[1] Bell gives a description of a method of committing murder which is probably a description of *ngwivi* sorcery (App. 1, p. 222). It is, however, certain that persons were sometimes smothered at night or had their bones broken (Murray, App. 1, p. 219), so that it is difficult to disentangle the diabolical reality from the belief, which fortunately corresponds to no such reality. Moreover, the distinction is a trivial one to the native.

able other ways in which an invisible man may inflict invisible wounds on another, so that there are innumerable possibilities for the *ngwivi* or the *tabusima* sorcery, although one variety is in particular favour on Rossel and others amongst the Massim. Unfortunately, the native does not co-ordinate his numerous items of belief about sorcery into any consistent scheme, so that the reduction of *ngwivi* methods to invisibility methods is an over-systematisation of beliefs which refuse to be classified by means of such categories. A perfectly visible dog may, in certain circum-stances, be interpreted as a *ngwivi*, and a *ngwivi* may be seen to enter a house, where he performs an action, at least some of the results of which are invisible. If we compare the occasion on which a dog is regarded as a *ngwivi* with an occasion on which it is regarded as merely a dog, we may find that the only difference in the two situations is in the state of mind of the observers of the dog. It is, therefore, not merely the external situation which is a *ngwivi* situation, in which case it would be theoretically possible to define precisely this type of sorcery, but it is also the situation relative to the state of mind of the persons in the situation. In a suitable situation a native will attribute almost anything to the operation of a *ngwivi*, if that is the most suitable peg on which, as it were, to hang his emotions. The same native, in a similar emotional situation, but in the neigh-bourhood of some *yaba*, would probably attribute anything he regarded as unusual to the action of that *yaba*. This does not mean that there is not a body of traditional beliefs concerning what are *ngwivi* manifestations, but it means that they are of a vague and fluctuating nature, and only obtainable after long and searching enquiry, and elimination of the innumerable spontaneities of belief of individuals.

The tentative unification of this type of sorcery given above makes the magical element the process of becoming invisible, the action of causing sickness or death being a more or less normal action, peculiar only because of its invisibility. The other types of sorcery on Rossel differ, in that the magical element lies in the actual procedure of causing sickness; they are mostly forms of sympathetic magic, made more effective by the physical and mental state of the sorcerer, who has to acquire power by fasting. This contrast is not made, however, by the native, the two types being interwoven and not regarded as distinct. This second type of sorcery has also its counterpart amongst the Massim. Hair, nail parings, faeces, urine, discarded husks of betel nut, banana skins, etc. may be utilised by the Rossel sorcerer in much the same way as they are by the Massim sorcerer, and indeed by sorcerers amongst primitive peoples throughout the world. The term *dwodia* is used to designate this type of sorcery: if hair is utilised, the victim suffers from *barapwo dwodia*; if nail parings, he suffers from *kandibi dwodia*, with slightly different symptoms, and so on. The sorcerer, however, will generally be called a *ngwivi*, whether or not he is supposed to combine this procedure by sympathetic magic with the process of becoming what is more strictly called *ngwivi*, a state of actual or potential invisibility, radiating dangerous power. *Dwodia* sorcery by means of the faeces was said to be very common, and I was given an account of some of the externals of the procedure by one of my informants. The faeces having been put aside, a number of plant and animal products are collected, the chief of which are a poisonous eel and a certain small black fish.[1] The poison from this fish and parts of the eel are mixed with the faeces and the plant products, some of which may have been obtained from *yaba*, such as that of Ye, though I could not confirm this. The substances are carefully handled with a stick or with tongs; for the operator would be injured by contact. The victim now suffers from diarrhoea, but the result need not be fatal, unless the sorcerer carries the process farther. If he desires the person's death he makes a fire and places the mixture on it. The victim becomes feverish by sympathy, and soon dies, unless the sorcerer relents at the last moment, and places what remains of the mixture in cold water. Apparently, heat is always associated with magical action, or is even to be regarded as a necessary rather than an accidental attribute of magical potency, and cold is a positive character which destroys or is destroyed by heat. This is similar to the Massim conception, where we find the term *gigibori* used as an adjective in all those cases where we should use the term 'hot', but also in all those cases where certain Melanesians

---

[1] This fish was said to be the one which recently caused the death of five visitors to Rossel, who were ignorant of its properties.

elsewhere use the term *mana*, or a term having a similar extension. The concept *mana*, as used for instance by Marett, if applicable anywhere in Melanesia, is applicable to Rossel and the Massim. Although this method of sorcery should, one would imagine, be independent of the state of the sorcerer, my informant insisted that the latter would first fast,[1] and thus become hot (acquire *mana*), which would facilitate the action. With regard to the spells in the above kinds of sorcery, I was only told that they are directed to Ye and not to Wonajö, who is not mentioned. In the above method no stone having special powers is utilised, but the action is directly sympathetic, for poison and heat are the only agents used. I was told that similar effects could be produced with parts of the body, or discarded portions of food, by placing these on certain stones.[2] These stones, presumably, contain *mana*, just as does the fire which consumes the object; while the victim also sympathetically has *mana*. Whether these stones are the stones of certain *yaba*, or stones secretly owned by certain individuals, I do not know.

A common form of sorcery amongst the Massim may be regarded as intermediate between the above two kinds, which we may label *ngwivi* and *dwodia* (although it must be remembered that these two terms are not used by the natives to make this distinction merely, which is quite an unimportant one to them). Owing, no doubt in part, to the fact that the spell emerges from the mouth, there is considered to be a potency in the process of spitting, if this is done in a certain way. Spitting to produce a magical effect is denoted by a different term amongst the Massim, and we find a similar term, in addition to the ordinary word for 'spit', on Rossel. By incanting over certain substances, which are then chewed and spat forth in the direction of a person, numerous forms of sickness may be produced, and the process may be utilised for more social purposes, such as *taboo*, diversion of squalls, and so on. The process, known as *pyukwe*, is therefore not confined to sorcery in the anti-social sense of the term. In so far as the *pyukwe* is a directing through perhaps many

[1] When a sorcerer fasts in order to become *ngwivi* he also frequently eats a certain centipede, which is common on Rossel. This centipede is about an inch long and smells strongly of prussic acid. I have noticed it only on Rossel. It is believed to turn the faeces white.
[2] Also mentioned by Bell (App. I, p. 226).

yards of space of an evil effect towards a person, it is nearer the *ngwivi* sorcery. *Ngwivi* sorcery may be combined with *pyukwe*; some substance is prepared and made dangerous by *pyukwe*; it is then, unwittingly, eaten by the victim or, in some way, brought into contact with him. This is practically the converse of what I have called *dwodia* above.

My information as to sorcery on Rossel is so fragmentary that it is possible that important beliefs have been overlooked; for little more than vague individual ideas on the subject can be collected until one has resided amongst a people for a long time. The spells used in sorcery and in magic in general, and inside information from the sorcerer himself, are naturally amongst the last aspects of culture to be revealed to an enquirer, who must have been long resident amongst the people. The present writer only pricked the surface of Rossel culture, and may, therefore, have missed whole complexes of important beliefs and behaviour, especially in this difficult region, studded with native reticences. Although these considerations indicate that there may be numerous other forms of sorcery practised by men, I am possibly right in saying that there is only one form of sorcery which is believed to be used by women. A stone, called *gömibe*, of which there appear to be a number on the island, is made to enter the body of the victim, who is crippled or even killed by it. My informant imagined that he knew the formulae used for causing the stone to enter and to leave the victim. In the former case, the stone is addressed as follows: '*Nidini andidini Luwe nidini Wonajö nidini Pere nidini*'; in the latter case thus: '*Niagebe andiagebe Luwe niagebe Wonajö niagebe Pere niagebe*'. The words are muttered with the mouth close against the stone. *Nidini* means, I believe, 'your food', while *andidini* means 'my food', according to the rule for possessive pronouns. *Ndiagebe* may mean 'stone', in which case '*niagebe andiagebe Luwe*' could be translated 'your stone, my stone, O Luwe'. My informant said that the first spell meant roughly, 'You eat this man, you go inside', while the second meant 'You leave this man'. It should be noted that the two snake gods, Luwe and Pere, are mentioned in the spells, as well as Wonajö. (The *yaba* of Luwe and Pere are referred to in Chap. XII, pp. 147 and 154.) Ye has nothing to do with these stones, which were given to women by Wonajö as their only weapon against man. The most likely motive for the use of this sorcery was said to be the rejection of sexual advances made by a woman towards a man. The effects are most varied, the more usual being some swelling or distortion of the limbs. The deformity shown in Pl. XXI *b* was supposed to be due to a *gömibe* stone. Although, in theory, the exclusive property of women, it was said that these stones were occasionally used by men. Although most of those I questioned about sorcery denied the existence of the *alawai* type, which they were fully aware existed on Sudest, investing that island with additional mystery and danger, I did receive one statement to the effect that a woman can practise sorcery by her own intrinsic power, if she takes off her petticoats. It is just possible that this is a form of sorcery which has spread from Sudest. Two forms were mentioned as having recently come from Sudest. In the one, the leaf of a certain tree, which occurs further east but not on Rossel, is treated, and waved about the victim's head in a way that will not attract his attention. Subsequently, a pointed stick is driven through the leaf, and sympathetically the victim's liver is supposed to be simultaneously pierced. In the other form, which has come in from Sudest, a man's footprint is treated with paraffin or petrol, and fired, the person whose footprint it is being stricken with fever as a consequence.

Divination of sorcery is sometimes resorted to. This appears to be of a type similar to that of the Massim, though the most usual method, known as *mbwoi*, is rather more complicated than the similar Massim method. I was told that parts of a number of different kinds of tree are collected, prepared with lime, and dried in the sun. This is held in the hand by the diviner, and a forked stick is fitted under the forearm. The names of people are uttered by the person employing the diviner, until, in response to a certain name, the arm on which the forked stick is fitted vibrates in a certain way. The guilty party is thus indicated. Murray refers[1] to a method of divination called *mbwo*, which is essentially the same as that described to me above.

A similar process of divination was actually observed by Bell, who was impressed by the sincerity of the diviner. Bell was told that there are only a few men who know how

[1] App. I, p. 219.

to perform this divination, and that the practice is handed down from father to son. In Bell's account[1] no forked stick was used, but two essential constituents of the ball of leaves, etc., were a black ant and the head of a black slug, a few inches in length and very fat, which discharges an acid fluid some distance if disturbed, and which is extraordinarily abundant on Rossel. When I enquired about this slug (really a millipede) I was informed that it was never used in connection with divination, and, following the matter up, was finally told that this divination was performed for Bell's benefit, by a man who was so scared by the request to perform his divination in public, and the fear of not satisfying the Government, that he invented these extras for effect. If that be the case, suspicion is thrown on some of my own data, which may have been similarly coloured in order to give me pleasure. But there is less opportunity in detailed investigation for the native to add picturesque untruths, owing to the possibility of accidental betrayal by other natives. Although there may be a few native inventions in the present book, they probably only occur in matters of detail, for even in the above case, Bell's diviner seems to have given a correct performance on the whole, if the general similarity of what he observed with what was described to me is to be taken as evidence. My informant was also under the impression that the person who had been divined as committing a murder by sorcery, had been sent to gaol on this evidence, which of course was not the case.

I did not discover any other forms of divination, though I have no doubt that they exist. I was told that divination is not used for *ngwivi* sorcery, but that persons are suspected from their behaviour, such as long absence from the village without adequate reason.

[1] App. I, pp. 226–227.

PLATE XXIII

(*a*) *Ptyilöwe* dancers.

(*b*) *Ptyilöwe* dance.

PLATE XXIV

(a) Pig fattened for feast.

(b) Smothering of pig.

CHAPTER XIV

Games and Songs

ONE has the impression that life is rather more serious on Rossel than elsewhere in New Guinea, but this may be due to the comparison one inevitably makes with the more irresponsible and laughter-loving Massim. I find I cannot remember what laughter sounds like on Rossel, and I recollect how the gloom of the natives used to fill me with uneasiness until I got used to it. One felt it was the appropriate attitude to life of natives who would murder their friends to satisfy religion or authority. But the children were like any other children of this part of the world, and had the simple games which are usual in New Guinea. A favourite game for small children is one in which a number sit in a circle and place their hands in the centre, alternately above each other. The last person to put a hand on this pile of hands in the centre has to say the following: '*Kwedidi kwedada na dangi bwa dongwa da dödöma do nangö iye, ko iye iy, jöbu jawa pwobwo dangwo gumaga madaga*', which, I was told, does not make sense, and contains unknown words. At the end of this talk, they put their arms around each other and press their heads together, swaying backwards and forwards.[1] Games of this sort are generally played in the evening, after the afternoon meal, the chief meal of the day. One small boy showed me a number of little tricks which are done with the hands and body, such as the production of a squeaking noise by pressing the hand under the armpit in a certain way. Although *mbo*, the dreaded blood-sucking ghosts, which wander about the bush, are not, one would imagine, beings to be trifled with, it is a common amusement of children to stretch the mouth with the hands into a hideous grimace, while the eyes are made to squint, this being a representation of a *mbo*. The audience must pretend to be seized with sudden terror, just as unsophisticated children amongst ourselves will respond to a similar

[1] This appears to be identical with a game found by Dr Haddon at Hula, *Journal of the Royal Anthropological Institute*, vol. xxxviii, 1908, p. 296.

jest of one of their number. Games are played with a toy bow-and-arrow, known as *dödö*, although the bow-and-arrow for serious use is absent from the island, as it is from the whole of Eastern Papua. More serious games are played at an early age, and, no doubt, help to familiarise the young with monetary procedure. Small stones are used to represent *ndap* and *nkö*, and sometimes opercula ('cat's eyes') for the higher values of *ndap*. A small house may be made and a feast imagined, the operations of the adults being copied in considerable detail. Even the morbid aspect of the dramatic sense is satisfied by detailed representations of funerary ritual. One child, for instance, will act the position of dead chief, while a small girl, as his widow, lies down by his side. One of the actors is accused of sorcery, and another is killed, in pantomime, to be cooked. The compensation of the relatives of the latter is not forgotten, though of less dramatic interest.

The Rossel children, and adults also, know innumerable string figures. One small boy showed me a dozen, some of considerable complexity, in a very short time. I failed, through lack of time, to record more than one or two of these, a very laborious business for one with my inexpertness. But through the medium of my Daui (mainland Massim) cook-boy, an expert in string figures, I obtained comparisons of some 30 Rossel figures with Daui figures. Of 26 Rossel figures tested, 21 had Daui equivalents, according to the judgment of my cook-boy, but of these only five had more or less identical interpretations—e.g. a crying baby, a red parrot, mosquitoes, a small crab, a crocodile. The majority of identical figures had, therefore, completely different interpretations—e.g. the figure which represents a squall on Rossel represents a bird in Daui, and the figure which represents a snake on Rossel represents pandanus fibre in Daui; the coconut on Rossel is taro in Daui; again, the representation of a sorcerer and certain of his activities is by totally different figures on Rossel and in Daui. A number of the figures observed appeared to be identical with some of those recorded in K. Haddon's *Cat's Cradles from Many Lands*.[1]

---

[1] It is hoped to record elsewhere the scanty material concerning string figures on Rossel, together with data from the Massim, in some other connection, and the subject is, therefore, not pursued further here.

Reference has already been made to two types of song or dance; one, the *ptyilöwe*, in which the dancers wear the petticoats of women,[1] and carry small baskets with long streamers (Pl. XXIII); the other, the *dama*, in which the dancers wear the ordinary male dress, decorating themselves with croton leaves, and, in some instances, carrying a croton branch (Pl. XXII *b*).

The *ptyilöwe* are similar in almost every respect, except that drums are absent, to that class of Massim dance in which the dancers don the petticoats of women. The dance element is very slight, being little more than the more or less symmetrical arrangement of the dancers, who indulge in slight swaying movements, with occasional movements of the feet, with very little rhythm.[2] Both *ptyilöwe* and *dama* are more correctly described as songs, for arrangement, movement, and decoration of the singers may be regarded merely as a setting for the singing. At the same time, when a *ptyilöwe* with many performers takes place, the appeal to the audience is not only, and perhaps not even principally, through the individual songs; it is the rhythm of a succession of verses, the monotonous persistence of the dancers. The charm lies in a sort of rhythmic monotony, a quality impossible to obtain through the medium of a song, symphony, or poem, which is some sort of individual entity, having emotional completeness, and equally impossible to realise through the medium of dance movements familiar to Europeans, for such rhythms are too active to be indefinitely prolonged. The rhythm is quickly absorbed and rapidly satisfies, and the dance has, therefore, a construction, and gives satisfaction as a single emotional unit that has beginning and ending. The Rossel song dance has no beginning and no ending; it gradually comes into being and gradually fades away.

The only full-dress *ptyilöwe* which I had the opportunity of observing, took place at an inland village during a pig feast (Pl. XXIII *b*). This dance has already been referred to in Chap. VII (pp. 90–91). As soon as the dance had got into full

---

[1] Noted by Murray (App. I, p. 220).
[2] There may be dramatic dances, with considerable movement, which I did not observe, for dramatic dances with elaborate figures occur amongst the Massim, in addition to the commoner dances, which are little more than songs.

swing, which was not for several hours, this rhythmic quality began to emerge. There is first the verse, sung either by one or by two men, with the characteristic Massim quality of insistence on a certain note, with rapid flights away from it, and final return to it or its minor third below, or sometimes above, in long drawn-out diminuendo.[1] Savage, though musically pleasant, yells of appreciation—'*Nye, nye, nye*'— follow, the performers swaying the body up and down. Other verses, each of which takes only a few minutes, may follow from the same singer or singers, each with the same conclusion, the yells of the other dancers, which seems to carry on the rhythm. At the beginning of each set of verses all the dancers, some fifteen or so, would sing the verse through on one vowel sound. The musical sequence of each verse, containing different words, appeared to be the same, though there were certain changes in some cases, when new singers carried on the solo or duet. When the soloist (or pair of singers) became tired, or exhausted his repertoire, or when his audience had had enough, there was a rhythmic clapping at the end of the verse, and a new singer would take his place. This continued for hours without a break, an indefinable continuity of rhythm being maintained throughout.

My informants gave me some idea of the meaning of the verses of '*Yemumu*', the particular *ptyilöwe* which was being performed in the village on this occasion. Yemumu is a *ptyilöwe* of recent invention. It was made by a man who had been fishing with a torch during the night; hence the name, Yemumu, by which is known the high tide of early morning that occurs at this calm period of the year, when fishing by torches is common. Every verse in this song dance is supposed to end with the word Yemumu.

A given *ptyilöwe* has an indefinite number of verses, for new ones are frequently invented, though each *ptyilöwe* has also its body of traditional verses, in many of which meaningless phrases occur. On this occasion the first verses had special reference to Kwangwe, the individual who was selling the pig, and who was regarded as master of the feast, or *tanuaga* as the Daui Massim would say. Kwangwe

---

[1] I do not feel certain about this interval and its generality. One frequently finds that a note is conclusive, though succeeded by an interval, which gives an even more satisfying conclusion.

was frequently mentioned in these first verses, which must, therefore, in all probability have been composed for the occasion—according to a traditional formula. Apparently, the phrases consisted of a number of truisms, with much repetition; e.g. ' This is your village, Kwangwe—you are making a feast—this is your village...'. Other verses followed, in which a number of trivial incidents were mentioned; e.g. the substance of one verse was the taking of a lamp from a Rossel cook-boy without his knowledge by his white master; the surprise of the cook-boy when he returned to the wharf where he had left the lamp; and the subsequent explanations of his master, when the latter appeared. Another verse was about the white man's tent, another about his trousers, and several about different kinds of boats, and in particular the whistle of a steamer that was seen near Loa some years before. Apparently, two men-of-war, supposed by the natives to be German, came within a short distance of the reef during the war: several verses of Yemumu commemorate this incident, and especially the heroes of a canoe which is supposed to have been bombarded by these ships, first from one side, and then from the other when that side of the warship grew tired, as my imaginative informant put it. One set of verses was quite new, for they concerned a man whom I had arrested only a day or two previously for murdering his wife. This individual, who, with a pair of handcuffs on one wrist only, accompanied me wherever I went, since there was no other way of disposing of him, could not avoid listening to these verses, much to the amusement of the other guests. The sentiments expressed in the song appear to have been somewhat as follows: 'Were you not aware that the Government and policemen were about? Why then did you kill your wife at such a time? Now you are handcuffed for being a fool. First of all, a piece of paper will go to Samarai. Later on you will go too, but we shall remain'. The verses seemed to cause a great deal of merriment.

Late in the evening food was brought for the dancers, and one of the latter produced a set of verses in which all the different kinds of food on Rossel were mentioned. Near midnight the rhythm was partially broken by an almost solemn ceremony, in which all the performers bowed their heads towards the centre of a circle after a verse in which the delights of the period of calm weather that follows the south-east season were extolled. The calm weather had arrived about the time of this feast, and I was told that dancers and non-dancers holding each other's hands came close together in a circle to hear the verse, very softly given, about the Jibe wind from the north-east, which is the pleasantest of all winds, and is associated with the Mbasi *yaba*. This subdued attitude may have been due to some reference to the Mbasi *yaba* in this verse.

Towards morning, the character of the dance again changed, the verses no longer being concerned with trivial and foreign matters; in fact I was told that there was a definite taboo on any references to 'dimdim' matters (i.e. matters connected with foreigners, such as the white men). The dance gradually came to an end after this, the last dancer removing his petticoat and ornaments, according to the ritual described in Chap. VII, some time after sunrise.

Ptyilöwe dances are held frequently, and I could discover no taboo as to time or place, such as we find amongst the Massim, where dancing is definitely connected with preparations for a '*Soi*', and is taboo at all other times. Even at an unimportant *dogomomo* that I witnessed, three dancers were employed to perform a *ptyilöwe*. The *ptyilöwe* is regarded as play, and anyone may sing a verse that he happens to remember at any time, even if it be the verse of a *ptyilöwe* of another district. Usually there is no reward when a *ptyilöwe* is performed by dancers in their own district; but if a chief invites a party from another district to perform their *ptyilöwe* in his village, the dancers will be given presents of baskets, tobacco, and so on, as well as of food, while dancers from his own district would not be recompensed in this way.

The second type of dance song, known as *dama*, differs considerably from the *ptyilöwe*. This, again, is performed only by males, who do not wear grass petticoats for this dance, but decorate themselves with croton leaves. The only *dama* that I witnessed (Pl. XXII *b*) was performed by three or four men, who carried on their shoulders croton branches; but I was told that a *dama* is correctly performed only in the neighbourhood of a *para nö* canoe. Either it is sung by the crew to the rhythm of their dipping paddles, or else, on land, the song is accompanied by the rhythmic scraping of the paddles against the sides of the canoe, which has been drawn up on the beach.

I could discover very little from the inadequate performance which was arranged for my benefit. The atmosphere was strained from the commencement, owing to the fact that my Massim cook-boy burst into loud uncontrollable laughter as soon as the song commenced. He found the singing ludicrous, merely because it was utterly different from what he had been used to: the *ptyilöwe* produced no such reaction, for they were obviously of the same type as his own songs. My cook-boy's reaction confirmed my own feeling, that in the *dama* one had to deal with a quite new form of music, having no affinity with any forms with which I was acquainted, whether Papuan or European. This effect may have been due to the inexpertness of the performers, but the gravity and apparent satisfaction of the Rossel audience makes this theory improbable, though politeness, in which the Rossel Islander is not lacking, would dictate such an attitude. I could perform no analysis of the music, beyond the fact that the performers sang in parts, producing a series of unresolving discords, and progressions that were ludicrous to my ear. Even rhythm was difficult to discover, though slight movements of the dancers' feet suggested that there was a rhythm, which would probably have emerged if the performers had continued long enough to 'warm up', which unfortunately was not the case. One noticeable element of the singing was the use of crescendo and diminuendo, a verse usually commencing very loud and fading almost to inaudibility well before the end. This effect is also utilised a good deal in the *ptyilöwe*. Frequent verses occurred, based on meaningless sounds having phonetic value merely, e.g. 'babuiabababuiababuiababuia...'. These are probably choruses, for they are said to be used by the crew of a *para nö*, especially in the races for which these canoes are utilised.

It has already been pointed out that each *dama* has an intimate relation with a *yaba*, though not every *yaba* has this relation to a *dama*. The *dama* may, then, be described as songs of the gods. At least two *dama* were composed by Wonajö. These are known as '*Wajamö*' and '*Dabubi*', of which the sense of the words of a few of the verses has been given in Chap. v (p. 60). The word *Mongwe*, which occurs at intervals, cannot be translated, and is, apparently, the counterpart of the shout, or possibly the clapping of hands, that separates verses or groups of verses in a *ptyilöwe* song, but I am not clear about this. Although at least one of the *dama* of Mbasi commemorates the making of *ndap* money and has a relation to the *ndap yaba* in Wolunga, the *nkö yaba* in Yongga has a *dama* called '*Agheenda*', which apparently has no such relation to Wonajö. The *dama* of Mbasi is known as '*Kobo*', that of the sun and moon '*Mwele*'. The *dama* of Loa (presumably of Lab) is '*Yöwe*', of Pere is '*Kwandim*', and the names of a number of others were given to me. The *dama* called '*Mbimadwa*', which belongs to Pchi, is supposed to be sung by the ghostly inhabitants of Pchi, who also give a feast whenever there is a new arrival.

I did not discover what were the occasions for the performance of *dama*. Some *dama* are supposed to have beneficial effects; for instance, the *dama* of Mbasi is prophylactic against shipwreck in a sailing canoe, for this commemorates Mbasi's voyage from Sudest through the Snake Passage to Rossel. The sun and moon *dama* will divert squalls, and may even be sung on a canoe for this purpose. It would seem almost as if the singing of *dama* is a sub-section of the ritual connected with securing the beneficent reaction of the *yaba*.

Every *dama*, unlike the *ptyilöwe*, is very ancient, for its invention is attributed to some god. The *dama* also appear to be the possession of individuals, unlike the *ptyilöwe*, which are, more or less, the common property of a district. Apparently, only a chief may own a *dama*, and whatever it is that entitles a person to own one entitles him also to own a *para nö*. Furthermore, my informants insisted that only the owner of a *yaba* could own the *dama* of the god of that *yaba*. A simple scheme, by which these relations are regulated, is obtained if we suppose that every clan has its *yaba*, on which resides a god, which is the fourth totem of the clan. Every clan has a chief, who is the owner of the *yaba*, its *dama*, and a *para nö*. The difficulties in the way of this scheme are the existence of patrilineal succession, and, to a certain extent only, patrilineal inheritance, alongside matrilineal descent, and the absence of localisation of the clans. The problem of the nature of chieftainship which thus arises will be discussed in the next chapter. Unfortunately, my data on this most important subject are inadequate; for I did not at the time realise the importance of this question.

CHAPTER XV

Chiefs

VERY little can be said on the subject of chieftainship
on Rossel.[1] It is, I believe, a field which would well
repay further investigation. The chief obscurity lies
in the fact that chieftainship is not simply hereditary, for
I was told over and over again that persons could become
chiefs by acquiring wealth or in some other way. Usually,
succession is patrilineal, and the rank passes to the eldest
son, though frequently this is abrogated in favour of a
younger son who proves himself more capable. In so far
as the rule of succession applies, the clan of a local chief
necessarily changes with each succession. A few instances
were given me of succession by the *jina* (sister's son): in
these cases the rank remains within a single clan. Owing to
these exceptions I do not feel absolutely confident in stating
that the general rule of succession is patrilineal, although it
is independently rendered probable by the fact that throughout the greater part (if not the whole) of Melanesia, where a
somewhat similar social organisation occurs, patrilineal succession prevails.

We have already seen that matrilineal inheritance of the
yaba is the rule, although no such rule regulates succession
to the priesthood. It is obviously only by matrilineal inheritance that the *yaba* could remain the property of the clan, the

---

[1] We find Macgregor, in 1888, tentatively denying the existence of
chiefs (App. I, p. 206); while Murray, in 1908, refers to a 'system of
chieftainship with one over-chief called Dabui, of Mogwö, on Mt Ngö'
(pp. 219–220). But it is the over-god who lives on Ngö (Ngwö). Bell implies that chieftainship is an important part of the social organisation and
that chiefs have an important power of taboo, which unfortunately I did
not investigate. He says, for instance, that a point of land might be
tabooed in such a way that women have to make a détour to avoid it
(p. 225). This is, obviously, quite different from the ordinary taboo
placed on food trees or reefs that is common enough in South-East
Papua. Bell also states that some boys, just returned from Sudest, had
to get a trader to take them along in his boat, as they had no native
money to pay the chief with in order to be allowed to pass (p. 225).
Whether the ground had been placed under taboo by a chief, perhaps
for the purpose of raising money, or whether the ground was simply the
site of a *yaba* is not quite clear.

fourth totem of which is a god of at least one of the *yaba* owned by some member of the clan. With regard to the priesthood, succession tends to be patrilineal, although fitness of the successor for the post is the more important consideration. A definite instance was given me of a priest of one of the most important *yaba* succeeding his cross-cousin.

Now, if chieftainship is not a definite office, but merely a quality admitting of an indefinite number of degrees, the above facts as to succession do not create any difficulties. All that we need to suppose is that the sons of a chief, even his principal successor, have less of this quality than the father, in so far as it is determined by relationship, so that the principle of patrilineal succession, acting by itself, would in the course of time destroy all distinctions of rank. We must also suppose that the sister's sons are elevated in rank to a slight degree by the principle of matrilineal succession, the degree depending on closeness of relationship. This principle also helps towards the degradation of rank. There are other factors, however, which tend in the opposite direction. In the first place, the ownership of *yaba* appears to be individual, and confers on a constant number of individuals a degree of rank which is dependent on the importance of the *yaba*. In the second place, the position of priest of a *yaba* is individual, and similarly confers on a constant number of individuals a degree of rank which depends on the importance of the *yaba*. Finally, the acquirement of wealth or even of skill in certain arts and industries[1] tends to confer rank on a person, and we have already referred to the effect of conspicuousness at feasts in creating prestige.

On this view of the determination of rank it will sometimes happen that an individual is the son of a chief and the nephew of a chief, both owner and priest of an important *yaba*, and a man of wealth. But such a degree of rank is

---

[1] There is, I think, rather greater division of labour on Rossel than amongst the Massim. For instance, a class of persons exists called *ndeb*, who are professional financiers, and do not work in the gardens, help in the building of houses, or go on fishing expeditions, except as a recreation. Others specialise in garden produce, when they are known as *ndibi*, while *nwibi* specialise in fishing and the making of fish nets. Carpenters are known as *yimebiu*, whether they be specialists in the making of houses or of canoes.

necessarily rare, owing to the different rules of succession and fortuitous acquirement of rank already mentioned. The majority of persons, to whom the term *limi* (chief) may be applied, will have far fewer claims to rank, and I was told of *limi* who could claim their rank for only one of the above reasons. This degradation of rank owing to succession can be illustrated by one example that I came across. An important chief, called Köbe, both owned and acted as priest of the sago *yaba*. This was the principal but not the only reason for his being regarded as a very big chief. On his death the individual who acquired most rank was a younger cross-cousin (*bje*), called Chita, who inherited the formula of the *yaba*, but not, of course, its ownership. Of less importance was a sister's son, who inherited the *yaba*, while Köbe's own sons inherited neither the *yaba* nor its formula, though I understood that they would be called *limi*.

There is probably another consideration that affects rank, namely, locality. A chief was often said to be the chief of a district having authority in the district over both his own and other clans. Whether the succession to this office depends on the degree of rank of the various persons who are called *limi* in the district I cannot say definitely, but I feel fairly certain that there are no absolute districts, and that the 'district of' a chief is a sequence of localities that overlap the 'districts of' other chiefs. At the same time, the district of an important chief may be regarded as more extensive than that of one of less importance. If the system is as fluid as I suppose, it explains why rival chiefs should sometimes appear in close proximity; in which case, so my informant maintained, each chief employs a number of *ngwivi* to destroy the other by sorcery.

In so far as there can be said to be an office of chief of a district, this is likely to depend on the relative positions of those who are called *limi*. In this sense, rank is likely to be, to a certain extent, dependent on locality; for in one district a person may occupy the office of chief, though having few claims, while a chief with greater claims in another district may be overshadowed by the even greater claims of another.

There is no doubt that the term *limi* denotes a larger class of persons than the very limited class who are entitled to own a *para nö* canoe. However determined, the title to a *para nö* is also associated with the title to a *dama*, which is intimately connected with a *yaba*. The possibility of its being simply a question of matrilineal succession and inheritance must be left open until the matter can be investigated, when light may also be thrown upon the *para nö* races, which take place between chiefs, and which are occasions for the singing of *dama* songs. I doubt whether it is possible to theorise further about these particular aspects of Rossel culture in the absence of more adequate material.

APPENDIX I

History and Bibliography

BOUGAINVILLE appears to have been the first to name the Louisiades if not the first to discover these islands, which he supposed to consist of continuous land from Rossel to New Guinea. His two ships were in some plight for want of food and water and had great difficulty in weathering Rossel; hence Bougainville, referring to the easternmost point of Rossel, says[1]:

This cape which we had so long wished for, was named Cape Deliverance, and the gulph of which it forms the easternmost point, Gulph of the Louisiade. I think we have well acquired the right of naming these parts.

Less than 30 years later, the Louisiades were more carefully observed by D'Entrecasteaux, in 1793, in his search for La Pérouse, but none of the inhabitants of Rossel are mentioned in the narratives of M. Rossel or M. Labillardière. Rossel, now recognised as an island, was named after the captain of D'Entrecasteaux' ship, M. Rossel, who writes[2]:

Les parties les plus élevées de cette île étoient alors cachées dans les nuages; mais on apercevoit, près du bord de la mer, des bois épais, séparés par des espaces revêtus d'une verdure très-agréable. Nous vîmes une petite île, au Sud de laquelle la côte formoit une belle baie, où il y avoit lieu de présumer qu'on pourroit trouver un excellent abri: malheureusement l'abord en étoit défendu par une chaîne non interrompue de brisans, qui se prolongeoient dans l'Ouest aussi loin que la vue pouvoir s'étendre.

In 1849, Captain Owen Stanley made a survey of the Louisiades in H.M.S. *Rattlesnake*. The *Rattlesnake* passed right along the northern side of the island in calm water, and a few natives were seen. Macgillivray, in his account of the voyage, says[3]:

Rossel Island (named after one of D'Entrecasteaux' officers) is 22 miles in length from east to west, and 10½ in greatest width; it is high and mountainous, and thickly wooded, with occasional large, clear, grassy patches. Towards the western end they become lower and more detached, but present the same features. The

[1] *A Voyage round the World*, by Lewis de Bougainville, 1766–69, translated by J. R. Forster, F.A.S., 1772, p. 312.
[2] *Voyage de D'Entrecasteaux*, rédigé par M. de Rossel, 1808, vol. 1, pp. 405–406.
[3] Macgillivray, *Voyage of H.M.S. 'Rattlesnake'*, 1852, vol. 1, pp. 182–185.

mountain ridges, one of which, but not the highest elevation
(which was obscured by clouds), is 2522 feet in height, form sharp
narrow crests and occasional peaks, but the outline is smooth and
the rock nowhere exposed, even the steepest ridges being covered
with vegetation. Some of the trees appeared to be of great dimensions, others were tall and straight, branching only near the top,
and many, probably *Melaleuca leucodendrum*, were conspicuous from
the whiteness of their trunks. Large groves of cocoa-palms scattered
about from the water's edge to half way up the hills, formed a
pleasing break in the sombre green of the forest scenery. The
shores are either bordered with mangroves with an occasional sandy
beach, or clothed with the usual jungle of the island.

As we advanced to the westward the reef gradually extended out
from the island with a short space inside, and this appearance
continued for several miles, until upon the land trending away to
the south-west, the line of reef left it and ran out to the westward
as far as the eye could reach, in an apparently unbroken line of
surf. This is Rossel Reef of the charts along which we ran for
35 miles, sounding occasionally, but although within a mile of its
edge, no bottom was got with upwards of 100 fathoms of line.
From the masthead we could see the surf of the southern border
of this great reef, the space between being a lagoon of apparently
navigable water. At the western extremity of the reef there appeared
to be a clear opening, but the day was too far advanced to admit of
entering it to search for an anchorage and the ship was hove to for
the night.

Rossel Island, judging from the little we saw of it, appears to be
well inhabited. The first natives seen were a party of five men,
apparently naked, who came out upon the beach from a grove of
cocoanut trees, and stood gazing at the unusual sight to them of
two vessels passing by. Opposite a pretty creek-like harbour, the
windings of which we could trace back a little way among the hills,
several canoes of various sizes were seen, with an outrigger on one
side, and one of them furnished with a large mat-sail of an oblong
shape, rounded at the ends. The people, of whom there were
usually about six or seven in each canoe, appeared to be engaged
in fishing in the shoal water. One man in a very small canoe was
bailing it out with a large melon-shell so intently that he appeared
to take no notice whatever of the ship which passed within a quarter
of a mile of him. We saw many huts close to the beach, usually
three or four together, forming small villages. They appeared to be
long and low, resting on the ground, with an opening at each end,
and an arched roof thatched with palm-leaves. The most picturesque
situations were chosen for these hamlets in the shade of the cocoa-
nut trees, and about them we could see numbers of children, but
no women were made out, and most of the men were fishing on the
reef. At one place we observed what appeared to be a portion of

cultivated ground; a cleared sloping bank above the shore exhibited a succession of small terraces, with a bush-like plant growing in regular rows.

A day or two later, while anchored in the Calvados, a canoe was seen, evidently of Rossel pattern. Macgillivray gives an account of this[1]:

Among the canoes which visited the ship one was of a different construction from the rest and resembled some of those which we had seen while passing along the northern side of Rossel island. It contained seven men, and came from the eastward—probably from Piron Island. The body of a canoe of this class is formed like the other, or more common kind, of the hollowed out trunk of a large tree, tapering to a point and rising slightly at the ends, which, however, are alike and covered over by a close-fitting piece of wood, each end being thus converted into a hollow cone. The sides are raised by a plank two feet high and end boards forming a kind of long box, with the seams pitched over. One side is provided with an outrigger similar to that already described, and on the other is a small stage, level with the gunwale, six feet long, planked over, and projecting four feet or thereabouts. The mast is a standing one stepped into a board in the bottom,—it is lashed to a stout transverse pole, and is further supported by two fore and aft stays. The halliards reeve through a hole in a projecting arm a foot long at the masthead. But the sail forms the most curious feature in the whole affair. It measures about fifteen feet in width by eight in depth and is made of rather fine matting stretched between two yards and rounded at the sides. The sail when not in use is rolled up and laid along the platform—when hoisted it stretched obliquely upwards across the mast, confined by the stays, with the lower and foremost corner resting on the stage and the tack secured to the foot of the mast. Both ends being alike, the mast central, and the sail large and manageable, a canoe of this description is well adapted for working to windward. Tacking is simply and expeditiously performed by letting go the tack, hauling upon the sheet, and converting one into the other. The large steering paddles are eight or nine feet long, with an oblong rounded blade of half that length.

In 1858–59, Rossel Island achieved notoriety owing to the wreck on the island of a ship, carrying over three hundred Chinese, bound for Sydney. All but two or three of these were killed and eaten, and in a way which reflects only on the humanity and not on the sagacity of the islanders. The reputation for cannibalism, of the most brutal kind, thus achieved, has biased, perhaps unduly, later observers against the natives.,

[1] *Id.* pp. 205–207.

although Sir Wm Macgregor gives the natives an excellent
character, by denying the whole story. The following account in
a magazine article by M. de Rochas,[1] who visited Rossel in 1859,
in the *Styx*, which rescued the only surviving Chinaman that
could be found, leaves little room for doubt as to what occurred,
and contains some interesting observations on the natives:

Au mois de décembre 1858, sept naufragés français recueillis par
le schooner anglais Prince-of-Danemark arrivaient à Port-de-France,
dans la Nouvelle-Calédonie. Le chef de ces infortunés, le capitaine
P..., se présenta devant les autorités de la colonie, où je me
trouvais alors, et leur fit un rapport verbal dont voici le résumé.

Le capitaine P... était parti dans le courant du mois de juillet
précédent de Hong Kong (Chine), sur le trois-mâts *le Saint Paul*,
avec vingt hommes d'équipage et trois cents dix-sept passagers
chinois, engagés pour l'exploitation des mines d'or d'Australie.
Longtemps contrarié par les calmes et menacé de la disette par la
prolongation anomale de la traversée, il s'était décidé à s'écarter de
la route ordinaire, qui lui aurait fait doubler les îles Salomon, pour
en prendre une qui devait l'amener plus promptement à Sydney,
son port de destination, et qui l'obligeait à passer entre ces dernières
îles et l'archipel de la Louisiade.

C'était, il est vrai, s'engager dans une voie plus périlleuse; mais
il obéissait à une impérieuse nécessité. Malheureusement, aux
calmes succédèrent bientôt les *gros temps*, et des brouillards épais
qui, durant trois jours consécutifs, empêchèrent le capitaine P...
de faire le point, c'est-à-dire de relever, par l'observation du soleil,
sa position exacte sur le globe.

Il fallait donc naviguer d'après *l'estime* moyenne de rigueur, trop
souvent trompeuse, et qui le fut tellement dans cette circonstance
que le troisième jour *le Saint Paul* faisait côte. Où? on n'en savait
rien, au moin d'une façon précise; ce que l'on voyait seulement
trop bien, c'est qu'on était en Mélanésie, et, par conséquent, sur
une terre inhospitalière, certitude qui ne rendait pas la position
plus gaie.

Le navire s'était échoué quelques heures avant le jour, et quand
le soleil vint éclairer la scène, on reconnut qu'on s'était jeté sur la
pointe extrême d'un immense récif de corail, qui se déroulait comme
un ruban à quelques milliers de mètres d'une terre montagneuse,
couverte d'arbres et très-vraisemblablement habitée. Triste con-
solation en de pareilles contrées que la possibilité de rencontrer des
hommes en mettant le pied sur une plage inconnue! Si l'on disait
à un voyageur qui se dispose à traverser des regions inexplorées,

[1] V. de Rochas, 'Naufrage et Scènes D'Anthropophagie à L'île
Rossell, dans l'Archipel de la Louisiade (Melanésie), [1858—texte et
dessins inédits]', in *Le Tour du Monde*, Tom. IV, 1861, 2e Semestre,
pp. 81–94.

des forêts vierges ou d'incultes pampas:—'Dans les immenses solitudes où vous allez voir engager, vous ne serez pas seul, les lions et les tigres y vivent en nombreuses troupes',—le pauvre voyageur, désagréablement ému, disait certainement qu'il se passerait bien d'une pareille société. Eh bien! lions et tigres ne sont pas plus avides de sang que les sauvages de l'île où l'on avait été jeté.

Le Saint Paul, battu par les vagues qui venaient déferler et se briser sur le récif, ne tarda pas à se défoncer: il fallut l'abandonner. Les canots dont dispose un navire marchand eussent été bien insuffisants à transporter trois cents hommes dans le court espace de temps qui devait s'écouler entre le moment du naufrage et celui de la destruction complète du *Saint Paul*. Heureusement l'écueil était guéable, si je puis m'exprimer ainsi, et les pauvres naufragés purent gagner à pied un îlot situé entre le lieu du sinistre et l'île qu'on apercevait plus loin. C'était un refuge qui permettait d'attendre quelque temps en sûreté le résultat de l'exploration qu'on se proposait de faire sur une terre plus habitable et plus fertile. Cette recherche était tout à fait nécessaire, car tout ce qu'on avait pu arracher aux débris que disputaient les flots, consistait en quelques barils de farine imbibée d'eau, deux ou trois quarts de viande salée, et un petit nombre de boîtes de conserve. Maigres ressources pour un si nombreux personnel! De plus, on manquait complètement d'eau douce.

Le capitaine P..., accompagné d'une partie de l'équipage et des passagers, débarqua sur la grande terre et y fit choix d'un campement sur le bord d'un ruisseau, à quelques pas du rivage et en vue de l'îlot que nous appellerons désormais *l'îlot du Refuge*.

Comme on s'y attendait, on trouva des habitants noirs, laids, nus, sauvages, mais de prime abord timides, ce qui était en semblable occurrence une qualité précieuse. On parvint même à se procurer quelques cocos, et l'on prenait les dispositions convenables pour recevoir la totalité des naufragés, quand on fut attaqué à la pointe du jour et à l'improviste par une nombreuse troupe armée de lances et de massues.

Les sauvages, comme il est d'ordinaire, s'étaient peu à peu enhardis, et, sans bien savoir compter, ils n'avaient pas tardé à s'apercevoir qu'ils constituaient une masse plus compacte que la petite troupe de ces êtres fantastiques, qui, sauf la bizarre couleur de leur peau, avaient d'ailleurs toutes les apparences d'hommes comme eux. Ils pensèrent qu'ils pourraient par conséquent les combattre avec avantage et subséquemment les manger, à condition cependant de les approcher en tapinois, et de tomber sur eux à l'improviste, avant qu'ils n'aient eu le temps de se mettre en défense. Donc, après s'être bien consultés, après avoir dressé leur plan avec cette sagacité du mal naturelle à tous les sauvages, ils attaquèrent les malheureux naufragés. Le combat ne fut pas long sans doute:

les uns périrent victimes d'un massacre plutôt qu'ils ne succombèrent dans une lutte; les autres parvinrent à gagner l'îlot du Refuge à la nage, ou furent recueillis par le canot du capitaine, qui commençait en ce moment même le transport des hommes restés sur l'îlot. Quand on en vint à se compter, on s'aperçut qu'il manquait huit marins et un certain nombre de Chinois. Avaient-ils tous péri dans l'attaque, ou avaient-ils cherché leur salut dans la fuite, et devait-on les retrouver plus tard? C'est ce qu'il était impossible de savoir pour le moment.

Devait-on se porter immédiatement à la recherche et au secours de ceux dont le sort inspirait tant d'inquiétudes et dans tous les cas prendre une juste revanche? Il parut imprudent de céder à cette tentation. D'abord on manquait de canots pour débarquer en troupe nombreuse: puis, les armes faisaient défaut, car on ne possédait que quelques haches et cinq ou six fusils; enfin les Chinois étaient presque tous pusillanimes et démoralisés.

On résolut donc d'attendre et d'aviser à quelque expédient.

Pendant ce temps les naturels vinrent rôder autour de l'îlot du Refuge. Quelques coups de fusil suffirent pour les éloigner. Pour comble de malheur, on n'avait point de capsules, en sorte qu'il avait fallu démonter les cheminées des fusils et mettre le feu avec un tison à peu près comme on le faisait, il y a quelques siècles, pour les mousquets. Deux hommes étaient employés à tirer un coup de fusil, l'un qui mettait en joue, et l'autre qui mettait le feu.

Le lendemain matin du jour où commencèrent les sinistres péripéties d'un naufrage aussi lamentable qu'il en fut jamais, le capitaine P..., profitant des premières lueurs du soleil et des dernières heures de sommeil des féroces habitants de l'île, débarqua au lieu du campement et fit dans les environs quelques recherches en faveur de ses malheureux compagnons. Il trouva le campement dévasté, et pas un être vivant, pas même un cadavre. Regagnant alors l'îlot du Refuge il exposa aux Chinois son avis sur la situation, et leur demanda s'ils ne jugeaient pas que le mieux était, dans l'intérêt commun, qu'il partît avec les onze marins qui lui restaient pour tâcher d'atteindre l'établissement Anglais d'Australie le plus voisin, et d'y fréter un navire afin de venir ensuite les recueillir et les sauver.

La proposition fut acceptée: il était difficile de faire prévaloir un autre avis. On convint ensuite que les Chinois resteraient en possession des vivres arrachés au naufrage et qui pouvaient les nourrir à la courte ration pendant une semaine au plus. Ceux qui partaient n'avaient à emporter qu'une douzaine de boîtes de conserve et la provision d'eau douce que pouvaient contenir trois paires de bottes de mer. Les fusils et les munitions restaient aussi entre les mains des Chinois.

Nous allons abandonner ces malheureux pour suivre le capitaine P...; plus tard on connaîtra leur sort....

Jusqu'ici, j'ai seulement rapporté ce que j'ai entendu dire par le capitaine P... ; je vais désormais prendre une part active dans les événements qu'il me reste à raconter ou du moins dire ce que j'ai vu. J'étais en effet embarqué sur le bâtiment de guerre expédié de la Nouvelle-Calédonie pour recueillir les malheureux qui attendaient, depuis cent jours, leurs sauveurs, sur le rocher de corail de l'île Rossell.

Nous partîmes de Port-de-France le 27 décembre, heureux et fiers de notre mission....

D'après les rapports du capitaine du *Saint Paul*, le naufrage avait eu lieu à l'extrémité orientale de l'archipel de la Louisiade, probablement à l'île Adèle.

Le 5 janvier, 1859, nous arrivâmes en vue de cette île, petite, formée de corail, couverte de bois, et sans traces d'habitation. Nous ne pûmes découvrir aucun vestige du *Saint Paul* et le capitaine P..., que nous avions à bord, déclara qu'il avait fait côte près d'une terre beaucoup plus élevée et qui pourrait bien être celle que nous apercevions un peu plus loin; c'était l'île Rossell que nous ne tardâmes pas à atteindre. *Le Saint Paul* laissait encore apercevoir son beaupré et sa poupe sur le récif qui, de même que dans la plupart des îles de l'Océanie, s'élève comme une barrière entre la haute mer et la terre dont il semble défendre l'approche. Quelques centaines de mètres plus en dehors, *le Saint Paul* eût doublé sain et sauf ce formidable écueil! Dieu ne l'avait pas voulu.

Nous aperçûmes aussi l'îlot du Refuge, mais pas un être vivant, pas un signal sur ce pâté de corail de vingt mètres environ de largeur sur trente-cinq de longueur.

Un officier descendit sur l'îlot et y remarqua une tente en lambeaux encore fixée sur deux arbres, des troncs d'arbres sciés à un mètre du sol et creusés comme pour servir de réservoir, deux cadavres ensevelis sous une couche de cailloux, des débris de toile épais sur le sol avec une grande quantité de coquilles, qui, ayant subi l'action du feu, avaient dû servir à la nourriture des naufragés.

La nuit survenant et aucun mouillage ne nous étant connu, il fallut attendre en dehors du récif la journée du lendemain.

Dès l'aurore notre commandant se mit en quête d'un mouillage. Cette officier, l'un des plus habiles de notre marine, avait observé dans ses longues pérégrinations en Océanie un phénomène si général qu'il pourrait être établi en loi: c'est qu'à l'embouchure de toute rivière il y a scission dans le récif de corail (récif-barrière ou pâté). Le mélange d'eau douce et d'eau salée semble antipathique aux polypes coralliens. Son premier soin fut donc de chercher une rivière, et, quand il en eut aperçu une, il fit sonder devant et trouva un espace libre où nous pûmes jeter l'ancre en sûreté. C'est le seul mouillage connu jusqu'ici à l'île Rossell, et la sagacité avec laquelle il a été trouvé fait certainement le plus grand honneur à celui qui en a doté la navigation.

A peine étions-nous mouillés, que les embarcations armées en guerre étaient détachées à la recherche des naufragés dont le sort nous inspirait déjà de vives appréhensions. J'étais dans l'une d'elles. Naviguant à quelques toises du rivage que nous avions l'ordre de parcourir dans la plus grande étendue possible pour tâcher de rencontrer soit des indigènes, soit des naufragés, nous ne tardâmes pas à apercevoir deux pirogues conduites par six naturels. En vain leur faisons-nous des signaux d'amitié et de ralliement, ils fuyaient au plus vite en poussant de fond avec une perche. Au moment où nous allions les atteindre, ils abandonnèrent leurs pirogues et disparurent dans les palétuviers qui forment un rideau impénétrable tout le long de la plage.

Ces pirogues, à peu près semblables à celles qu'on voit dans toutes les îles de la Mélanésie, se composent d'un tronc d'arbre creusé. Elles sont munies d'un balancier destiné à maintenir leur équilibre. Ce balancier se compose d'un cadre flottant à droite ou à gauche et solidement fixé par un de ces côtés au bordage de la pirogue. Comme on le pense bien, de pareilles nacelles sont fort étroites; elles ont de trois à quatre mètres de longueur. Il en est d'accouplées et alors l'une plus petite que l'autre joue le rôle de balancier. Les indigènes les font naviguer à la perche, à la rame et à la voile, espèce de natte de jonc portée par un mâtereau et fixée par des cordages faits avec diverses fibres végétales, comme celle de la noix du cocotier.

Nous n'eûmes garde de détruire les deux pirogues tombées entre nos mains, car nous tenions dans l'intérêt de ceux que nous étions venus secourir, à ouvrir des relations amicales avec les indigènes. Nous continuâmes donc notre route, et bientôt nous aperçûmes un petit homme nu, dans l'eau jusqu'à la ceinture, et qui nous faisait des signes de ralliement, sans proférer une parole, sans pousser un cri. Cette conduite si réservée nous donna tout d'abord à penser que c'était un fuyard qui n'osait pas crier et par conséquent un des naufragés. C'en était un en effet, mais non un compatriote.

Le pauvre petit Chinois se jeta dans les bras du capitaine P..., et ses premiers mots furent: *All dead!* (tous morts!) Qu'on juge de notre consternation! Nous ne pouvions pas nous figurer que trois cent dix-sept hommes avaient pu devenir la proie de sauvages mal armés et malingres comme ceux que nous avions vus tout à l'heure. Les assertions du Chinois qui se traduisaient autant par des signes que par quelques mots de mauvais Anglais ne nous laissaient cependant que peu de doute sur une aussi épouvantable catastrophe. Il parvint à nous faire comprendre qu'il restait seulement quatre de ses compagnons à terre, dont un appartenait à l'équipage du *Saint Paul* et était probablement le maître charpentier! (D'après le rapport du capitaine P... cet homme était un Prussien embarqué à Hong Kong, colonie anglaise en Chine.) Suivant le Chinois ce malheureux était gardé à vue dans les

environs, garrotté, réduit au dernier degré de marasme. On lui
avait passé dans la cloison du nez la tige d'os que les insulaires de
Rossell et de toutes les terres environnantes considèrent comme le
plus bel ornement. Sans doute le charpentier avait été adopté par
quelque chef comme le petit Chinois lui-même, qui portait un
collier et des bracelets. L'un des premiers mouvements de ce
pauvre garçon, quand il fut en sûreté dans notre embarcation, fut
d'arracher et de jeter avec indignation ces colifichets de la vanité
des sauvages.

Nous poussâmes un peu plus loin et nous nous engageâmes dans
une crique où notre nouveau compagnon nous annonçait l'existence
d'un village. Il y en avait un en effet, et nous nous trouvâmes de
suite en présence d'une trentaine d'indigènes. Nos armes étaient
cachées dans le fond des embarcations pour ne pas être un sujet
d'effroi et par conséquent de méfiance; cependant les naturels se
tenaient à une distance plus que respectueuse, en sorte que nous
ne pouvions entamer de négociations. Les plus hardis de la bande
s'approchèrent enfin, armés de lances, et firent immédiatement
toutes sortes d'avances au Chinois pour l'engager à revenir parmi
eux. Ils lui énumeraient tous les mets, toutes les jouissances qu'ils
lui réservaient, mais notre compagnon, qui nous traduisait leurs
propositions, y restait tout à fait indifférent.

Après s'être tant occupés du Chinois qu'ils paraissaient véritable-
ment aimer, les sauvages finirent par s'occuper un peu de nous
qui leur présentions de belles cotonnades rouges, du tabac, des
pipes, et qui en jetions même à leurs pieds, mais en vain car ces
barbares ne daignaient pas les ramasser. Ils ignoraient jusqu'à
l'usage du tabac, ignorance fabuleuse et qui ne peut s'expliquer
que par leur séparation complète du genre humain. Les traitants
Australiens ont en effet propagé l'usage du tabac dans toutes les
îles de l'Océanie qu'ils fréquentent. Si M. de Rienzi avait vu les
Rosseliens, il aurait peut-être cru trouver dans cette ignorance une
preuve à l'appui de son originale comparaison, car il est probable
qu'on n'a jamais vu d'orang-outang fumer la pipe.

Les sauvages firent une manœuvre pour nous cerner, mais ils
reconnurent à notre mouvement que le leur était déjoué. Ils
employèrent nonobstant tous les efforts mimiques de leur rhétorique
pour nous engager à retirer de l'étroit goulet qui donnait accès dans
la crique une de nos embarcations qui gardait le passage et en
prohibait même les abords. Il était impossible de leur donner
cette satisfaction. A la fin, convaincus que nous ne réussirions à
rien obtenir de ces misérables à qui nous demandions par l'intermédiaire du Chinois les quatre prisonniers qu'ils détenaient nous
partîmes pour aller tenter ailleurs de nouvelles négociations.

Nous nous arrêtâmes à l'embouchure du ruisseau près duquel le
capitaine P... avait établi son camp lors du désastre.

Là un spectacle horrible s'offrit à nos yeux. Des monceaux de vêtements et de queues de Chinois (on sait qu'ils étaient plus de trois cents) marquaient la place où les malheureux avaient été massacrés. Un tronc d'arbre renversé avait servi de billot où l'on appuyait le cou des victimes. Les meurtriers avaient arraché la queue de chaque Chinois encore vivant, puis l'avaient égorgé à coup de lance et enfin s'en étaient partagé les lambeaux palpitants.

Ces affreuses explications que notre compagnon parvenait à nous faire comprendre sur le théâtre même de l'événement nous furent confirmées et développées plus tard à Sydney par un interprète. Voici exactement ce qui avait eu lieu:

Tant que les pauvres naufragés avaient pu se sustenter sur l'îlot du Refuge, ils étaient restés sourds aux invitations insidieuses des sauvages, qui étaient venus rôder en pirogues autour d'eux les convier à passer sur la grande terre pour avoir de l'eau et des vivres. Par un de ces prodiges d'industrie, je voudrais dire d'ingéniosité, dont la nécessité seule peut donner le secret:

'Nécessité d'industrie est la mère',

les Chinois étaient parvenus à se faire de l'eau potable au moyen d'appareils distillatoires improvisés avec de grosses conques marines et des bouts de manches de cuir provenant du *Saint Paul*. Ils avaient en outre coupé et creusé les deux arbres un peu plus gros que les broussailles dont le sol était couvert pour en faire des réservoirs de l'eau pluviale qu'ils recevaient sur la toile des tentes. Mais enfin ayant épuisé les quelques vivres arrachés au naufrage et les bancs de coquillages qui avoisinaient l'îlot; ayant déjà vu deux de leurs compagnons mourir de faim; les plus hardis ou les plus désespérés accédèrent aux perfides avances des sauvages et s'embarquèrent avec eux. Ceux-ci, qui ne pouvaient et ne voulaient d'ailleurs prendre qu'un très-petit nombre de passagers à la fois, les emmenaient trois par trois, à l'ancien campement, où les Chinois demandaient à être conduits. Là, une troupe nombreuse fondait sur ces malheureux exténués et les sacrifiait de la façon la plus barbare, puisqu'elle poussait la rage de la férocité et d'une sensualité horrible jusqu'à les rompre de coups pour amollir la chair vivante dont elle se préparait à se repaître.

Les cris des victimes ne pouvaient parvenir jusqu'à l'îlot, distant de un à deux kilomètres, et quelques arbres touffus dérobaient le massacre à la vue des infortunés demeurés sur le rocher. Ce fut ainsi que successivement trois cents et quelques hommes purent être massacrés sans combat. Quatre seulement, ai-je dit, furent épargnés parce qu'ils avaient été *adoptés* par des chefs.

Le théâtre de cette boucherie humaine soulevait nos cœurs. Nous eûmes hâte de le fuir, et bientôt, reprenant notre marche vers le navire nous arrivâmes à l'embouchure de la rivière devant laquelle il était mouillé. Une colonne de fumée s'élevait à une grande distance dans le bois qui couvre les bords de ce cours d'eau; il était donc probable que nous trouverions des habitations en ce lieu. Nous nous engageâmes dans la rivière étroite, mais profonde. Une végétation luxuriante l'ombrageait au point de nous plonger dans une obscurité qui, tout en nous permettant de continuer notre navigation, nous empêchait de distinguer clairement ce qui se passait autour de nous.

Cependant un matelot crut apercevoir un homme perché au sommet d'un arbre. Des hurlements affreux et une grêle de pierres qui succédèrent presque immédiatement, prouvèrent qu'il ne s'était pas trompé sur la présence de cet éclaireur. Nous saisîmes précipitamment nos armes, qui consistaient en armes blanches propres à défendre un abordage, et en quelques fusils et pistolets. Les premiers coups de feu n'éloignèrent pas nos agresseurs, qui se tenaient en très-grand nombre, à quelques pas de nous, s'abritant derrière les arbres, mais ils ne tardèrent pas cependant à prendre la fuite, et nous n'entendîmes plus que leurs hurlements qu'on ne saurait comparer qu'à ceux des bêtes féroces. Deux ou trois de nos hommes seulement avaient reçu des horions. Nous continuâmes d'avancer, mais la rivière cessant d'être navigable avant que nous ne fussions en vue du village supposé, nous fûmes obligés de nous retirer, d'après la défense expresse qui nous avait été faite d'entreprendre aucune attaque, et nous dûmes regagner le bord.

Toute la nuit qui suivit, nous entendîmes des cris et des sons de trompe que les sauvages produisent en soufflant dans une conque marine percée à la pointe. J'avais trouvé une trompe semblable au campement de la *rivière du Massacre*. Des feux s'allumaient de tous côtés aux alentours de notre mouillage. Tout cela nous faisait supposer des signaux de ralliement, suivis peut-être d'affreux festins.

Le lendemain matin, nos embarcations retournèrent à l'endroit où nous avions rencontré le Chinois, et au village où nous étions entrés en pourparlers; mais, attaquées, elles durent se défendre, et revenir à bord sans résultats satisfaisants, car on ne pouvait pas même considérer comme une représaille suffisante la mort de trois ou quatre sauvages tombés dans cette affaire.

On se dirigea vers un deuxième village construit sur la plage du côté opposé et à un ou deux milles du navire. De nombreux indigènes nous firent un accueil hostile, mais sans tenter contre nous aucun acte de violence. On ne put rien obtenir d'eux. Alors notre commandant, persuadé que toute nouvelle démarche serait de même sans résultat, ne songea plus qu'aux représailles. Les embarcations bien armées retournèrent d'abord au village dont il vient d'être parlé et où un plus grand nombre d'indigènes se trouvaient réunis. Nous fûmes accueillis cette fois à coups de pierres qui eussent pu nous faire des blessures graves; elles étaient en basalte, très-dures par conséquent et angulaires. Mais, comme elles étaient lancées à la main, sans l'intermédiaire de la fronde, qui est inconnue des Rosseliens, et par suite douées de peu de vitesse, il était assez facile de les voir arriver et de les éviter à l'aide de quelques mouvements appropriés à la circonstance. Deux de nos hommes seulement furent atteints légèrement. Un matelot placé à l'avant de l'embarcation où je me trouvais eut l'idée de ramasser un de ces projectiles et de le renvoyer à son propriétaire qui semblait être le plus courageux de la bande et s'était avancé le plus près de nous. Le guerrier fit un geste d'estime et d'approbation en faveur de cet ennemi qui, seul au milieu de ses compagnons, avait enfin le courage de saisir une arme et de répondre aux coups qui lui étaient portés. Outre ceux qui s'avançaient pour nous jeter des pierres, une bande de gaillards armés de lances faisaient des prouesses de gymnastique sur la plage, où ils nous attendaient. Les femmes, semblables à des furies, excitaient les guerriers, auxquels elles s'étaient mêlées, battant la surface de l'eau de longues gaules et hurlant comme des possédées.

Pendant ce temps nos embarcations se disposaient de la façon la plus propice à balayer la plage, après s'être avancées jusqu'au point où elles ne flottaient plus qu'à peine. Chacun prenait son fusil caché jusqu'alors et on démasquait un obusier dissimulé sous un *capot*. A la vue de ce bloc emmaillotté dont ils ne connaissaient certes pas l'usage, mais qui, nonobstant, ne leur disait rien qui vaille, les guerriers commencèrent à reculer, puis à déguerpir et dès lors commença le feu. L'explosion de notre petit canon provoqua un cri de détresse inimaginable, bien que, par une circonstance fatale, il n'eût pu produire tout l'effet qu'on en attendait. Nous débarquâmes aussitôt au nombre d'une vingtaine d'hommes, pendant qu'une dizaine d'autres gardaient les embarcations afin de les empêcher d'aller à la dérive ou de s'échouer.

Inutile de dire que nul ne s'opposa à notre débarquement. Nous incendiâmes le village complètement désert. Une perche plantée en terre et portant à son extrémité une petite tige transversale sur laquelle étaient peintes des barres rouges et noires attira notre attention parce qu'elle figurait une croix. Nous nous dirigeâmes de ce côté; nous visitâmes la cabane près de laquelle elle était placée, de même que nous avions du reste fureté dans toutes les autres avant de les incendier; nous fouillâmes en outre les environs du village, mais, hélas! sans trouver trace d'aucun des compatriotes auxquels cette sorte de croix nous avait fait songer. Enfin nous regagnâmes nos embarcations, chargés des vêtements de Chinois que les sauvages avaient entassés dans leurs greniers sans daigner s'en servir, et emportant aussi quelques-unes de ces bagatelles qui ne sont précieuses que pour les ethnologistes et les amateurs de collections.

Du village incendié nous allâmes dans la rivière où nous avions été attaqués la veille, mais sans pouvoir rencontrer un seul indigène, dont nous n'entendîmes que les cris éloignés et, cette fois, plutôt gémissants que menaçants.

Bientôt enfin le navire leva l'ancre, et nous fîmes route vers Sydney pour y déposer les naufragés que nous avions à bord, y compris le capitaine P... qui avait pris part à nos expéditions, investigatrices et vengeresses.

Certes, le résultat obtenu était médiocre, et le lecteur jugera que les représailles avaient été peu en rapport avec les sanglantes horreurs qui les avaient provoquées, mais on avait fait ce qu'il était possible de faire avec les forces très-restreintes d'un équipage d'aviso à vapeur, contenues d'ailleurs dans une prudence forcée par des instructions très-sévères données avant le départ de la Nouvelle-Calédonie.

Il me reste à donner quelques détails sur l'île Rossell et sur ses habitants. Le lecteur curieux de géographie ne me pardonnerait pas de l'avoir conduit si loin pour ne lui rien faire voir, et d'avoir parlé si longuement de ce triste épisode de naufrage sans tracer au moins l'esquisse de la scène où il s'est passé.

L'île Rossell est la plus orientale de l'archipel de la Louisiade, dont elle fait partie. Cet archipel est lui-même situé au sud-est de la Nouvelle-Guinée, dans cette partie de l'Océanie qu'on a désignée sous le nom de Mélanésie.

On n'avait, avant notre expédition, aucun renseignement sur l'île Rossell, non plus que sur la plupart des îles du même archipel. D'Entrecasteaux et Dumont d'Urville en avaient relevé la position et les contours, mais sans y laisser tomber l'ancre.

Les marins Australiens, qui connaissent le mieux et parcurent le plus souvent l'Océanie dans tous les sens, n'ont pas encore osé entamer de relations commerciales avec les féroces habitants de ces îles.

Le priorité qui nous appartient donnera peut-être quelque intérêt à la courte description que je vais faire.

L'île Rossell est montagneuse et de formation volcanique. Son sommet le plus élevé doit atteindre neuf cents à mille mètres environ. Son plus grand diamètre, qui l'emporte peu sur les autres, est d'à peu près douze milles. Ses montagnes s'élèvent en pentes roides, ne laissant entre leur base et le rivage qu'un étroit cordon de terrain plan, marécageux et envahi par les palétuviers.

A en juger par les nombreux cours d'eau qui viennent déboucher au rivage, on peut dire que l'île est parfaitement arrosée.

La *rivière du Mouillage*, celle où nous avons été attaqués, étroite mais profonde, serpente dans une belle vallée couverte d'arbres gigantesques. L'aspect général du pays est magnifique; les forêts s'élèvent jusqu'à la crête des montagnes, qui ne laissent à decouvert sur leurs flancs que des cabanes entourées d'une pelouse verdoyante et ombragées d'arbres fruitiers. Au pied des coteaux sont épars de petits villages comme les deux que nous avons vus, au milieu d'arbres à pain, de cannes à sucre et de bananiers.

Le cœur saigne quand on songe que cette splendide nature

n'élabore ses productions que pour des êtres aussi dégradés que ceux qui habitent cet admirable pays.

Le village que nous avons détruit, et dont j'ai examiné avec curiosité les habitations, se composait de six cabanes seulement. Ces cases sont d'une construction fort originale et très-appropriée au climat. Ce sont de grandes cages en claies de jonc, munies d'une porte et d'une fenêtre à battants, et soutenues par des piquets à soixante centimètres environ au-dessus du sol. Leur toiture à double plan incliné déborde de beaucoup les murailles, de façon à former une galerie autour de l'habitation ; elle est faite en feuilles de canne à sucre ou de cocotiers et élégamment soutenue par des poteaux indépendants de la muraille et placés aux quatre coins.

Ces cases ont, en moyenne, une dizaine de mètres de longueur sur trois en largeur et autant en hauteur. Élevées comme elles sont au-dessus du sol, il n'est facile d'y pénétrer qu'à la faveur d'un escalier rudimentaire fixé en permanence devant la porte. C'est un morceau de bois bifurqué dont la fourche sert d'échelon.

Elles sont passablement aérées par la porte et la fenêtre, qui sont, à vrai dire, très-exiguës. Il est facultatif de les ouvrir ou de les fermer au moyen des battants dont elles sont munies.

Au milieu se trouve un foyer circonscrit par des cailloux. On y entretient sans doute la nuit un feu permanent pour écarter les moustiques, qui pullulent sur le rivage. Pareille disposition et pareille coutume existent en Nouvelle-Calédonie, aux îles Fidjis, et probablement ailleurs, mais je ne parle que de ce que j'ai vu.

En résumé, la construction de ces habitations est fort bien entendue pour procurer à leurs hideux propriétaires un abri contre les ardeurs du soleil de feu qui les éclaire et qui ferait mieux de les brûler, en même temps qu'elle les met à l'abri de l'humidité du sol, avantage précieux durant l'hivernage.

Les Rosseliens sont loin d'apporter en toutes choses la même industrie, car, si j'en juge par les objets trouvés dans leur village et enlevés par nous à l'improviste, de telle sorte que les fuyards n'eurent le temps d'en rien emporter, ils n'ont d'autre instrument d'industrie qu'une petite herminette. C'est une pierre de basalte articulée en coude avec le manche. La sagaie et la pierre sont leurs seules armes de guerre. J'ai fait connaître la trompe (conque marine) dont ils sonnent pour se rallier. C'est quelque chose d'analogue à ce qui sert dans nos campagnes, *à offrir* un charivari à la dame qui convole à de nouvelles noces.

On connaît leurs pirogues ; ils les manœuvrent très-bien.

Ils fabriquent des nattes et des paniers avec des lanières végétales. Leurs couteaux sont des valves d'huître finement dentelées sur les bords.

Arrivons enfin au portrait de ces affreux personnages. Ils ont la peau d'un noir mat comme la suie, le nez écrasé, la bouche large, l'œil noir et injecté, les pommettes saillantes, la chevelure noire, longue et crépue, la barbe rare et frisée, le front un peu fuyant. Leur taille et leur musculature sont très-médiocres.

L'usage du bétel donne à leurs lèvres et à leurs gencives la couleur de l'écrevisse cuite; leurs dents sont noires et corrodées.

Les femmes sont obèses, avec des traits grossiers, une chevelure semblable à celle de leurs maris, un sein exubérant et piriforme.

Les élégants se font des favoris avec de la chaux et se passent transversalement dans la cloison du nez une tige d'os grosse comme une plume d'oie. C'est la même tige que les matelots de Cook remarquaient avec étonnement au nez des Australiens et qu'ils appelaient comiquement la *vergue de beaupré*. Le costume des hommes consiste en une poche faite avec une feuille d'arbre.

Les femmes ont pour tout vêtement une ceinture à franges, en fibres d'écorce, et qui retombe jusqu'à micuisses.

Les deux sexes font un fréquent usage du bétel. A chaque instant, on les voit mordre un morceau de noix d'arec (fruit du palmier arec) et de feuille d'un poivrier (piper bétel), et porter sur les gencives, au moyen d'une spatule en bois, la chaux qu'ils puisent dans une calebasse. C'est ce mélange qui constitue le bétel; mélange qui se fait dans la bouche des sauvages, et n'est pas préparé d'avance comme dans l'Indo-Chine et à Java.

J'ai rapporté en France tous ces objets, pris soit dans le village, soit entre les mains de notre Chinois, qui nous arriva avec un costume et un appareil de toilette complets.

Le climat de Rossell est très-chaud.

Si tout le littoral est peuplé comme la partie de la côte que nous avons parcourue, il doit y avoir plusieurs milliers d'habitants dans l'île.

The wreck of the *St Paul* and the fate of its passengers is referred to in an Admiralty publication a few years later[1]:

On the 30th of September, 1858, the ship *St Paul*, bound from Hong Kong to Sydney, with 327 Chinese passengers on board, was totally wrecked on this island, when all hands reached the shore. The captain and eight of the crew then left in a boat to obtain assistance, and on the French steamer, *Styx*, arriving at the spot from New Caledonia early in January 1859, it was found that the whole of the passengers and remainder of the crew, with the exception of one Chinese, had been horribly massacred by the natives. The survivor stated that the natives feasted upon the bodies of their victims.

Twelve years later the *St Paul* incident is referred to in a letter from G. P. Heath, who had served in the *Rattlesnake* during the survey of the Louisiades by Captain Owen Stanley. This letter

[1] *Australia Directory*, vol. II, 1864, p. 400.

is probably responsible for the view, widely current amongst the white population in Papua at the present day, that the Chinese were deliberately fattened up by the Rossel Islanders for subsequent consumption. Referring to the treacherousness of the Louisiade Islanders, Mr Heath says[1]:

...Then, if I remember rightly, a vessel with Chinese emigrants was wrecked somewhere at the Louisiades some years ago, and it was reported that the natives penned the Chinese up like sheep, and daily came to select the one in best condition for the table, the last survivor being rescued by some passing vessel....

Rossel does not appear to have been visited again, except by 'blackbirders' recruiting labour for the Queensland sugar plantations, until 1885, when Captain Bridge of H.M.S. *Dart* reports as follows:[2]

...Rossel Island was reached in the evening. I landed at a village, where two canoes were seen, to communicate with the natives, who were extremely shy. At first they kept out of sight altogether, and when they did appear, although I was alone, they remained for some time on the other side of the stream. Confidence was soon established, and they approached, offering cocoa-nuts and receiving a few presents, which Lieutenant and Commander Moore, who had joined me, helped me to distribute. One or two of them knew the words 'tobacco' and 'pipe', to the use of which most of them were evidently unaccustomed; beyond this they were quite ignorant of English. I succeeded in making them understand that in the morning the flag would be hoisted, and believe that they had a fairly clear idea of the meaning of what we had come to do. The next morning the Protectorate was proclaimed and the flag hoisted. A copy of the Proclamation, to be shown to any white visitor, and the flag, was placed in charge of an elderly native, named Nao, pointed out as the Chief, and a medal was given him.

A few words, of little value and therefore not quoted here, were collected.[3]

In the official correspondence for this year it is also reported that certain recruiting boats, mostly of evil reputation, visited Rossel to obtain labour,[4] e.g. the *Ceara* in 1883–84, probably the *Lizzie* in 1884, and the *Hopeful* in 1884, the latter, possibly owing to the success of the earlier boats, obtaining no recruits.

Two years later, in 1887, the island was visited by the Hon. John Douglas, for the purpose of returning some of the recruits

---

[1] *Correspondence respecting New Guinea*, July, 1876, p. 17.
[2] *Further Correspondence respecting New Guinea and other islands in the Western Pacific Ocean*, August, 1885, p. 101.
[3] *Id.* p. 551. [4] *Id.* p. 617.

who had survived the Queensland plantations. The journal of the Hon. John Douglas, then Special Commissioner for British New Guinea, contains the following account:[1]

...[We] steamed...to an anchorage in four fathoms in Cannibal Bay, as we named it, a little to the westward of the 'Swingers' anchorage as marked on the chart. Rossel presented to me a sombre, gloomy, and uninviting aspect from the side on which we approached it. The hill sides are very steep, and covered with dense vegetation; profound silence reigned around, broken only by the occasional scream of a cockatoo frightened by the movement of the natives, whom we did not see, though they no doubt saw us. The first glimpse of human life which we caught was that of two natives emerging from a hole in a rock off a point immediately abutting on [our] own anchorage. Rossel is not an inviting solitude. This morning we became a little better acquainted with its inhabitants. A canoe came alongside of us with five natives. Before breakfast, Cholmondeley took two of our boys in the whale-boat to land them at their native cocoa-nut grove about a mile from our anchorage. A dozen truculent and hungry-looking dogs came down to meet them, but our poor 'boys' were frightened out of their seven senses, for they were informed, it seems, with great candour, that their own relatives—six in number—had been killed and eaten. The gentlemen who had cleverly accomplished this gastronomic triumph were very anxious that our 'boys' should land, but they did not seem to see it, and Cholmondeley very properly brought them back to the vessel. We took them on to High Island, where the rest of our Rossel contingent were landed at their native *habitat*, and they seemed to be satisfied that here they would be sufficiently strong to hold their own. I confess I felt some compunction in landing them at all, for I feared that they and their boxes might become the prey of some of the revolting-looking Anthropophagi who floated around us in their canoes this morning. I was glad, at 11 a.m. this morning, to know that we were leaving behind us this atmosphere of this most unalluring fastness of the Giant Despair—the Ultima Thule of the Louisiade Archipelago.

Sir Wm Macgregor, visiting the island in the following year, 1888, with a party of 21 miners, who did not remain, gives the following account of the island:[2]

The island is composed of slaty formation, very similar to that of Sudest, varying in hardness from the consistency of clay to the density of basalt, with small veins of quartz running through it in all directions....Accompanied by my staff I crossed the island

[1] *British New Guinea: Report of the Special Commissioner for 1887*, p. 29.
[2] *Annual Report on British New Guinea*, 1888–89, pp. 3–4.

from sea to sea, and returned the greater part of the way by a different route, but unfortunately saw very little of the natives, who were extremely shy, probably being so naturally, but likely also timid as being afraid of punishment for the massacres they are supposed to · have committed on white people wrecked there. During the journey we saw only six towns, one of which had evidently been deserted for some time. They would average about six or seven houses each. On the southern side of Dixon Bay I saw four more towns of about the same size, and on High Island two similar towns. Enough was seen to enable me to say that the population is very scanty for the size of the island, probably not exceeding a total of 1000 or 1200....

...As far as I could make out they have no chiefs, though the old men appear to have some authority in their own towns; but the different small districts seem to live in a state of hostility with each other....

...We found two men who could speak a little English, which they had learnt when at work on the sugar plantations of Queensland; but neither would accompany us across the island, fearing they would be killed and eaten after we left, if they conducted us to any other towns in the centre or on the other side of the island. Before we got into any village, after leaving Dixon Bay, the natives always fled into the bush.... No violence or obstruction was offered to us, however. We saw none of the women and children.... One remarkable feature of the villages visited by us was their cleanliness. The houses are chiefly built on posts, about five feet high, and the ground below and between the houses kept swept and perfectly clean. The houses are entered by trap-doors through the floor, and are when in good repair, dry and comfortable to sleep in. Cooking is done by small heated stones, and seems to be carried on under the houses. They have no pottery and no domestic animals, except an occasional pig and a few dingoes.... Their food consists of taro, sago, via, bananas, pandanus, cocoa-nuts, papaya, sugarcane, forest nuts of several kinds, mangoes, jaica, arrowroot, and bread-fruit, with fish, wild swine, dugong, turtle, prawns, and sometimes pigeons or other birds....

...For covering they use a cord twisted round the waist several times, and a perineal band of a single pandanus leaf. They are not tattoed. The spear appears to be their only weapon. The stone adze seems to have fallen into desuetude amongst them, as they are well supplied, presumably from wrecks, with iron to make adzes, which they shape like a plane iron, and mount as the stone adze is mounted in other islands. Their gardens on the west side are on steep ridges, and are not well kept, and contain but little, chiefly taro. On the east side the gardens are on level rich patches of ground, and contain choice kinds of taro. I did not see on the island a single representative of the orange family, nor any pineapple, but I noticed one small clump of rather slender bamboo. In each village there was one human skull, but sometimes as many as three or four, placed in a conspicuous spot on a shelf or plate. The skulls are evidently those of natives, being of small size, and decidedly prognathous, and from their position are probably the skulls of deceased leaders, and not trophies of cannibalism....

B. A. Hely[1] notes in the same *Annual Report* that 16 men went to Rossel, prospecting, and stayed four weeks. This would be in 1889, after the above visit of Sir Wm Macgregor.

Sir Wm Macgregor visited Rossel again in 1890, on this occasion getting into communication with the natives, now regarded as 'perhaps the most harmless and inoffensive in the Possession':[2]

On the 10th of July we anchored at Roua (Rossel Island) in Mebi Bay, opposite Wüli (High Island). In my despatch of 18th October, 1888, it was pointed out that it was very desirable that Roua should be visited again at an early date.... As related in my despatch mentioned above, we were not successful in our endeavours to establish friendly intercourse with the natives, although we crossed the island from sea to sea and walked back again. We naturally left the island with some prejudice against the Roua tribes. It was, therefore, a matter of no little surprise and satisfaction to find that the Roua natives are perhaps the most harmless and inoffensive in the Possession. A rumour had become current that there were two Chinese, survivors of the *St Paul*, somewhere on the north coast. I therefore determined to visit that part myself....

Accompanied by the Rev. A. Maclaren, I went round the northern coast in a whale-boat with a coloured crew in two days, nearly as far as the Cape Deliverance of Bougainville, the most easterly point of the island. We had not much difficulty in getting into communication with the occupants of the first two or three villages, and after that there was practically no difficulty whatever.... They [the villages] are generally built close to the sea, surrounded with small clumps of cocoa-nut trees. So close are they to the water that the village divan, consisting of a number of flat stones laid down as seats on the top of a low cairn with back supports, is generally on the foreshore, a foot or two below high-water mark. The villages are small, averaging probably six to eight houses. There are, however, many of them, and they evidently live at peace among each other. A good proof of this is seen in the fact that we surprised a number of canoes out fishing, and in all these there was not a single fighting spear. No native met us armed, and indeed one could hardly see any arms in the houses. They accompanied us freely from village to village and, quite contrary to what is the

[1] *Id.* p. 50.
[2] *Annual Report on British New Guinea*, 1890–91, pp. 3–4.

general rule in the Possession, they never spoke of any danger to them or us in going to some village further on. The women and children were kept out of our sight, but the men did not appear to entertain much suspicion of us, even at first. The cultivation of the land on the north side of the island is not well performed reminding one of the state of matters in Tagula, being much inferior to what we saw on the east side of Roua. Land is seldom cleared for planting; the bush is thinned and burned, but most of the large trees are left standing....Houses on the north coast are often very inferior; numbers of them are not built on posts and have the earth for a floor. They do all their cooking by means of hot stones; they take only one meal a day, towards evening. They seem to catch many fine fish by means of nets, and by the use of plants that stupefy the fish. The men wear probably eight or ten turns round the waist of cord as thick as one's little finger, and a pandanus leaf as a covering. They have the customary earrings, nose and neck ornaments, but do not wear much jewellery. They are not tattooed, but suffer much from *Tinea desquamans*. It is usual to remove all hair from the face, except the eyelashes; for effecting depilation they use a small piece of pumice-stone. The women are very clever at basket-making, and turn out some fine worked specimens of their skill. Each man carries one of these on his arm in which he has the ingredients for betel-nut chewing, and almost invariably a piece of fine sponge. The use of this sponge on the north coast of Roua is so unique and remarkable in this country that one would have had some hesitation in believing, without ocular proof, that it is actually used for washing the face....
One striking peculiarity seen by me for the first time on this coast, but described many years ago, I believe, by the Russian naturalist, Mr Miklouko Maclay, as occurring on the Maclay coast of the mainland, was the extraordinary development of the incisor teeth. The man in whom this was first observed was from fifty to sixty years of age. The left central incisor tooth was the largest. It was more than an inch broad, about an inch and a quarter long, and about a fourth of an inch thick. Its colour was that of the teeth of confirmed eaters of betel nut. The central right incisor was as long and as thick, but only about half as broad. It probably arises from a deposit of tannic acid from the betel-nut, combined with the lime eaten with it, and from the absence of teeth in the lower jaw....
...In one village several skulls were noticed. These they said they had recently dug up; they were the skulls of relatives, and seemed to be kept in connection with some form of ancestral worship....
...I could not obtain any information whatever that would support the rumour of any Chinese survivals of the *St Paul*, although the natives remembered distinctly that two vessels had been wrecked in the vicinity of Cape Deliverance....

From One-tree Point on the south to Ola on the north the protection for small vessels is perfect, and this space is constantly traversed by the Roua canoes. Of these they seem to possess none fit for the open sea; but for coasting they are superior, resembling a Rob Roy canoe in form and structure, and well and securely caulked with gum.

The Hon. F. P. Winter,[1] who accompanied Sir Wm Macgregor on this visit, collected a vocabulary of about fifty words of insufficient value to be quoted.

Sir Wm Macgregor paid a third visit to the island in 1892, in connection with the murder of a Frenchman, Lucien Fiolini, by the natives. It is interesting to note that Sir Wm Macgregor, presumably unacquainted with the evidence given above, suggests that the Chinamen of the *St Paul* were not eaten by the natives, who deny it and furnish a different story. He finds, moreover, 'no proof whatever that they were cannibals'. Sir Wm Macgregor reports as follows:[2]

On the 1st of August the steamer anchored at the head of Yongga Bay, and preparations were made for visiting the south coast of the island next day. Mr Moreton, the magistrate of the district, and the Commandant with some police, were directed to march across the island to near the place where it was understood the murder had been committed. I went round the west end of the island in a whale-boat with a native crew, in the hope of gaining over the different tribes along the coast. In this we were completely successful. The co-operation of every tribe was secured up to Tama, where 'Lucien' was killed. My boat was beached about two miles west of that place, so that it was not seen by the Tama people, and my crew, with a number of volunteers from Bamba and Kwanija, went on to the first Tama houses, and were successful in at once arresting one of those implicated in Lucien's murder. The rest of the Tama tribe fled to the mountains without offering resistance. The Kwaija tribe, near neighbours of Tama on the west side, were naturally very shy and timid, but they were soon secured for the Government side. About fifteen or sixteen men and youths received me in their village, but in a somewhat peculiar way. Under the largest house, which was built on six posts about five or six feet long, they had put up a sort of fence of leaves of the cocoa-nut palm laid on their edges and about a yard high. When I appeared the chief and three or four of the leading men were seated inside this enclosure, but before I reached the place the other grown-up men all went inside it, and remained there during my visit. The

---

[1] *Annual Report on British New Guinea, with Appendices*, 1890–91, p. 157.
[2] *Annual Report on British New Guinea*, 1892–93, pp. 5–7.

idea seemed to be that it was a sacred spot where they would be safe from molestation....

...On the way back [from an unsuccessful attempt to reach the island of Loa] we met three canoes at the head of Nyebe Bay, which had come down the Nyavo Creek to fish. They were of the usual peaceful and friendly character of the Yela people, and carried no spears or other arms in their canoes.

On returning to Tama I found that the volunteers of Bamba, Kwanija, and Kwaija had captured two of the principals in the murder. Unfortunately the securing of one of them had a fatal result. It appears that two men found one of the criminals and tied him up by cords put round his legs, thighs, arms and forearms. I could not find that any ligatures were applied so as to compress the chest. I am unable to say whether the unfortunate man died from natural causes, from fright, or from the constriction of the bands used to confine him. There was certainly no intention whatever on the part of the men that secured him to inflict any injury on him; they were, I believe, entirely unarmed....

There seems to be no doubt as to what was the cause of his murder. The same reason for it was given me by the natives at the east end of Tagula, and from Yongga Bay to Tama, or Yela; they all maintained that Lucien was killed because of his being 'after their women'. The Yela people are peculiar in many ways, as I shall show further on, but in nothing are they more different from their northern neighbours of Kiriwina, etc., than in their scrupulous care of their women. I have not yet seen a native woman on the island, so jealously do they guard them from strangers....

...There was every reason to be pleased with the attitude and conduct of all the tribes on the coast. They unanimously condemned the Tama people for killing Lucien, and fully approved of their being punished. They assured me there was no intertribal fighting on the island, and all the men and canoes we met carried no arms....

At one of the villages on the north coast a boy brought me a Mexican dollar of 1852, with three Chinese stamp impressions on it. I was informed that this was from the large ship that was wrecked on the reef near Loa (Adele Island). This no doubt referred to the *St Paul*, which was wrecked there in September 1858. I had made enquiries respecting this occurrence of all the elderly men on the west and south of the island, and had received in general terms the same account there as on the north coast. The story as given in the *Pacific Directory*, vol. I, p. 194 (second edition, 1890),[1] is that the *St Paul* struck at Rossel, and 327 Chinese, who were being taken to Sydney, were left temporarily at the island. A relieving vessel found only one Chinese there in the following January, and

[1] This is the account reproduced from that in the *Australia Directory*, vol. II, 1864, quoted above, p. 203.

apparently on his representation it was accepted that the other 326 men were killed and feasted on by the natives in less than four months.

The native account of it is that the Chinese landed and obtained water, sugar-cane, cocoanuts, and all the food they could find, and then left in boats or rafts, proceeding northwards, the only direction they could well take at that time of the year in such craft. The natives described how they were afraid to go near the wreck after the people left. When they got up near to it someone suggested that the foreigners were hiding in the wreck to catch them and kill them, and they turned back and did not actually enter the wreck for some days after the Chinese had left. I told a native that it had been said they killed and ate all the Chinese. His reply was that he supposed some white man must have seen skulls in their houses and thought that these were from people that they had eaten; but these skulls, he stated, were those of their own people. It is their method of disposing of the dead to keep the body until the flesh falls off and disappears, then to keep the bones in or near their houses. That this is true I had an opportunity of verifying. At Wöla (High Island) I saw a dead body tied up in a reclining position in a shroud made of the leaves of a species of fan palm. The house was closed up, and evidently left for the time to the sole tenancy of its ghastly occupant; and at Bibe the head of a man recently deceased was seen buried in a basket in a dwelling-house. Probabilities are altogether in favour of the native account. The natives are the mildest, quietest, and most inoffensive in the Possession. I have no proof whatever that they are cannibals. The tribes all along the southern coast are very small communities, and by no means of a warlike disposition. Their only weapon seems to be the spear. I have seen only one club on the island. There is no tribe on the island that could not be conquered by fifty Chinese armed with stones, which abound everywhere on Yela. A rough stone is but little inferior to the Yela spear as an offensive weapon. Three hundred Chinese could undoubtedly have conquered the island with such weapons as they could pick up. But the natives seem to think they had some firearms. In consideration of all these circumstances it seems to me incredible that the 326 Chinese were killed and eaten at this island, and I therefore accept the native account as being correct. They are well acquainted with the main facts. There is no village on the south coast that does not contain iron from this ship, and some of her blue enamelled plates and dishes.

Although we have now met many of the Yela tribes, there yet remains much to learn about them. I should say they distinctly belong to the Papuan race, the average type of face and form clearly belonging to that stock. But it may even be inferred that they are the purest blooded Papuans we have in the Possession.

They do not intermarry with any other islanders. Tagula is their nearest neighbour, and until very recent times they have had but little intercourse with that island. Even now they do not intermarry with Tagula. One of the results of their recent communication with Tagula has been the introduction thence in Yela of that loathsome ringworm, *Tinea desquamans*, which with its usual eastern name of *Sipoam* [? Sipoma], they received a few years ago. The Yela people are great eaters of lime, betel-nut, and pepper. They grow small quantities of taro, sugar-cane, bananas, sweet potatoes, a variety of edible hybiscus, and some yams. They eat a large amount of sago and many nuts from forest trees. Half a dozen different varieties of sugar-cane were noticed, and two or three of their bananas are decidedly superior. There are no extensive sago tracts on the island, the largest perhaps being near Dao, on the north coast, but the island produces enough for the wants of its scanty population. One of the most objectionable habits of these people is that they cut down a number of cocoanut trees when a person dies. In proceeding along the coast one can always tell from the cocoanut trees when a death has recently occurred. They do not shave any part of the head, nor pull out the eyebrows, but they keep the beard cut very short. Each man carries a small basket of fine workmanship, containing shells to be used as knives and spoons, a piece of sponge for cleaning the face, and the betel-nut gear. The pandanus leaf they wear is twisted round behind, flat and high in front, and fastened to a girdle of six or eight turns of twisted rope, about half an inch thick. They perforate the septum of the nose, and wear nose-pencils of clam-shell. They also pierce and distend the lobe of the ear, and wear armlets of shell and of mat-work, but they do not tattoo. They do not employ a shield with the spear, and are ignorant of the sling and bow and arrow. They cook with heaps of hot stones, and do not know how to make pottery, but have got a few clay pots from Tagula. They have sails for their canoes, but they are small craft, fit for use inside the reef only, and not capable of undertaking sea voyages. They have taken kindly to tobacco, and will consequently be willing to trade. Tobacco is not grown on the island. All the young men wear their hair in thin, matted tufts; the old men cut it shorter. The language of Yela is of great interest on account of the all but complete isolation of the island. Several hundred words of the vocabulary of the west end and south side have been written down, and will, when supplemented by another visit, be worth printing. It abounds in double consonants, especially 'gg', 'mb', and 'ng', but its vowels are extremely perplexing. One of these is nearly equal to the German 'ö', and this is of frequent occurrence; but there are shades and gradations of the Greek 'u', the French 'u' and 'eu', and the German 'ü', that cannot possibly be written in any known alphabet. There are guttural sounds quite as puzzling as these complicated vowels; nearly all the consonants are used before some of these guttural sounds. So far as can be judged from the materials collected, the language differs greatly from those of Kiriwina, Murua, and even from Tagula, the nearest island. The provincial differences between the language, as spoken in the north and south of the island, are so great that it is hardly comprehensible in both districts to one interpreter. As might perhaps be expected, there seems to be but a slender tie between the Yela tongue and the Polynesian dialects. Such common words of constant use as father, mother, water, yam, butterfly, breadfruit, etc., which are generally traceable from Honolulu to the east side of the Gulf of Papua, are either not found at all on Yela, or are so changed and disguised as to be of doubtful recognition. All this will tend to make Yela a place of the greatest interest to the student of mankind. The name of this island in their own tongue is Yela; in the Tagula language it is Rova, or Roua. Tagula is called 'Yemba' at Yela, a word which seems to be the 'berg', 'dun', or 'kremlin' of their language. The tops of the Tagula hills are visible at Yela....

The vocabulary above referred to was published in the following year,[1] and is not quoted here (see Chap. 1, p. 6).

The canoes referred to in the above report are described by Sir Wm Macgregor as follows:[2]

The canoe of Rossel Island is different from all others, and is undoubtedly the most skilfully made of any in the Possession. They are not made for sailing, and are not of large size, some 20 to 30 feet long, and from 1 to 2 feet broad in the middle part, which occupies about a third of the whole length. A third or a fourth part of the hull at each end gradually narrows towards the extremity. It is straight above, and reduced to a flat surface before the process of digging out is begun. The central part is oblong in shape, and is closed in, sides and ends, by boards a foot or more in height, sewn and well caulked with lime and different kinds of gum. The end parts are dug out through a slit, about 2 or 3 inches broad on the upper side. When the hull is hollowed out to the end, a board is carefully fitted along the whole length of the slit, and is caulked watertight. It thus becomes a Rob Roy canoe, which cannot be sunk or filled so long as water does not get over the top of the central citadel. They are provided with an outrigger, and are pushed or paddled according to the depth of the water.

For seven years after this last visit of Sir Wm Macgregor the island appears to have been unvisited by officials, although recruits have evidently been obtained from the island, as is

[1] *Annual Report on British New Guinea*, 1893–94, pp. 116–120.
[2] Macgregor, *British New Guinea*, London, 1897, pp. 58–59.

shown by the following report of Mr G. R. Le Hunte, who paid Rossel a visit in 1899:[1]

...We sailed on the morning of 25th for Rossel Island.... I came here especially on account of what Mr Campbell, the Resident Magistrate, informed me had occurred here recently in connection with the recruiting of men for carriers to the Mambare Gold Field. I enclose a copy of his report.... We... steamed along the coast for about twenty miles, touching at one or two places to land a man, or some sticks of tobacco for the wages due to one of those who had deserted or died at the goldfield, which would be given to their relations. Mr Campbell informed me that those whom we were returning were in some apprehension of what the relations of those who had died might do to them; satisfaction must be got somehow out of somebody for a lost life. We visited one village, Lowa, situated in an unhealthy swamp. In a small peculiar-shaped house we saw four smoke-discoloured skulls, which we were informed were those of departed relatives. Their immediate burial was ordered by the magistrate....

...The soil appears to be very poor, and what is not rugged mountain is swamp. The people are poor and wild; the population is estimated at between 2000 and 3000....

Mr Campbell in the report referred to above says:[2]

...I visited Rossel in October last year, just after the last recruiting vessel had left, and from what I then heard, I was certain in my own mind that the natives had been deceived.... The returned carriers stated that fifty-four natives were taken from Rossel to Mambare; of this number about twenty died, and ten deserted owing to the severe nature of the work required of them....

Mr Campbell in his report on the South Eastern Division states in reference to his October visit:[3]

In October last three natives of Rossel Island were arrested on a charge of being concerned in the murder of a man and a woman at that place. The reason given for killing the man was, because he set to work building a much larger and better house than any other in the town, whereupon the town rose in its wrath and speared the pretentious fellow. The woman was killed because an old man having fallen sick told some youngèr man that if he died it would be owing to this woman having bewitched him. He did die, and the woman was promptly clubbed by her brother.... During this expedition a number of spears were taken and destroyed.

Mr G. R. Le Hunte again visited Rossel with Mr Campbell two years later, early in 1901. He reports as follows:[4]

[1] *Annual Report on British New Guinea*, 1898–99, pp. 29–30.
[2] *Id.* p. 34.   [3] *Id.* p. 86.
[4] *Annual Report on British New Guinea*, 1900–1, pp. 21–22.

...We anchored at the head of the long inlet, Wonga Bay, which runs about six miles inland. Mr Campbell and I landed at a village on the south side...finally two men came...; after a little the women and children came, and when we left we were on the best of terms....

The next morning the *Merrie England* dropped us...off Wola Island, where Mr Campbell was informed they had a man from one of the hill villages in custody for him, having killed a man of another hill village, in accordance with their custom on the death of his own chief. The islanders now know that this is wrong and wish it put a stop to. His own people had made a prisoner of him and sent him down to the coast to be handed over to the magistrate....We went along the coast calling in at various villages, and finding the people in them most friendly, except at one which we found completely empty, but at this place a man is wanted for murder, which quite accounts for its being deserted. The same story: the chief had died, and one of his men had gone off to another village and killed a woman; he will be captured later. We also found on a rock a skull, evidently of an old person, with a piece of broken pottery beside it; the head was complete, with the lower jaw in its place, and there was no sign of any hurt or fracture of any part of it. We visited the village of Banyu, which I had visited in 1899....They had buried the skulls as I had directed, and had, besides, given up burying their dead in their village....One small girl had a most beautiful red parrot with a blue breast on the top of her head; the bird was quite tame and allowed its wings to be opened. The feathers were cut. It came from Sudest Island, where one of the villagers had bought it....

Mr Campbell and I landed next morning to visit a village, Doroa, farther to the eastward....It was composed of a few wretchedly built houses, as all the Rossel ones are (they are all the 'turtle-back' pattern), under a clump of cocoanuts. The chief's wife and one or two other women were there, protected by a small sized but very belligerent pig—the only one Mr Campbell has ever seen on the island—which was only kept back by vigilant prevention from an onslaught on us....

We then left for Sudest, stopping off the Swinger opening to take on board the prisoner, who was brought off securely tied up. He pleaded guilty when charged before Mr Campbell, and was sent on for trial. His Honour sentenced two men from this island when we were at Nivani for the same customary offence to a few years' imprisonment....

...With regard to Europeans, the natives have for a long time been inoffensive, and they repudiate the story of their having eaten the Chinese who were shipwrecked off the island in 1858—a supposition of those that left them there. The Rossel Islanders say that the Chinese made a raft and went away....

Mr Campbell reports another visit to Rossel in February, 1901 :[1]

...We proceeded round the north coast, and about midday reached a point some three miles below the village of Dagoa, where a murder had been committed by some of the villagers....Here I landed a party of police and some friendly natives as guides, to cross overland and approach the village from the inland side, while I with the other party proceeded up the coast in the boats to surprise it from the sea frontage.

Both parties arrived at the village simultaneously, but the people having apparently been apprised of our coming had fled into the bush. There were a number of spears lying about, which we collected and destroyed.

...We again landed a party at a place called Sibu, to march overland to the village of Leadino, situated near the head waters of the Foa-mo-sia River....No natives had apparently been there [at the village] for some considerable time.

In one of the houses we found the body of a man strung up to the beams supporting the roof. It was very carefully wrapped up in native mats and dried grass, etc. Another corpse was lying in a hole in the ground underneath the house. No earth had been thrown on it; only some dried grass and leaves covered the body. A few planks, evidently taken from an old canoe, had been placed on top of the hole.

What struck me as being remarkable was the entire absence of any offensive smell from either of these bodies, although there could be no doubt that they had been there for some time.

I presume one was the corpse of the head man of the village, who had presumably died from natural causes, and the other that of the man killed to accompany him in to the land of the spirits....

During my visit to Rossel Island I made particular enquiry as to the cause of the murders occurring on that island, and the natives tell me that it is the custom of the place, whenever the head man of a village dies, for his relations then present to at once start out in search of some one to kill. The first person met with is speared. Thus it often happens that a brother kills his sister (as a matter of fact we arrested one youth, who, when out on one of these expeditions, had speared his own sister whom he met returning from the gardens with food), a father his son, or a son his father.

This custom has nothing in common with that in vogue in other parts of the division, where one particular person would be singled out and accused of having caused the death of the chief by sorcery. Here it is the first person the killers meet, or rather, succeed in spearing, that falls a victim. There is no thought on the part of the relations of a person despatched in this way to avenge his death.

Mr Campbell's prediction that the Rossel Islanders were likely to give up their custom of murder on the death of a headman is

[1] *Annual Report on British New Guinea*, 1900–1, pp. 24–25.

not fulfilled, for the Hon. M. H. Moreton, Resident Magistrate
of the South-Eastern Division, had to visit the island in 1902 for
the usual reason. He says:[1]

..At Rossel I had to arrest several natives for murder, the outcome of a custom among these natives, which is that, when the
headman of a village dies, his wife has to be killed and eaten, but
should he have no wife, then the first small boy belonging to
another village that is met by the murdering party is the victim.
As the villages on Rossel are all small, consisting of, on an average,
about five houses, there must be rather a large number of headmen. It
cannot, therefore, be a very enviable position for a woman to be in.
There is only one village of any size, and that contains but ten to
twelve houses. The custom is more prevalent towards the east end
of the island than at the west end, the latter having had more attention paid it, the east end being rather inaccessible to a sailing vessel.

On the 16th September, 1902, the s.s. *President* arrived at Tryon
Bay, Rossel Island, with the Rev. W. E. Bromilow, Mrs Bromilow,
and several other members of the Methodist Mission Society....

In April, 1903, I visited this island again, and purchased four
sites for Mission Stations, which had been chosen at the time of
the Mission visit. I also at the same time purchased some 200 acres
of land for cocoanut planting....

Apparently, the Mission enterprise got no further than the
purchase of sites, and no attempt to introduce Christianity seems
to have been made since.

The purchase of land for Mr F. Osborne probably occurred
about the time of an incident, which nearly cost him his life.
He appears to have endeavoured to clear a portion of ground in
which was a *yaba* (see Chap. XI): this the natives naturally
resented. The outcome was a siege which lasted four days,
Mr Osborne being confined in a small hut with his dog. The
watchfulness of the dog appears to have made the natives lose
patience and come to a compromise, for every attempt to seize
Mr Osborne, who was armed, while he slept was frustrated by
the barking of his dog.

Mr Frank Osborne has been on Rossel almost continuously
since this date, and his sympathetic treatment of the natives has
had a most beneficial effect. This civilising influence increased
with the development of two or three plantations, and the arrival
later of Messrs Harry and Eric Osborne, and Mrs Eric Osborne.

In the *Annual Report* for the following year Mr M. H. Moreton
makes the following statement:[2]

[1] *Annual Report on British New Guinea*, 1902–3, p. 29.
[2] *Annual Report on British New Guinea*, 1903–4, p. 29.

On Rossel Island, the most easterly island in the Possession, they
still go in for cannibalism, one of their customs being that, when
the head man of the village dies, some one had to be killed and
eaten; there is some law as to who it is that has to suffer. This
custom is not as prevalent on the western end of the island as it is
on the eastern, and it is to be hoped that this custom will shortly
become a thing of the past. The Mission has applied for four
blocks of land as sites for Mission Stations; these have been
granted, but as yet only on the ten years' lease system, and £10
improvements, and they have not up to the present commenced
operations.

The villages are all small, only from two to five houses in each,
except at the village of Dau, which is the largest, containing twelve
houses, or so; they are also much scattered, and I am afraid that
the Mission will have much trouble in gathering the people.

At Yeve, on the south coast of the island, Mr Osborne applied
to purchase 300 acres of land for cocoanut planting, and his application was approved; but I think that the land that was bought
will not amount to more than 200 acres. Mr E. H. Lamb has also
applied for 160 acres, but this has not yet been granted.

In his report for 1905, Mr Moreton says he thinks that the
custom of mortuary homicide is gradually disappearing, and also
suggests that 'these natives are not as black as they have been
painted'.[1]

The Acting Administrator, J. H. P. Murray, obtained some
fresh information on a visit to the island in 1908. He gives the
following account:[2]

...This news [of two murders on Rossel] confirmed the intention
I already had of visiting Rossel....

Four murders in all had taken place recently on the island.

The population of the island is very scattered and is split up
into a number of very small villages, some containing hardly more
than one family. It is hard to form an estimate of the number of
inhabitants. Mr Osborne estimates it at 1500. In their gardens
they grow sugar-cane, taro, and bananas. Some of the houses are
built on the ground, some on piles with a clay floor underneath,
on which they do their cooking. They cook with hot stones and
leaves. The houses are divided into partitions, the married people
being divided from the single. They do not manufacture pottery,
but get it from Sudest.

The East and West speak different dialects, which, however, are
now becoming assimilated. The language is extraordinarily un-
musical in sound; it is full of nasals and gutturals, and cannot be

[1] *Annual Report on British New Guinea*, 1904–5, p. 31.
[2] *Annual Report, Papua*, 1907–8, pp. 14–16.

better described than as resembling the snarling of a dog interspersed with hiccoughs. The women wear the ordinary grass petticoats; the men a rope nine or ten feet long, which is twined round the loins and passed through a pandanus leaf. The rope is very skilfully made out of pandanus fibre.

There are wild pigs on the island, but no wallaby. There is also an animal which the natives describe as 'cat he walk on top of stick', and which Mr Osborne says is an opossum. It is called Möh in the West, Uoa in the East. Apparently, the only weapons which the natives possess are a few spears, but they have no need of them, for apparently inter-village warfare is a thing of the past, and, though murders are frequent, they are nearly always committed by smothering the victim—rarely with the spear. The practice seems to be for a number to set on one man whom they wish to kill, to hold his nose and mouth, and either smother him outright, or, if they wish him to die a lingering death, to kneel on him and break his ribs, and sometimes his arms and legs. So in hunting they smother or strangle the pig which they catch, instead of killing it with the spear. I am told also by Mr Osborne that they catch pigeons and seagulls by climbing noiselessly up the trees or rocks where they roost and smothering them one after another so quietly that none of the rest awake. They were cannibals until recently, but seem now either to have given up the custom or only to practise it in secret.

They may, I think, be classed as being about as murderous a lot of people as you can find in Papua, and there are not many who, according to our ideas, are more repulsive in appearance. On the other hand, they by no means neglect the aesthetic side of their nature, and are not without sympathy with animals. For instance, they plant flowers and bright shrubs in their gardens, carry sponges about with them wherever they go to wash their faces with, and have hosts of tame cats which they seem to treat kindly instead of eating them as most natives would do. And—the strangest trait of all in their somewhat complex character—they spend their spare time in teaching one another English.

They seem to have a rudimentary, and, to our eyes, not very logical system of administering justice. A thief is punished by killing the woman who cooks his food; this causes great inconvenience to the thief, and the incidental suffering to the woman is 'thrown in'. There is a form of trial called apparently something which I can best represent by the letters 'Mbwo'. The sorcerer takes several (it is said seven,) different kinds of leaves, rolls them up together in his closed hand, and the names of the various persons who could have committed the offence are called over to him; when the name of the guilty person is called out his arm and hand tremble violently, the fingers open, and the trial is over.

There seems to be a system of chieftainship, with one over-chief called Dabui, of Mōgwŏ, 'on Mt Ngŏ'. They have no drums or musical instruments; dancing is practised, but only by men who are dressed in the grass petticoats of the women.

They have betel nut—the small kind known to the Motuan as Viroiro, and found in the Gulf of Papua—and call it Kiamp, Kiamma, or Mboa. On a visit we paid to the village of Wabiaga, up Yeve Creek, near Avalletti, we found an old woman, widow of a chief, with what looked like a growth coming from the front of the upper gum, and protruding between her lips when the mouth was shut. We were told that this came from the excessive use of betel nut, and was called Nyorro (Nyo means a tooth). It is confined, we were told, to the chiefs and their wives. On examination, it proved to be not a growth but a mass of betel nut and lime which had got stuck firmly to the teeth and gums, and which grew by continual fresh accumulations of the same materials. A commoner must remove such a thing if it makes its appearance; one commoner told me in confidence that he was glad that the Nyorro was confined to chiefs—'all the time he smell too much that fellow'.

There are traces at the East end of the island of the existence of a different language for men, and a different language for women; e.g. 'No' is the man's word for a canoe, 'Didi' the woman's. This is, I believe, not uncommon in the South Pacific, but I know of no other instance in Papua.

Women are not allowed to land on the small uninhabited island of Loa—off the East end of Rossel—in fact they are barely allowed into a canoe at all, and when in a canoe they must not speak. The men go to Loa to fish, but they have to be careful. There are octopus on the island, of small size under normal conditions, but, if they hear the human voice, they grow to enormous proportions— 'We fellow kaikai (eat) him along Yela (Rossel); along Loa he kaikai we fellow'. Also, they must not talk the usual language on Loa; at least, they must, in many instances, use different words. They count in the same way on Loa as on Rossel, except that on Loa they must not say the word for 7; they have no word for it that they can use on Loa, so, while they are there, they simply have to do without that numeral. If they did use the word, there would be a storm of rain and wind which might destroy the island.

They seem to have an idea, according to Mr Osborne, of a deity who resides at the summit of Mt Rossel, and of a home for the souls of the dead on Mt Bö at the West end, which they say is really covered with beautiful gardens and houses, though we can only see rocks and scrub. On the same or a neighbouring mountain there is a snake called Gwöle or Kwölle, which swells to an enormous size if it sees a man, and attacks and kills him. There are, however, certain men who can go up the mountain with impunity, as they know how to talk to the snake; I did not meet any of these favoured individuals. . . .

In 1908, Mr Bell conducted a patrol of about three weeks on Rossel, mainly on account of the numerous alleged murders on the island. Mr Bell obtained a considerable amount of information, which is given below:[1]

...This morning, the 23rd, the police arrived with Tabwoi, the leading chief of the island. I had sent for this man, as the natives seemed to regard him as a person of unlimited power, and were quite satisfied that he was directly or indirectly connected with all the murders that had taken place recently on the island.

Buli, one of the chiefs had died, and some of the natives believed he had been murdered. He had several wives, one of whom was named Kuilimo, and who, it was stated, he was always on bad terms with. Kuilimo, after Buli's death, was assaulted by a woman named Gwaube, and cut severely about the head with a scrub knife. Gwaube was Buli's sister. Kuilimo, after a time, was reported to have got better, but one morning was found to have died from internal injuries. Then followed the death of Kai-o, a native who, it was alleged, had been murdered for informing the Osbornes that Kuilimo had been murdered.

The *Merrie England* arrived, and his Excellency heard of the murders....

I ascertained it was here a native custom on the death of a chief to kill either one of his wives, or some small boy or girl to accompany him to the next world, which they believed was a mountain at the south-west end of the island, and there to look after him to cook his food.

The next case was where a man named Buliwom was stated to have gone fishing with another native named Tiene....Buliwom... was afterwards found...dead. His friends of course considered him murdered. His Excellency had arrested two men on suspicion, named Tiene and Unbundi....A man named Idingu helped a village constable to arrest the men, and when the *Merrie England* had left, the friends of the chief Unbundi were to have killed his brother, Kupa, out of revenge.

Another alleged murder reported to me was that of Pindu, a small boy.

These Rossel Island people are not a fighting race. It appears that from time to time the Resident Magistrate and the *Merrie England* had gone to Rossel and taken men away charged with murder, etc. Their methods were the usual ones of killing a person with a spear, and of course in these cases there were generally witnesses. One or two men getting acquitted made them think apparently that 'no witnesses' would probably mean 'no gaol'. I made certain of this, as what I am now going to describe as their

[1] *Annual Report, Papua*, 1908–9, pp. 104–109.

methods of killing, they assured me are not what their fathers did before them.

If a chief or any other person desires to kill someone, they invariably do it now at night. It depends on the strength of the person to be killed whether the party consists of one or more. They enter his house, and if four are in the party one will hold the lower limbs, another grasps the throat, another holds his hands over the person's mouth to prevent him calling out, and the other breaks two or three ribs with his hands. It appears the trachea or the gullet in most cases is injured as well, as the person complains of his throat afterwards. They do not attempt anything beyond this, apparently being quite satisfied the person must die, which of course must take place, the native himself realising it. Death occurs usually the next day, the man suffering great pain and unable to take any food. The internal injuries received do not seem to affect the man immediately—it is not till a few hours afterwards....

I examined to-day Tabwoi, the chief. He was very reticent and nothing was obtained from him of any importance....

...We camped in the afternoon, nearly half way across the island, where there were three or four houses which the natives called Mopa. It was here Tabwoi, the chief, lived....

The 28th was spent at Mopa....The houses were very poorly built. The style favoured seemed to be that of a huge 'lean-to' made of sewn sago leaf, and a floor of hard clay banked up, even a foot high. They drain the water off by a gutter a foot wide. The women seen were very poor in physique, and covered with skin disease....

...A little inland from Lailigmai are a few houses called Iama, and it was here that the woman Kuilimo was alleged to have been murdered. I examined the house and saw that it was at the present time not occupied. There were two graves in the house. One, they informed me, was where Buli, the chief, had been buried, and the other contained the woman Kuilimo.

The disturbed ground had started to settle down, and the cracks showed the dimensions of the graves, which were about four feet long, by two feet wide. They bury the dead only 2 ft. 6 in. down. On top of the chief's grave flat boards had been placed. The house had all its four sides enclosed with sewn sago leaf. The people in some of the houses sleep on the clay floor.

At Lailigmai one of the houses had the ordinary sago roof. It was about sixty feet long and twenty feet wide, and open at all sides. The chief, Newa, of this small place came to see me. He is an old man, and was attended by his five wives....The nose-bone he wore was like all the others on the island, thin and ground down from a clam-shell, and shaped the same as a bull's horns....

A man named Daqua, whom I had sent for, arrived with a village constable, and confessed that he and the other prisoners I had, murdered the native Kupa.

To-day, I further examined the witness, Tabwoi, and after some time he admitted having given a Darp (native money) to a man named Damia. At first he stated he did not know what it was required for, but afterwards stated he gave it to Damia as he wanted one to give payment to the brother of the murdered woman.. . .

. . . They [the Rossel Islanders] are small in size, and dark. They are not a fighting race, and possess no weapons of war outside of a poor class of spear and a wooden club, which has no stone fastened to it, as in other parts. These weapons are now very seldom seen amongst them. They know nothing of the bow and arrow. The only time they paint their faces is when they dance. The dancing is very poor compared with other parts. They have no drums. They decorate themselves with croton leaf stuck in the belt at the back and in the plaited cane armlets. The men dance in grass dresses made by the women for the occasion, and payment is made after the dance is finished.

The hair of the men and women is generally cut short, especially the latter. The women outnumber the men, and I regret to say a great deal of immorality takes place.

The majority of the women are of very poor physique, and skin disease has a very large hold. They wear the grass petticoat. It is very often the case the best of the young girls are sold by the parents as courtesans, the native name being Jelibio. I came across men married, and possessing in addition these women. Young fellows, not having reached puberty, had clubbed together in parties of three and four, and bought young girls from the parents to make courtesans. At feasts, these girls are used for the purpose of enriching themselves and their owners. The present population of the whole island I would not estimate at more than 1500. I judge from what I have seen, the natives of the island were at one time very considerable, but intermarrying, abortion (especially amongst the Jelibios), and other practices have probably for a century been causing them to degenerate. The people, Mr Osborne informs me, are decreasing. They very rarely marry outside of the island, and then only the men of Sudest. They are cannibals, but no one has been eaten now for a very long time. The men wear the pandanus leaf. In front it comes up higher than the navel, and is bent inwards to the waist. Both ends are curled, and a piece of string tied round the waist keeps it in position. Native rope, about the thickness of one's small finger, is passed through the centre of the two curled ends, and falls in eleven rows at different depths half way to the knee on each side of the leg. It presents quite a singular appearance.

There is very little tattooing done. It appears to be only on the men. There is no design, only straight lines. A very handy basket, neatly plaited, is made of coconut leaf split into several strings, and dried slightly before being plaited by the women. The shape of the baskets is like native cooking pots, and are made in nests. A few are made also of pandanus leaf. Cooking pots are brought from Sudest. For mourning, the men wear a single piece of string tied round the neck, the women rows and rows of thin string tied over each shoulder, and loosely under the opposite armpit.

The bamboo pipe (Baubau) is used, but it is supposed to have been introduced from other islands.

Feathers of birds and shell armlets are occasionally seen worn as personal adornment.

The septum of the nose of the men is pierced, and a thin bone, ground down from a clam shell, is inserted as a nose jewel. The ordinary person must wear his very short, as it is only the chiefs who are permitted to wear it long. The bone is a little less than the thickness of a lead pencil.

The chiefs have what looks like at first a small piece of wood inserted under the upper lip, but it is nothing more than an accumulation of betel-nut on the upper front eight teeth. The betel-nut is allowed to accumulate until it becomes level with the lip, slightly beyond sometimes, and pressing it a little upwards. It is a strange sight, and, when the man smiles, more so, as the upper lip moves and curls inward on the betel-nut, which remains firm. No other person than a chief is permitted to accomplish this.

The average canoe is 21 feet long. It is a small tree, dug out and decked fore and aft about 4 feet from the ends. The centre 17 feet has sides 9 inches high, running fore and aft, at the ends of which a flat board is placed in the canoe at right angles to them, and forms a rest for the back of one of the persons paddling the canoe. These back ends are about 4 inches higher than the sides, and with them give the shape of a narrow oblong box. The enclosed rough sketch, showing the design carved on the sides, will, perhaps give an idea. The sides are caulked with banana fibre, etc., to the body of the canoe, and held in position by means of cane and cross pieces of wood about 1½ inches in thickness, likewise the backs. When the canoe is light she floats below the caulking, but when loaded the water is generally flush with it. The canoes are very frail. The paddles are long and narrow. Some of the natives will squat down on their heels on the decked part and paddle, whilst others will sit in the canoe, the top of the sides coming almost under their armpits. They paddle in jerks, and can lift the canoe along at a good pace. Apart from the design carved, the only other decoration is a few cowrie shells tied forward and aft and on the outriggers. The outrigger consists of five or six saplings running from the main body to a soft wood runner in the water, and fastened to it by means of hardwood sticks driven in and tied with cane. On the top of the outriggers flat boards and plaited coconut leaves are placed to carry goods and chattels.

The inner reefs are all marked off with sticks and are regarded as the property of certain individuals. Only the outer reef is public property.

Gardens are sometimes fenced. Pitfalls for pigs are made with leaves on top and spears underneath.

Taboo is very common. Coconuts are sometimes tabooed. A stick is stuck up in the ground, and on the branches small leaves inside large ones are tied on. One point of land will be tabooed. Women desiring to go round it stop and cut away inland, coming out the other side. While I was at Rossel, some boys returning from Sudest were obliged to get a trader to take them along in his boat, as they had no 'Darp' (native money) to pay the chief with in order to be allowed to pass. Certain things are tabooed to women and not to men. A Darp is a hard shell, slightly concave. The back is red, and the inside white. It is ground down about 2 inches long and 1½ inches wide. It represents the most valuable of native money on Rossel. It is shaped like a heart. Most of them are possessed by the chiefs. The man who makes a Darp has to fast a certain number of days before so doing. They are used as payment to a murderer by a chief, purchase of a Jelibio, etc. Ker is another valuable piece of money. It is a string of ten thick red and white shells (clam). It is ground down like 'Sapisapi', but about six times as thick. It is used for buying wives.

Pigs are sometimes caught by rope tied in a slip knot on the track over which they pass. They catch birds in trees in the same way.

They have native poets. Black ants are put on the forehead to cure headache. The forehead is scratched for grief. When a man dies his house is closed up, and often a plaited mat put on the grave.

Elephantiasis is rare.

When one man buys another's daughter for a wife, the girl is not informed by the father till towards evening. She cries, and runs into the bush, and the prospective husband goes to his village. Afterwards, the next day, she follows her husband, sometimes accompanied by other women.

A woman has never left the island, and the one I took to Samarai as a prisoner was the first to have done so.

The language is slightly different at both ends of the island.

The Annual Report for 1893–4 contains a vocabulary. The greatest difficulty is the pronunciation, and to get the necessary consonants together to produce it.

Women are only allowed to go in canoes up rivers and along the mangroves in the sea, and not near the reef. They are not permitted to enter the canoe which is sent by the chief to announce special feasts and to collect Darps. Many of these canoes are about 30 feet long, some larger. About five men paddle, and one steers. They are very fast, and go round the island in a day and a half.

It is noticeable that brothers never mention the names of each other's wives, referring to her as 'the wife of my brother'. Away to the east of Rossel is an island marked on the map Adele Island. The women call it Bola, and the men Loa. It is about 44 acres, and has been cleared and planted by the two Osborne Brothers with coconuts. Although birds, fish, etc., are in many cases the same as on the mainland, the natives of Rossel supply different names.

Sorcery is very common, and the people have a dread of the people who practise it. Hair, parings of finger nails, and betel-nut of a person whom it is desired to harm is put on a certain stone, and, as it rots away, so the person will become ill and die. Natives going to other villages and receiving food will eat it and carry away the scraps to throw in the salt water to prevent the sorcerers getting it. When a coconut husk is thrown overboard it must be immersed, so as it may not float ashore dry and reach the hands of the sorcerers.

Stealing is looked upon as a very serious offence, and in some cases death is regarded as only just punishment. In other cases, a warning is first given, and, if ignored, the wife of the man is killed.

Yumbwa, at the western extremity, is the mountain the natives believe they go to when they die. When ascending this mountain I noticed the carriers spoke little, and only in whispers. I asked one of the natives to shoot a bird, but he desired not to. A large snake living on the top is believed to control their future destiny. In knocking off a piece of stone with a tomahawk for a specimen, I was asked to desist. They have many peculiar stories in connection with the mountain. In planting taro they go through a great amount of whispering to it to grow and jump up like the Gunga (Kingfish), who does so to view the two largest mountains on Rossel.

They have the rain man, whose duty it is to bring rain when wanted, for which he receives payment. A certain stone is taken by him and wrapped in a leaf and put into a creek in a shallow spot. The leaf is believed to annoy the stone by its offensive odour, and the stone will bring the rain. The rain maker blackens himself immediately he has done this, and allows it to remain on till the rain comes.

They have two ideas concerning their origin. Some think they originally came from an island to the eastward. Others told me the following, and brought me the two plants to see:—A woman was the first person on Rossel Island. She gave birth first to the two plants, then a pigeon, a male child, and afterwards a female one, and thus population came.

A man having a friend or relation murdered, and not knowing the guilty party, goes to a man who is supposed to have 'medicine' to find out. This man makes a collection of about twenty-five leaves of various descriptions from the bush, and with the soles of his feet and a little water works them up into a ball, then places them in the sun for about half-an-hour to dry. Afterwards, he puts inside one black ant taken alive and the head of a black slug, the body of which is from 4 to 6 inches in length, and found nearly all over Papua, the natives being very afraid of it, as it discharges a fluid some distance which, if it reaches the eye, is alleged to cause blindness. Then he takes the ball in the palm of his left hand, and closes his fingers on it, and the people gather round and ask—'Was it so and so who killed so and so?' Everybody's name is called, sometimes over and over again. This goes on some considerable time, the man with the leaves working the fingers and muscles of his arm, causing the latter to contract, apparently, which in time must make the arm stiff and painful. When he reaches this stage he moans, and the voice of the questioner rises, his eyes still on the man's hand. Slowly the fingers open and the leaves are put aside, and the name of the guilty man is known. The palm is then gently pressed where the leaves had been, and smoothed out by the questioner, the fingers pulled apparently to get the stiffness out of them, and the arm jerked several times. The man states himself that his arm gets 'like stone and hot' when the guilty person's name is called.

I saw the thing done, and I think the man honestly believes himself. There are a few other men on the island, I am told, who know how to do it. The practice is handed down from father to son, or to relations.

One of the chief industries of the island is that of obtaining a shell of a rich red colour, from which native money used in other parts of Papua is made. This shell is like an oyster in appearance, the inside being white, with the lips of bright and dark red colours. Below the white lining the shell is red. Four 'Sapisapi', as a rule, can be cut from the average shell. The shell is obtained on the northern side of the island, on the inside of the reefs near the mangroves, and is dived for in shallow and deep water by the natives. The fish inside the shell is eaten, and the shell is bagged and sold to the traders, who get £7 to £10 a bag for it at Samarai. The 'Sapisapi' here is well known as being the best obtainable in Papua, owing to its particularly rich dark-red colour. The shell has to be ground down, and there is, of course, a great waste in the breaking of them up at the present time with hammers, but, even so, with shells averaging four 'Sapisapi' each, and the price of sixteen on a string to tie to the lobes of the ears at 10s. in Samarai, the profits must be very large. Mr Craig, of Sudest, informs me he is importing a machine from London to perform the task of grinding the shell, also boring it in the centre.

Copra is made by the natives, and sold to the traders, the output of the island per month, I am told, is 4 tons. Dugong are plentiful, many being seen from my camp. Goldlip shell is found only in very small quantities. Blacklip shell is found in large quantities, but does not pay to work at only £10 a ton in London, I am informed. Small pieces of wreckage are strewn over the island. I saw many pieces of Oregon pine. Small pieces of copper occasionally are washed ashore from some old wreck. Lately, a Fife-rail stanchion of Oregon pine came ashore. On the reefs on the south side of the island are two large anchors and fathoms of cable. One anchor is of the old-fashioned type, with the stock, fluke, and blades immovable; the other the modern anchor.

The Lieutenant-Governor, J. H. P. Murray, paid a visit of inspection to Rossel in 1911, and gives the following account:[1]

The chief industry on Rossel Island is making native money, Sapi Sapi, or, as it is called on Rossel, Bau, which is manufactured from shell which the Motu call Bodea. Sapi Sapi is the same as the Ageva made by the natives of Tatana Island, in Port Moresby, and of Vabukori, just outside. Bau was made on Rossel Island before the arrival of the white man, and was sold in Sud Est; the hole was bored by putting a sharp stone like a nail at the end of a stick, and turning it between the hands. Ndarp—an orange-colored flat shell—was used as money, not, apparently, Bau. The Ndarp is now worked out, that is to say, there is none left in the shallow water. The Sapi Sapi or Bau is very valuable throughout the east of New Guinea, and the price is said to be rising. The Ndarp apparently was never worn as an ornament, the Sapi Sapi is.

Before the advent of the white man, the only connexion the Rossel Islanders, or Yela Jemba, as they call themselves, had with the outside world was with Sud Est, and that was always a peaceful intercourse. No man, they told me, ever came to Rossel to fight; the Brooker Islanders and other head-hunting pirates who ravaged the coasts of Sud Est were too far away, and the people of Sud Est came only in peace and friendship. Bau was exported from Rossel to Sud Est, and lime-sticks, Dien (pronounced to rhyme with the French lien), made from a tree with a dark wood, which appears to be called Mwo, and, in return, pots were imported and also parrots, to which they apply a word which appears to me to sound something like Ngam. The parrots the men of Rossel give to their wives, who, when they are not working in the garden, appear to spend most of their time in mute admiration at the Ngam (handsome birds), which are seated each on his mistress's hand. The women will not sell these birds for anything you may offer. 'Mary he no want to sell him', said the interpreter, 'he like him too much. Suppose he die Mary he cry'.

Canoes were built on Rossel and Sud Est sufficiently strong and seaworthy to stand the passage across, sometimes a very stormy one. The Rossel Island canoes are built up with boards sewn together and well caulked, and the ends of the canoe, fore and aft, are decked.

[1] *Annual Report, Papua*, 1911–12, pp. 19–20.

The canoe has an outrigger, and the most peculiar part about the structure is a sort of platform which is built up from the canoe at an angle, and affords seating accommodation for passengers. A detailed description of these canoes is given by Mr Bell, in his report of his patrol in Rossel in June and July, 1908. The Sud Est canoes are now built at Panaiet; my informant, Aleck, a village constable of Sud Est, says that formerly fine canoes were made on Sud Est, but now the man who made them is dead, and, if he wants a really good canoe, it must be imported, preferably from Panaiet. This is apparently a reversion to an old custom, for Mr David L. White, in the Annual Report for 1893–4, speaking of these natives, says—'At one time nearly all the canoes were made at the Island of Panaietti. . . ; but now they are making them here themselves'. The people of Sud Est, less isolated than their neighbours of Rossel, traded with the adjoining islands, even with their enemies of Brooker Island, from whom they bought pots in exchange for sago.

Cannibalism is practically extinct in both islands at the present moment; in Rossel one sees the remains of Jabbega, or 'sitting down places', made of flat stones in a more or less circular form, once the scenes of cannibal feasts, and the fact that these Jabbega are falling into decay may, I think, be taken as a hopeful sign.

Various old men were seen who said that they remembered that the Chinese survivors of the *St Paul* were eaten, but they were all too young at the time to have taken part in the feast. The interpretation was not clear enough to enable me to obtain a clear account of the manner in which the Chinamen were enticed off their island. The ordinary way of preparing them, I was informed, was to cut them up and disembowel them, and to cook them on stones covered up with leaves.

They made stone tomahawks on the island, though they have no knowledge of stone clubs; they used the spear (a very clumsy one) for fighting. Pigs and dogs were on the island before the arrival of the white man. Presumably they came from Sud Est, but there seemed to be no tradition of this, nor could I find any as to the origin of the Rossel Islanders themselves, except a very tentative theory that they came from over the sea.

The only words in which I could find a real resemblance to the Melanesian languages were Limi for five and Mbwomma for pig. The latter word was probably introduced with the animal, and the language is, no doubt, properly classed as non-Melanesian.

There are totems on both Rossel and Sud Est. On both islands they descend through the mother, and in both it is forbidden to eat the totem bird, and to marry within the totem. In Sud Est each man has a bird, a tree, and a snake, the combination being in each case inherited from his mother. In Rossel it is the same, except that the snake is absent.

The Resident Magistrate of the South-Eastern Division visited Rossel in 1913, for the purpose of checking the outbreak of dysentery in that island and the island of Gawa (Marshall Bennets), the epidemic having accounted for 120 deaths in these two islands. The Resident Magistrate remarks:[1]

> This fact is much to be deplored, but not surprised at when the loathsome habits of the people at the former place (Rossel) are taken into consideration. In this connexion I may mention the interment and subsequent exhumation of the dead. The general habit of depositing excreta anywhere and everywhere in the vicinity of the villages must also be a predisposing cause of dysentery, whenever a drought occurs....
>
> ...When a death occurs, burial is effected in the village, usually under the house which has been occupied by the deceased. The hole in the ground is lined with leaves, and the corpse placed in it in a sitting position, with the head resting on the knees. The hole is then covered with cocoanut and banana leaves, with a light layer of earth on top. The body is left for a period for the flesh to decompose. The hole is then uncovered, and the body exhumed. The head is removed from the trunk by the women of the village, and taken to the nearest water, where all the flesh adhering to the skull is removed by hand. The skull is then taken to the salt water and washed, afterwards being left on the sand to dry, carefully watched over by all interested. When the skull is returned to the village, a general lament is indulged in by the relatives and friends. The skull is given a place of honour in the house of the parents or son or daughter, as the case may be. The trunk of the body is wrapped in a covering of sago leaves, and lashed in the fork of a tree, and left for sun, rain, and air to complete the process of cleaning the skeleton. In course of time the lashings give, and the bones fall to the ground, where they are allowed to remain—the spot being religiously shunned by all. This custom, in vogue from time immemorial, will take a considerable period to abolish....

A census of Rossel was made in 1920, giving the following results:[2]

> 145 villages, 406 male adults, 436 female adults, 312 male children under 16, 261 female children under 16, total population 1415...11 men with 4 children, 12 with 5, 10 with 6, 2 with 8, 1 with 9, 31 men with 2 wives, 3 with 3, 1 blind, 1 deaf and dumb, 2 cripples, 10 otherwise unfit.

No further first-hand accounts of Rossel occur, as far as I am aware, other than my own articles as follows: 'Anthropology of

[1] *Annual Report, Papua*, 1912–13, p. 112.
[2] *Ibid.* 1920–21, p. 25.

the South-Eastern Division',[1] 'Rossel Island Religion',[2] 'Rossel Island Money: A Unique Monetary System',[3] and 'Shell-Money from Rossel Island, Papua'.[4]

[1] *Annual Report, Papua,* 1921–22, pp. 26–37, reprinted in *Papua, Native Taxes Ordinance,* 1917–22; *Reports on Anthropology, No.* 2, pp. 1–31.
[2] *Anthropos,* 1923–24, pp. 1–11.
[3] *Economic Journal,* 1924, pp. 423–429.
[4] *Man,* 1924, pp. 161–162.

Physical Measurements

MEASUREMENTS[1] of 26 Rossel natives are given in the table below, linear measurements in centimetres, weight in kilograms. Ages are approximate. Height is given to the nearest centimetre, the possible error with the primitive means employed being in the neighbourhood of ·5 cm. Weight was taken with a crude spring balance and is given to the nearest kilogram. The figures for hair represent roughly the average diameter of the spirals—' < ·5 ', therefore, represents very frizzy hair. Skin colour (taken on the body just below the arm-pit) was measured by means of the scale given by Hrdlička in a Bulletin of the Smithsonian Institute.[2] The numbers in Table I refer to this scale. Nos. 21, 22, 37, 43 form a series of darkening browns. No. 36 is close to No. 37, but rather greyer. No. 30 is a little lighter and contains more orange than No. 21, and No. 40 is lighter still and contains more yellow. Where the skin colour was judged to lie between numbers on the scale, both numbers are given. The remaining measurements recorded in Table I were taken to the nearest ½-millimetre, for the possible error was found to be in the neighbourhood of ¼-millimetre. The cephalic index is, therefore, given to the nearest ·5 per cent., and the facial and nasal indices to the nearest 1 per cent., for the measurements on which these latter depend are smaller than those on which the cephalic index depends: moreover, the naso-alveolar diameter, from which and the bizygomatic diameter the facial index is calculated, is an awkward measurement on the living; and the nasal width loses some significance, owing to the practice of wearing a nose-stick or nose-plug from quite an early age.

In Table I the males are seriated by their cephalic indices. The final column gives the median figure for each measurement, independently seriated for the 23 males; the median cephalic index is, thus, the cephalic index of No. 12 (or No. 11, as it happens), while the median nasal index is the nasal index of No. 6 (or Nos. 7, 8, 22). The arithmetic mean differs slightly

---

[1] See W. L. H. Duckworth, *International Agreements for the Unification (a) of Craniometric and Cephalometric Measurements, (b) of Anthropometric Measurements to be made on the Living Subject*, Cambridge, 1913.

[2] Hrdlička, 'Directions for Collecting Information and Specimens for Physical Anthropology', Part R of *Bulletin of the United States National Museum*, No. 39, Washington, 1904.

from these figures, e.g. the average cephalic index is 78·7 (as compared with 78 for the median); the average facial index is 50·0 (the median is 49); the average nasal index is 86·1 (the median is 85); the average stature is 155·4 (the median is 156).

Seven other measurements were taken on each person, which are not recorded in Table I, for it is doubtful whether they are of sufficient value. They were, necessarily, only approximate, owing to the wealth of hair of the Papuan, the difficulty of obtaining the mouth in repose, and the practice of distending the lobe of the ear. The medians were as follows: horizontal circumference of head across glabella and inion, 54·6; longitudinal circumference of head from glabella to inion, 33·7; transverse circumference of head from points of maximum width, 34·3; width of the mouth, 5·9; bilabial height, 1·8; maximum length of ear 5·5; auricular width, 3·5.

The colours of hair and eye have not been tabulated since the variation is slight; the hair black, occasionally grey, or brown, or even orange, the latter tints resulting generally, if not always, from the use of lime; the eyes dark brown to almost black with usually a greenish tinge.

Tables II, III, and IV show seriations of stature, facial index, and nasal index, the first two columns seriating these figures for lower and higher cephalic indices respectively. No correlation is revealed between facial index or nasal index and cephalic index, but Table III shows that a lower cephalic index is associated with slightly higher stature. This is also revealed by taking the arithmetic mean of stature for Nos. 1–12, which gives an average of 158·7, and comparing it with the mean for Nos. 12–23, which gives an average of 152·25, almost pygmy.

These results are further analysed below and comparisons made with the nearer Massim.[1] The observations on females are neglected, since too few to be of much value. The following scales are adopted:

C. I. Dolichocephaly (–77), Mesocephaly (77–82), Brachycephaly (82 +).

N. I. Mesorrhiny (70–85), Chamaerrhiny (85–100), Hyperchamaerrhiny (100 +).

St. Pygmy (–148 cm. = 58¼ in.), Short (148–158 cm. = 58–62¼ in.), Medium (158–168 cm. = 62¼–66 in.).

[1] The figures in this section on Rossel and the Eastern Massim, unlike those in Table I, have not been corrected for 'greatest possible error'.

Appendix II

ROSSEL (23 males).

C. I. 70·4–88, median 77·8.
N. I. 70–112 (but the next highest is 98), med. 85.
St. 132·1–167·7 cm. (52–66 in.), med. 155·6 cm. (61¼ in.).

5 dolicho.	= 21·7 %,	av. N. I.	89·4,	av. St.			1·556
13 meso.	= 56·5 %,	,,	86·7,	,,			1·587
5 brachy.	= 21·7 %,	,,	83·6,	,,			1·460
8 mesorrh.	= 34·7 %,	av. C. I.	78·8,	,,			1·553
14 chamae.	= 60·8 %,	,,	78·5,	,,			1·540
1 hyperch.	= 4·3 %,	,,	80·0,	,,			1·639
3 pygmy	= 13·0 %,	,,	84·3,	av. N. I.			83·1
12 short	= 52·1 %,	,,	77·9,	,,			86·9
8 medium	= 34·7 %,	,,	77·9,	,,			87·8

The dolichocephals are of short stature (the average being the same as the median of the whole group) and chamaerrhine.

The mesocephals are of low medium stature (5 short and 1 pygmy) and mesochamaerrhine (1 hyper. ch.).

The brachycephals are mainly of pygmy stature and are more chamaerrhine than mesorrhine.

There is no appreciable difference between the meso- and chamaerrhines in regard to their C. I. and stature, though the latter are 13 mm. (½ in.) shorter.

The hyperchamaerrhine is broader headed and taller.

Those of pygmy stature are brachycephalic and meso-chamaerrhine.

Those of short stature are dolicho-mesocephals (3 brachy.) and chamaerrhine (4 meso.).

Those of medium stature are rather low mesocephals and are meso-chamaerrhines (1 hyper.).

SUDEST AND SABARI (14 males).

The nearest large island to Rossel is Sudest (Tagula) and north-west of this is the Calvados Chain. The following are particulars of 8 Sudest men and of 6 from Sabari Island, Calvados Chain. The measurements from these two islands are so similar that they may be taken together, and thus they represent the most southerly of the Massim (Papuo-Melanesians), except the Rossel Islanders, who, if we include them among the Massim, are clearly differentiated culturally from the other Massim.

C. I. 71·8–85·7, med. 80·4.
N. I. 79·6–104·3 (but the next highest is 97·8), med. 86·6.
St. 146·1–167·7 cm. (57½–66 in.), med. 152·7 cm. (60⅛ in.).

3 dolicho.	= 21·4 %,	av. N. I. 88·2,	av. St.		155·2
5 meso.	= 35·7 %,	,,	90·6,	,,	150·9
6 brachy.	= 42·8 %,	,,	88·4,	,,	156·6

5 mesorrh.	= 35·7 %, av. C. I.	78·5, av. St.	154·6
8 chamae.	= 57·1 %,	„ 80·6,	„ 154·6
1 hyperch.	= 7·1 %,	„ 81·9,	„ 152·4
2 pygmy	= 14·2 %,	„ 78·5, av. N. I.	83·1
8 short	= 57·1 %,	„ 79·3,	„ 93·1
4 medium	= 28·5 %,	„ 82·0,	„ 84·2

The dolichocephals are of short stature and are chamaerrhine.
The mesocephals are of short stature and are chamaerrhine.
The brachycephals mainly have a medium stature and are chamaerrhine.
The mesorrhines are short and half of them are really dolicho-brachycephals (2 of each).
The chamaerrhines are short and half of them are brachycephalic.
The hyperchamaerrhine is short and just brachycephalic.
The four with broadest noses have an av. C. I. 80·7 and St. 150·9
Those of pygmy stature are mesocephalic and mesorrhine.
Those of short stature are mesocephalic (4 brachy.) and chamaerrhine.
Those of medium stature are brachycephalic (1 dolicho.), and meso-chamaerrhine.

There are 6 men (3 each from Rossel and Sudest + Sabari) who may be classed as of pygmy stature, though it does not necessarily indicate that they can be considered of pygmy race. They are brachycephalic and barely chamaerrhine (N. I. 85·6), average stature 143·9 cm. (56½ in.).

C. I. 78·4, 78·5, 79·5, 82·4, 85·5, 88.
N. I. 86·7, 79·6, 73·1, 97·7, 85·4, 90·9 (in same order as C. I.).

There are 11 men (5 Rossel, 6 S. + S.) who are brachycephals, av. C. I. 84·2 (82·1–88), low chamaerrhine, av. N. I. 87·1 (70·4–97·8) and short in stature, av. 151·3 = 59½ in. (132·1–167·7 = 52–66 in.). If the 3 of pygmy stature be excluded the average stature of the remaining 8 is 155·7 = 61¼ in. (149·9–167·7) so they thus remain short though 3 are of medium stature.

Table I. *Measurements of 23 males, seriated by*

No.	1	2	3	4	5	6	7	8	9	10	11	12
Age and sex	18♂	25♂	30♂	16♂	30♂	25♂	20♂	20♂	45♂	40♂	20♂	40♂
Height	157	159	151	154	157	167	157	159	156	168	163	156
Weight	40	34	35	33	43	41	39	39	40	45	40	40
Hair	<·5	·5–1	·5–1	<·5	<·5	>1	·5–1	·5–1	·5–1	·5–1	·5–1	·5–1
Skin	22	21	21	21/36	22/37	21	21	22/37	30/37/37	21	21	22
Maximum length of head	19·6	19·0	18·1	19·0	19·3	19·1	18·5	19·0	19·1	19·5	18·9	18·9
Maximum width of head	13·8	13·9	13·4	14·1	14·7	14·7	14·3	14·7	14·8	15·25	14·7	14·7
Cephalic Index	70·5	73	74	74	76	77	77·5	77·5	77·5	77·5	78	78
Maximal frontal width	11·3	11·5	11·3	10·3	12·2	11·9	10·8	11·8	10·8	11·7	11·7	11·0
Maximum bimastoid diameter	12·0	12·3	11·5	12·9	13·2	13·4	12·7	13·9	12·1	13·1	13·3	12·3
Bizygomatic diameter	13·1	14·2	12·6	12·15	14·1	14·3	13·05	13·7	13·7	13·7	13·0	13·5
Bigonial diameter	9·2	11·6	9·1	9·9	11·1	10·6	10·5	10·3	9·9	10·2	9·6	9·2
Naso-mental diameter	11·0	11·5	10·3	10·45	11·8	10·8	11·3	11·9	11·4	12·3	12·1	10·6
Naso-buccal diameter	7·9	7·6	6·8	6·7	7·7	7·1	7·15	7·4	7·45	8·3	8·2	7·5
Naso-alveolar diameter	7·0	7·0	6·15	6·3	6·8	6·6	6·3	6·7	6·6	7·55	7·7	6·9
Facial Index	53	49	49	52	48	46	48	49	48	55	59	51
Nasal height	5·45	4·6	4·4	4·6	5·2	4·85	4·8	4·95	5·1	6·0	5·05	4·65
Nasal width	3·95	4·2	4·1	4·5	4·8	4·1	4·1	4·2	4·1	4·7	4·6	4·5
Nasal Index	72	91	93	98	92	85	85	85	80	78	91	97

Table II. *Distribution of C. I. (23 males).*

C. I.	No. of cases
70·5–72	1
72·5–74	3
74·5–76	1
76·5–78	7
78·5–80	6
80·5–82	2
82·5–84	1
84·5–86	1
86·5–88	1

Table III. *Distribution of Stature of males in relation to C. I.*
and absolutely.

Stature	No. of cases		
	1–12	12–23	1–23
< 140	0	1	1
141–145	0	1	1
146–150	0	2	2
151–155	2	3	5
156–160	7	4	10
161–165	1	1	2
> 165	2	0	2

Cephalic Index, and 3 females.

13	14	15	16	17	18	19	20	21	22	23	24	25	26	Medians of seriated measurements of males
40♂	40♂	35♂	40♂	22♂	17♂	17♂	30♂	25♂	50♂	25♂	25♀	30♀	21♀	
154	160	147	164	156	159	150	154	152	132	143	142	159	140	156
37	38	33	52	34	38	38	34	34	19	35	32	37	36	38
·5–1	·5–1	·5–1	·5–1	>1	·5–1	·5–1	·5–1	·5–1	·5–1	·5–1	·5–1	·5–1	<·5	·5–1
22/37	36	22/37	22/37	21	37	22/37	21/36	22/36	21/40	21	30/37/37	37/43	22/37	about 22
18·5	18·5	17·6	18·7	17·8	17·8	17·9	17·4	17·6	16·6	16·7	17·5	17·2	16·7	18·5
14·5	14·7	14·0	15·0	14·3	14·3	14·7	14·3	14·8	14·2	14·7	13·3	14·5	14·1	14·7
78·5	79·5	79·5	80	80	80	82	82	84	85·5	88	76	84	84	78
10·9	11·7	10·7	12·1	10·6	11·4	11·1	11·0	10·8	10·1	10·7	10·1	10·4	11·5	11·1
12·1	12·2	11·9	12·5	12·1	12·5	12·35	12·1	12·2	12·9	11·6	11·2	12·0	12·3	12·3
13·2	13·4	13.1	14·4	13·0	13·5	13·2	13·4	13·2	12·4	13·0	12·6	12·7	12·5	13·2
9·5	9·9	10·0	10·4	9·65	9·0	9·1	9·8	10·1	8·6	9·1	9·0	9·0	9·1	9·9
11·0	11·0	11·0	11·8	10·1	10·1	10·9	10·7	10·85	8·75	9·75	10·75	10·1	9·45	11·0
6·5	7·5	7·35	7·6	7·1	6·55	7·0	7·1	7·3	6·4	6·7	6·7	6·1	6·5	7·1
6·0	7·0	6·5	6·8	6·7	6·0	6·4	6·5	6·75	6·0	5·9	6·1	5·6	5·55	6·6
45	53	50	47	52	44	48	49	51	48	45	48	44	44	49
4·6	5·1	5·2	4·7	4·7	4·9	4·9	5·1	4·9	4·8	4·4	4·65	4·5	4·4	4·85
4·4	3·9	3·8	5·05	4·1	3·6	4·4	4·15	3·45	4·1	4·0	3·7	3·5	3·2	4·1
96	76	73	112	87	82	90	81	70	85	91	80	78	73	85

Table IV. *Distribution of F. I. of males in relation to C. I. and absolutely.*

F. I.	No. of cases		
	1–12	12–23	1–23
43–44	0	1	1
45–46	1	2	3
47–48	3	3	6
49–50	3	2	5
51–52	2	3	4
53–54	1	1	2
55–56	1	0	1
57–58	0	0	0
59–60	1	0	1

Table V. *Distribution of N. I. of males in relation to C. I. and absolutely.*

N. I.	No. of cases		
	1–12	12–23	1–23
< 75	1	2	3
76–80	2	1	3
81–85	3	3	6
86–90	0	2	2
91–95	4	1	5
96–100	2	2	3
> 100	0	1	1

General Theory of the Classificatory System of Relationships

ACCORDING to Rivers,[1] the essential feature of the classificatory system is the extension of the use of relationship terms to all the members of a clan of a given generation: 'Wherever the classificatory system is found in association with a system of exogamous social groups, the terms of relationship do not apply merely to relatives with whom it is possible to trace genealogical relationship, but to all the members of a clan of a given generation, even if no such relationship with them can be traced...'.

According to this statement, if A uses the relationship term R to B, then A will use this term, R, towards all the members of the clan of B, who are of the same sex and generation. Also, by the same statement, B uses Ř (the converse of R) not only to A, but to all members of the clan of A who are of the same sex and generation. Rivers's statement may therefore be put as follows: 'Where we have a classificatory system in association with exogamous groups, a relationship term used between any two persons, A and B, is also used between all members of the exogamous group of A of the same generation and sex, and all members of the exogamous group of B of the same generation and sex'. This is equivalent to the statement that classificatory relationship is a relation between classes, which are exogamous and determined by unilateral descent, for members of the same generation of a clan or other exogamous group are all those persons who are related by unilateral descent to a common ancestor by an equal number of generations. The relationship classes above referred to within the clan or other exogamous group are thus simply the generations, each consisting of two classes, male and female.

It will now be shown that Rivers's interpretation of 'classificatory relationship' implies one of the three following facts about any people who have a so-called classificatory system:

(1) The classes, as defined above, practise group marriage, or a form of individual marriage equivalent to it (by which I mean that if any member of one class marries any member of another class, then no member of the one class marries outside the other class; i.e. the classes are grouped in endogamous pairs) and the

---

[1] W. H. R. Rivers, *Kinship and Social Organisation*, 1914, pp. 70–71.

classes intermarry in a systematic way, which will be investigated below. Any such system will be called an 'open class system'.

(2) The classes, as defined above, are grouped into a limited number of classes that practise group marriage, or individual marriage that is equivalent to it in the above sense. These intermarrying classes contain an indefinite number of generation classes, the principle of grouping being that of a separation by two or more generations, so that a given marriage class contains all generation classes related by a given interval of descent, the distinction between generations being thus partially lost in a way that will be investigated below. Any such system will be called a 'closed class system'.

(3) The classes disappear, and every member of the inter-marrying exogamous groups is related to every other member by every classificatory relationship consistent with exogamy and the sex of the members. Such a system will here be called a 'classi-ficatory system'; for most so-called classificatory systems probably belong to this type.

That one of the above alternatives must hold, if we adopt Rivers's description of 'classificatory relationship' may be shown by the following considerations.

All the classes of an exogamous group,[1] on this view, are related in a simple way by unilateral descent. The classes of other exogamous groups, on the other hand, become related to the classes of the first only through intermarriage of these groups.

If marriage be individual, the possibility of marriage of the members of any one class with members of more than one other class is not excluded. Let us assume, then, that one class marries into more than one other class. For instance, let an A (where A is a male class) marry a b (where b is a female class). This by the classificatory principle places every b in the classificatory relationship of wife to every A. Let an A now marry a c (where c is some other female class); every c becomes, as a result, a classificatory wife of every A. b and c become one class from the point of view of relationship, whether in relation to the class A, or any other class which is related to A. Further, by the same principle, each class that has a certain relation to b becomes identified with that class that has the same relation to c. Lastly, b and c may themselves have a certain relationship to one another —if there are only two moieties, they are necessarily related by matrilineal or patrilineal descent—and from this results a more widespread classification of classes. If R is the relation which

---

[1] The exogamous groups with which we are concerned are those in which descent is unilateral, such as clan or moiety.

b has to *c*, then that class which has R to *b* becomes identified with *b*, and also that class which has R to this one, and so on; these classes, similarly, become identified with the class to which *c* is R, and so on. This may be illustrated by the following example. Let us assume that members of one class marry into a given class of another exogamous group, in which we will suppose descent to be matrilineal, and also into the class of mothers of that class. The effect of this is to reduce the classes of that group to two, the class of males and the class of females, for mothers become classed with daughters, and, therefore, daughters with daughter's daughters, and so on. Similarly, brothers become classed with sister's sons, with mother's brothers, and so on. In other words, the classes disappear and we have left only the exogamous groups, each divided into two groups, male and female. This is a condition in which, if classificatory relationship persist, everyone is related to everyone else by every classificatory relationship, consistent with exogamy and the sex relation.

If, however, we assume that the second class into which the members of a given class marry is the class of mothers' mothers of the first class, instead of the class of mothers, four classes in each exogamous group will result instead of two; if the second class be that of mothers' mothers' mothers, then six classes will result. This condition, as we shall see presently, is that in which the distinction of generations becomes only partially lost, so that any two persons are related by classificatory relationship in some only of the possible ways.

The above argument has proved that, where we have a classificatory system in Rivers's sense, (1) generation classes practise group marriage, or equivalent individual marriage, or (2) the generation classes are grouped together into classes in a systematic way dependent on descent, the resultant classes practising group marriage or equivalent individual marriage, or (3) everyone is related to everyone else by every classificatory relationship consistent with the sex relation and exogamy. It still remains to prove the other element in the alternatives given on pp. 238–9, namely, that the classes must intermarry in a certain systematic way.

The necessity on alternative (1) (pp. 238–9 above) of systematic intermarriage between the classes, will first be proved, and, in order to be as general as possible, exogamy of the unilateral descendant groups will not at first be assumed.

In order that a system of group marriage (or the equivalent individual marriage), may work, it is obvious that there must be a rule determining what groups shall intermarry, that is to say, it must be customary for a class to marry that class to which it is related in a certain way, and such that for every class there shall be one and only one class which is its class of mates. If the marriage be individual, no other system is conceivable than the injunction to marry a certain relative, if the class system is to be preserved. It follows, therefore, that, if the unilaterally descendant group is not exogamous, it is completely endogamous. This follows from the fact that all the classes of such a group are already related, apart from their marriages, so that if any class marries within the group, it is marrying a class to which it is already related. This must, for the reason given above, constitute a rule, so that if any one class marries its class of sisters, then every class marries its class of sisters. The possible marriage rules, given that the descendant groups are not to be exogamous and that matrilineal descent is assumed—the rules on the basis of patrilineal descent are equally simple—are only three, namely, that every class marry the class of sisters, or that every class marry the class of sisters' daughters, or that every class marry the class of sisters' daughters' daughters; later generations may be excluded, for the average difference of age would be too great, and the ascending generations of females are excluded for the same reason. If a class system ever originated amongst a people consisting of more than one unilaterally descendant group, which is almost bound to have been the case, the exogamy of the groups could, for the above reasons, be explained as a device to allow intermarriage, rather than a device to prevent incest, although it does, incidentally, prevent certain forms of incest.

Applying the same principle, which makes exogamy a practical certainty, further limitations follow. Marriage between any two classes previously unrelated, establishes a relationship between all the classes of the two exogamous groups. A second marriage between classes of these two groups is, therefore, a marriage between groups already related, and therefore establishes a marriage rule. If A, a, etc., and N, n, etc., are the classes of the two groups α and β (where A, N, etc., are male, and a, n, etc., are female classes, and descent is matrilineal, so that a is the class of mothers of B and b, n the class of mothers of O and o, etc.) the first marriage may be shown by the line connecting B and o in the accompanying figure.

The first limitation on other marriages between α and β imposed by this first marriage may be expressed as follows: 'If K, any male class of α, marries x, a female class of β, and if R is the relation of K to B, and S the relation of x to o, then the R of K marries the S of x, and the R of R of K marries the S of S of x, and so on; also, that class of which B is the R marries that class of which o is the S, and so on. Further, x must be separated from B by an equal number of generations in the same direction as separates x from o'.

The first part of this limitation follows directly from the principle that marriage between the classes must be determined by relationship. If, for instance, in the diagram below, C marries p, i.e. the class of mothers' brothers' daughters of C, then it follows that D marries q, the mothers' brothers' daughters of p, and so on.

The second part of this limitation follows from the fact that if an equal number of generations did not separate the intermarrying classes from B and o respectively, there would be an increasing discrepancy of age between the intermarrying classes,

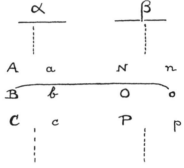

which would make the system unstable. Furthermore, it is easy to see that a number of female classes must remain unmarried, if an equal number of generations did not separate the intermarrying classes from B and o respectively. In the case of a dual organisation, this is obvious at a glance. If, for example, we suppose C to marry q, then all the male classes of a marry half the female classes of β, while all the male classes of β marry half the female classes of β; half the females are, therefore, without mates. Introducing a third exogamous group does not get over this difficulty; for, although the male classes of the third group may be supposed to marry the remaining female classes of one of the first groups, this could only be at the expense of having all its female classes unmarried. The proportion of female classes without mates must clearly remain the same, however many exogamous groups we introduce.[1]

[1] If we express the class relationships by means of diagrams, as in the accompanying figures, the above limitations imply that all lines which

These two principles of limitation of possible marriages on a generation class system enable us to see at a glance the possible systems of marriage, provided the number of exogamous groups is small. Take, for instance, the simplest case, that of a dual organisation with matrilineal descent. The marriage of any one male class of α with a female class of β determines all the marriages between the male classes of α and the female classes of β; for, if B marries o, then, since C must marry into β, C must marry p, by the above principles, and, therefore, D must marry q, and so on. It will be noticed that this means that a man must marry into the mother's brother's daughter class, no matter what class we suppose B initially to marry. The classificatory relationships, wife and mother's brother's daughter, must inevitably coincide. Given the marriages of the male classes of α with the female classes of β, there still remain a number of different possibilities for the marriages of the female classes of α with the male classes of β. The possibilities may be put at three or at most four in number, a result that is easily demonstrated. Given $B \times o$ (i.e. B marries o), and therefore $C \times p$, etc., then, either $O \times a$, or

---

are drawn from the male classes of one group to the female classes of some one other group must be parallel—this symbolises the latter part of the principle laid down above—and any interval thus established between parallel lines must be repeated indefinitely—this corresponds to the first part of the principle—e.g.:

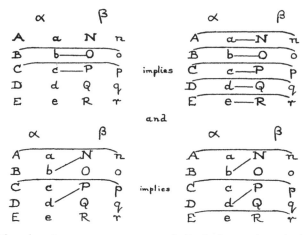

Although only two groups are symbolised above, the principle is exactly the same for any number of groups.

$O \times b$, or $O \times c$, or $O \times d$, and, of course, if $O \times a$, then $P \times b$, etc., and similarly for $O \times b$, $O \times c$, and $O \times d$. It is clear that O could not marry an earlier class than a, for this would mean that men on the average marry women more than half a generation older than themselves, while if O were to marry a later class than d, this would mean that men on the average marry women more than a generation younger than themselves. This conclusion may be expressed diagrammatically as follows:

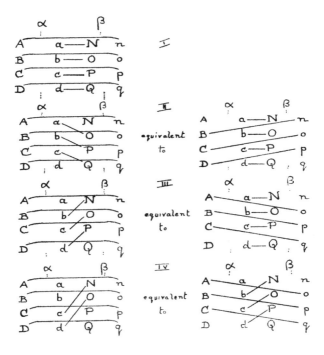

The Diagrams I, II, III and IV represent the four possible forms of matrilineal dual organisation with a regulation of marriage by generations. In all cases a class of males marries the class of mother's brother's daughters; in Type I this class is also that of father's sister's daughters; in Type II it is the class of father's sisters; in Type III the class of father's sister's daughters' daughters; in Type IV the class of father's sister's daughter's daughter's daughters.

It should be noted that the principal classifications necessary to any matrilineal dual organisation, given the preservation of generation classes, are as follows:[1]

wife	= mother's brother's daughter
husband	= father's sister's son
mother's brother	= wife's father
father's sister	= husband's mother
	etc.

The principal additional classifications given by the completion of the marriage system as one of the four above types are given for reference in a note below.[2]

[1] English relationship terms other than cousin always define the sex of the second term of the relation, but only rarely of the first; where the first term is female the relationship term is in darker type in the present work, thus making all the relationship terms used unique.

[2] Type I, which must be regarded as the most probable, since the intermarrying classes will be of the same average age, gives the following principal classifications:

wife	= mother's brother's daughter
	= father's sister's daughter
	= sister's husband's sister
husband	= father's sister's son
	= mother's brother's son
	= brother's wife's brother
mother's brother	= wife's father
	= father's sister's husband
	= sister's husband's father
father's sister	= sister's husband's mother
	= mother's brother's wife
	= wife's mother
	etc.

Type II gives the following principal classifications:

wife	= mother's brother's daughter
	= father's sister
	= sister's husband's mother
husband	= father's sister's son
	= mother's brother's daughter's son
	= brother's son
mother's brother	= wife's father
	= father's father
	= sister's husband's mother's father
father's sister's son	= sister's husband
	= mother's brother's daughter's son
	= son
	etc.

Type III gives the following principal classifications:

wife	= mother's brother's daughter
	= father's sister's daughter's daughter
	= sister's husband's sister's daughter

Open class systems having more than two exogamous groups have a proportionately greater number of possible forms, which may be simply discovered by applying the rule for diagrams given in a footnote on pp. 242–3.

The second part of alternative (1) (pp. 238–9 above), has now been elucidated. If generation classes practise group marriage, or equivalent individual marriage, the classes must intermarry in a systematic way which is strictly limited. If there are only two moieties and descent is matrilineal, the number of possible systems is four only.[1]

husband	= father's sister's son
	= mother's mother's brother's son
	= brother's wife's mother's brother
mother's brother	= wife's father
	= father's sister's daughter's husband
	= sister's husband's sister's husband
father's sister's son	= sister's husband
	= mother's brother's wife's brother
	= wife's mother's brother
	etc.

Type IV gives the following principal classifications:

wife	= mother's brother's daughter
	= father's sister's daughter's daughter's daughter
	= sister's husband's sister's daughter's daughter
husband	= father's sister's son
	= mother's mother's mother's brother's son
	= brother's wife's mother's mother's brother
mother's brother	= wife's father
	= father's sister's daughter's daughter's husband
	= sister's husband's sister's daughter's husband
father's sister's son	= sister's husband
	= mother's brother's wife's mother's brother
	= wife's mother's mother's brother
	etc.

[1] Rivers does not seem to have fully realised that, if we are to explain the classificatory system by a former condition of marriage between groups, the groups must be generations (or possibly groups of generations). In an essay on the 'Origin of the Classificatory System' (reprinted in *Social Organization*, App. 1) Rivers postulates a condition of group marriage between classes which are determined by age and matrilineal descent. Now it is obvious that a class which is an age grade cannot, except possibly for the first one or two generations starting from a single female ancestor, coincide with a generation class. Such a class must contain members of several generations, and only some of the members of a single generation can be members of the class. Rivers admits later that it is difficult to see 'how the relationships set up by these age grades developed into those regulated by generations such as we find among most people of low culture at the present time' (*ibid.* p. 189). This is surely to admit that the classificatory system receives no explanation

Let us now suppose that marriage inconsistent with an open class system takes place, and that classificatory relationship terms are still used in the sense defined by Rivers. As has already been shown (pp. 239–40 above), this implies either that generation classes are grouped together into a closed class system, or that everyone is related to everyone else in every possible way consistent with sex and exogamy. To take the former alternative first; then, for a given interval of generations classed together within the moiety— to take a dual organisation—there will be a limited number of solutions; e.g. if a female class, where descent is matrilineal, is classed with the class of daughter's daughters, we have:

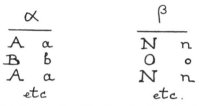

i.e. we have eight classes, for, if a female class is classed with the daughter's daughter class, the brothers are thereby classed with the daughter's daughter's brothers. Two possible systems of group marriage, or the equivalent individual marriage, result from this, as follows:

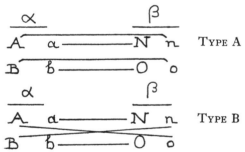

Type A may be regarded as the partial break-down of Types I or IV of the open class system; Type B as the partial break-down of Types II or III of the open class system.

until this transformation has been effected. If the classification based on age grading has to be replaced by a totally different classification based on generations, it seems superfluous to introduce group marriage between age grades to explain a system which can only be derived from group marriage (or the equivalent individual form of marriage) between generations.

In Type A:[1]

        wife = mother's brother's daughter
            = daughter's daughter
            = father's sister's daughter
            = sister's husband's sister
            = father's mother
            etc.

In Type B:

        wife = mother's brother's daughter
            = daughter's daughter
            = father's sister
            = sister's husband's mother
            = father's mother's mother
            etc.

If generation classes, separated by three generations, be classed together, we have the following possible 12-class systems:

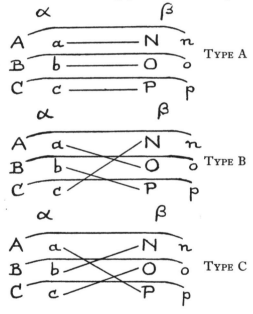

[1] The so-called 4-class systems of Australia are of Type A, whether descent be matrilineal or patrilineal. Apparently there are no class systems in Australia where the class of sisters does not marry the class of wives' brothers, so that a class of brothers and sisters may be treated as a unit. Australian 4-class systems are, therefore, what I am calling 8-class systems, and Australian 8-class systems are what I am calling 16-class systems.

in which

    the wife = mother's brother's daughter
         = daughter daughter's daughter
(and in Type A)   = father's sister's daughter, etc.
(in Type B)   = father's sister, etc.
(in Type C)   = father's mother, etc.

The classing of every fourth generation together gives four marriage systems, which may be regarded as simple forms of break-down of an open class system. A more complex break-down would result in that type of 16-class system which may be attributed (though the classes are unnamed) to certain Australian tribes, such as the Dieri.[1] This system is as follows:

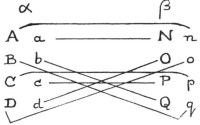

and, unlike all open class systems with two moieties and matrilineal descent, a man does not marry into the mother's brother's daughter class.

The closed class systems, in which there are more than two exogamous groups, are proportionately more numerous, and may be investigated on the above lines. One such system of more than two exogamous groups may be mentioned, owing to its occurrence in Australia at the present day. This is a system of four exogamous groups with patrilineal descent, known generally as the 8-class system. It is one in which alternate generations are classed together, and brothers and sisters, in the classificatory sense, marry sisters and brothers, so that one line in the diagram below serves to show the marriages of both brothers and sisters. The system may be represented thus:

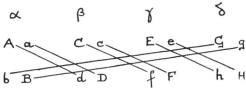

[1] *Vide* Rivers, *Social Organization.* p. 197, and A. R. Brown, 'Three Tribes of Western Australia', *Journal of the Royal Anthropologica Institute*, vol. XLIII, 1913, pp. 190–194.

The system is equivalent to the hypothetical Dieri system above, for there are two exogamous matrilineal groups, and four exogamous patrilineal groups in either system, and the relationships between the classes are the same. The one may, therefore, be derived from the other by emphasizing a different line of descent. It should be noticed that the Australian 8-class system may be regarded as a form of dual organisation, for two moieties are recognised consisting of α and γ on the one hand, and β and δ on the other.

While it is possible that the Australian 4-class and 8-class systems are not the only existing closed class systems, their existence in any other part of the world has not yet been demonstrated, and, for reasons which will appear presently, it is useless to look for such a system, and even less for an open class system amongst the majority of those peoples who have a so-called classificatory system.[1] If, however, neither an open nor a closed class system can be found we are reduced to alternative (3) for the majority of peoples who use classificatory relationships in Rivers' sense. This is, for instance, the state of affairs on Rossel, which has neither an open nor a closed class system.

We have seen that a classificatory system can be derived from a class system by a process of break-down, but this does not mean that a classificatory system could not originate in some other way. There is, however, one feature of the classificatory system of Melanesia which points strongly to their origin in some form or forms of class system. I refer to the classing of mother's sister's children with father's brother's children. Rivers found this classification to be widespread, but does not, to my mind, draw the correct conclusion from it. He says[2] that there is 'no direct reason why this feature of relationship should exist where there are more than two social groups. There is then suggested an origin of all forms of the Melanesian system in a dual organisation of society, such as is still found in several parts of Melanesia. The nomenclature for the father's brother and mother's sister, their consorts and children points to the dual organisation having at one time been universal in Melanesia'. This classification is bound to occur, as we have already seen, on any class system, no matter how many intermarrying exogamous

---

[1] It must also be pointed out that the relationship-terminology in Australian closed class systems is more complex than is required by the classes. We find, for instance, that the distinction between older and younger brothers and sisters is of considerable importance and that there are marriage rules depending upon this.

[2] W. H. R. Rivers, *History of Melanesian Society*, vol. II, 1914, p. 16.

groups there be. It is, therefore, evidence of the former existence of a class system rather than of a dual organisation, although, on other grounds, the probabilities may be in favour of a class system with two moieties only.

If class systems were once widespread in Melanesia, their disintegration may readily be interpreted as the result of marriage with the mother's brother's wife, which is incompatible with a class system. Not only is this marriage in existence in parts of Melanesia at the present day, but in other parts there is a terminology of relationship together with avoidance customs between these relatives, which Rivers has shown to be survivals, in all probability, of an earlier custom of marriage with the mother's brother's wife. Another common feature of nomenclature which is very general makes a distinction between elder and younger brothers, which is also incompatible with a class system if such distinction affects the relationship terminology. We also find in some parts, e.g. Rossel, an avoidance between a man and his brother's wife's sister, which is equally incompatible with any class system. Although class systems are, therefore, necessarily absent from the greater part of Melanesia, this may be because of the introduction of certain forms of marriage inconsistent with a class system. This is a possibility worth while considering; firstly, because it would explain the classification of mother's sister's children with father's brother's children, and secondly, because it would explain certain other features of social organisation, such as grandmother and granddaughter marriage, for which Rivers gives a quite different explanation.[1]

Pursuing the above suggestion, some slight probability may be attached to the following mode of development. Firstly, a condition of group marriage between generation classes of two or more exogamous groups; secondly, the development of individual marriage between members of the intermarrying classes; thirdly, owing to individual marriage the occurrence of certain marriages outside the appropriate class, causing either a break-down of the system, or a reduction of the classes to a closed class system. That marriages outside the appropriate class on an open class system should occur as soon as individual marriage has become established is only to be expected; for the members of a generation class are likely to vary considerably in

[1] Recognising the incompatibility of marriage with the mother's brother's wife (which is associated with grandmother and granddaughter marriage) with a class system, such as the Australian, Rivers neglected this line of enquiry. *Vide*, Rivers, *History of Melanesian Society*, vol. II, p. 67, also 'Pentecost' in vols. I and II.

age amongst themselves, and the members of the classes are likely to vary in numbers, so that sometimes the men of a class will be more numerous than the women, who are their potential mates, and sometimes the women will be the more numerous. There will, therefore, be occasions when the last members of a class to attempt to marry are unable to do so, and must either remain unmarried or break the marriage rule. A system which necessitates that a small proportion of males, through no choice of their own, shall go through life unmarried, inevitably breaks down. As soon as group marriage gives place to individual marriage an open class system necessarily gives place either to a closed class system or to a classificatory system. Which of these two latter takes place depends on the aberrant marriages which follow the disappearance of group marriage, and it would seem, at first glance, that the stranded males would take their wives from the class adjacent to their correct marriage class. This, however, is no more likely than that they should take their wives from the class two or even more generations removed, for the following reasons. If the generation classes have persisted for some time the few youngest members are not likely to be much older than the average members of two or three generations later. If all but the youngest members of a class have married, then a great many of the women of the next class are likely to have married, while in the class two generations removed the majority of women may still be unmarried. For the residue of unmarried males of a class the choice of suitable mates of more or less the same age is small in the class next to the appropriate marriage class, but is likely to be larger in the class below that. After two or three generations, more or less according to circumstances, the choice again becomes restricted. As soon as a closed class system or a classificatory system has been produced by a few marriages of the above kind, the difficulty which forced the revolution on the community is solved. There is no reason why a closed class system thus produced should not persist until the introduction of a new mode of marriage incompatible with it, such as marriage with the mother's brother's wife.

The above considerations show how the so-called grand-daughter and grandmother marriage of parts of Melanesia may be explained, without the difficulties inherent in Rivers' scheme. On the above view, a dual organisation with matrilineal descent and an open class system would tend to give place, owing to marriages into the granddaughter class at the critical moment, to an 8-class closed class system, or with perhaps less probability to a 12-class or 16-class system, or else simply to a classificatory system. In the supposed 8-class closed class systems resulting, we have a system in which men class their granddaughters and their grandmothers with their wives, without necessarily marrying their genealogical brother's granddaughters, whereas on Rivers' view it is necessary to suppose that these marriages are actual in the sense that a man marries his close brother's actual granddaughter. In fact, on Rivers' view, a man necessarily marries a woman who is of the same age on the average as an own granddaughter. Rivers does deny this,[1] but I think without reason. He points out that the disparity of age between grandparent and grandchild may be very slight. This is perfectly true, and, it may be added, the grandchild in this classificatory sense may be an old man, while the grandparent is a young girl. But Rivers' whole scheme implies that such marriages are systematic, so that every man who selects a granddaughter of his own age is dooming one of his brothers to marriage with a granddaughter who will probably not be born until he is dead. This is so, because members of generations two generations apart are necessarily, on the average, two generations apart in age, even though there may be many members of the older generation who are considerably younger than many members of the younger generation. It might, however, be contended that the above misleading statement of Rivers is due to his abandoning his earlier description of classificatory relationship. That Rivers still adheres to this description is shown by the following passage: '...the monopoly of women by the old men which I assume must have existed in a community already divided into two exogamous moieties; it involves the clear recognition of generations and the existence of the classificatory system of relationships'.[2]

The explanation of granddaughter (and grandmother) marriage by means of a closed class system is one which does not necessitate there being any discrepancy of age between those who marry, and does not require that a man ever marries his genealogical brother's granddaughter, though he will always marry his classificatory granddaughter. Since granddaughter marriage in Melanesia is associated with marriage with the mother's brother's wife, a marriage which is inconsistent with a class system, we cannot test the hypothesis directly, for owing to this latter marriage some transformation of relationship terminology must have taken place and the class system must have broken down. The former existence of a closed class system in those parts of Melanesia where apparent granddaughter marriage takes place

[1] Rivers, *History of Melanesian Society*, vol. II, p. 57.
[2] *Ibid.* p. 69.

can, therefore, be regarded as probable only if Rivers' interpretation appears sufficiently improbable.[1] If, however, this can be done, the probability of the former existence of a class system in other parts of Melanesia, e.g. Rossel, is increased.

It is obvious that marriage with own granddaughter or genealogical brother's granddaughter cannot be at all systematic; less than half the marriages can be of this form. If a number of brothers marry each others' granddaughters we must not forget the wives by whom the granddaughters were procreated. According to Rivers, as soon as the old men marry their granddaughters the old wives are, or were at one time, passed on to their sisters' sons. The granddaughters, however, will be young when the grandfathers die, and of suitable age for the grandfathers' nephews, and so they may become, by a second marriage, the wives of their mother's father's sister's sons, the men, therefore, marrying their mother's brother's daughter's daughters. The latter then marry their daughter's daughters, and their mother's brother's daughter's daughters are passed on to their nephews, so that in the next generation a man's first wife is likely to be his mother's brother's mother's brother's daughter's daughter, and so on for later generations.

If we could imagine these marriages becoming systematic, we should have the curious result of all the males of one moiety marrying alternate generations of women of the other moiety, i.e. all the men would marry half the women. This could only be avoided by marriage with a mother's brother's daughter, or mother's brother's daughter's daughter's daughter, or some more remote relation. In other words, systematic marriage with the mother's brother's wife and the brother's granddaughter cannot take place. The most we can say is that a man marries either his mother's brother's wife or his brother's daughter's daughter or a woman not standing in any close genealogical relation.

Of course if we use the term in the classificatory sense, the wife will always be the brother's granddaughter, for in the absence of

---

[1] Although the daughter's daughters appear to be classed with the wife's sisters on Pentecost, it is not clear that the wife's mother's mothers are classed with the wife's sisters, which is equally demanded on a closed class system. I think it will be admitted that Rivers' evidence is insufficient to reveal how the Pentecost system works, so that the absence of a statement that the wife's sisters are classed with the wife's mother's mothers is no serious objection to the view of the former existence of a closed class system. Of course, if the terms are used in the classificatory sense, as Rivers seems to imply, then wife's sisters are classed with wife's mother's mothers, with daughter's daughters, and so on. *Vide* Rivers, *History of Melanesian Society*, vol. I, Chap. VIII.

a class system everybody is in every classificatory relationship, consistent with the dual organisation if this coexists, to everybody else. Similarly, the wife will always be the mother's brother's wife. The marriages are significant only if between persons who are closely related by the required relationships.

There is, it may be mentioned, one way in which it would be possible for the majority of women to be both wife and mother's brother's wife of some man. This could happen if a man always passed on a wife, who was not the wife of his mother's brother, to his nephew in a short space of time, only retaining as permanent wife one passed on to him by his mother's brother.

We may, therefore, conclude that from the point of view of genealogical relationship the probabilities are against a woman's mother being her husband's daughter or husband's brother's daughter on a system of marital gerontocracy, but it is conceivable that a man's child should generally be the mother's brother's child (i.e. the mother's brother's former wife's subsequent child), although this would imply the peculiar custom of passing on the first wife quickly to the sister's son, a most unlikely procedure.

It might be maintained that it is not necessary for most persons to become related in the required multiple ways in order to affect appropriately the relationship terminology, but that terminology is directly affected by (1) the native view that certain forms of marriage are best, and (2) the conscious realisation of the effect of such marriages in placing persons in certain multiple relations to one another; e.g. the potentiality of the mother's brother's wife as wife might make a man call her children by the term for children, since, if subsequently she became his wife, they would attain the status of his children. If, as seems probable, marriage with the mother's brother's wife has usually been no more than inheritance of the mother's brother's widow, such an explanation seems to be required.[1]

These considerations suggest that while part of the relationship terminology in the area of granddaughter marriage may be the result of mother's brother's wife marriage, it is more difficult to suppose that any part of the relationship terminology should result from granddaughter marriage, for the latter cannot be systematic. Since the existence of a former class system in Melanesia is already made probable by the very general classing of mother's sister's children with father's brother's children, the difficulty of explaining such systems as that of Pentecost, with its so-called granddaughter marriage, is additional and inde-

---

[1] Driberg gives instances of such anticipation of relationship from the Lango of Uganda (J. H. Driberg, *The Lango*, 1923, p. 181).

pendent evidence of the former existence of a class system in Melanesia.

As we have already seen, a classificatory system is readily explained as a breakdown of a class system. In a class system a term applied to one person for genealogical reasons may be applied to another for non-genealogical reasons, e.g. A may call B by the term for brother, because A calls C and C calls B by this term. This way of determining the use of relationship terms is also common in classificatory systems, such as we find in Melanesia.[1] But since the classificatory relationships which hold between persons do not, on a classificatory system, depend on generations (although it is true that a given classificatory relationship must hold between pairs of generations, for the simple reason that it holds between wider groups than generations), neither will the use of relationship terms depend on generations. If A uses the term R to B, it does not follow that A will use the term R to C, who is of the same generation and sex as B; further, if A uses the term R to B, A may use the term R to C, even though C is of a different generation from B. The reasons for this will become clear below, but it may be pointed out here that, if the view is correct, Rivers' description of a classificatory system tells us nothing about the use of classificatory relationship terms, and is without significance as a description of the classificatory relationships themselves. In the case of a class system this distinction between the classificatory relationships and the use of classificatory relationship terms is not, of course, required, except in so far as the terminology of an open class system might persist in the closed class system to which it gives rise.

This distinction between relationship and the use of the relationship term is of considerable importance in a classificatory system, as distinct from a class system, owing to the variety of classificatory relationships which hold between any two persons.

[1] It may here be pointed out that this is also one way in which a genealogical relationship system (in which genealogical relationships only are recognised) could become a classificatory system. If the reason for regarding a relationship R to hold between two persons A and B is the fact that A and B have certain relationships to C and D between whom R holds, then either a classificatory or a class system would necessarily result. If R is not a relation holding between persons of either the same or different sex, then more than one such relation would be required. But it is difficult to see what function such an innovation could serve, and, therefore, why it should ever take place. This difficulty does not arise if we regard a classificatory system as derived from a class system. We have, moreover, other reasons, already mentioned, which tell in favour of the latter view.

A further distinction of importance must be made between the kinds of relationship terms that we find in actual classificatory systems, namely, that between classificatory relationship terms and other relationship terms. This distinction is usually one of degree (at least, this is so in South-East New Guinea), and, judging from the use of the terms, we generally find that the relationship terms for brother and sister are the most classificatory; for most of the members of one exogamous group use these terms between each other, unless they happen to be in some other very ose genealogical relationship. On Rossel we find certain relationship terms which are not classificatory and are not *simply* genealogical. In all probability such terms occur elsewhere in Melanesia.

We have seen that on a classificatory system every person is related to every other person by every classificatory relationship, consistent with exogamy and the sex relation. Why, then, it will be asked, do we find that a person regards himself as being in a certain relationship to another, and why is he also regarded by other persons as being in that relationship? This can best be answered by denying the generality of the fact implied by the question. It is only in the case of near relatives that there is the constancy implied in this question. In the case of more distant relatives a person may sometimes regard himself as in one relationship, sometimes in another, and by some of his friends and relatives he may be regarded as being in yet another relationship, which he has not contemplated. This variability seems to have been overlooked by most ethnologists, but the evidence of its occurrence in South-East New Guinea is conclusive, and is, moreover, exactly what one would expect on theoretical grounds. Its importance in applying Rivers' genealogical method is considerable, for the relationships obtaining between persons may not be the ones corresponding to those revealed by the selected pedigrees, except in the case of very close relatives. This does not mean that the genealogical method is useless, except when we are dealing with close relatives, but it means that pedigrees must be treated statistically, or that the reasons given by an informant for a given relationship must be discovered. Rivers does not seem to have realised this, owing to his misunderstanding of the nature of the classificatory system, otherwise he would not have been satisfied with the investigation by means of pedigrees only.

The factors which determine the use of a particular relationship term between two persons, who are, as a matter of fact, in all possible classificatory relationships to one another will now be considered. In the case of close genealogical relatives it is almost certain to be the case that one relationship is *nearer* than any other; in other words, there is one route by which relationship can be calculated, which is shorter than any other. We have, therefore, in such cases a very good reason why one relationship term should be used between these relatives, and why this relationship should be regarded as *the* relationship holding between these relatives by other members of the community who know anything about them and their families. This priority of one relationship becomes less as we take for consideration more remote genealogical relatives, so that it may be difficult to discover which is the nearer of two or more ways of determining the relationship. Let us suppose that by the nearest genealogical relationship route A is the R of B, and by that route which is next in order of nearness A is S of B, then it is probable that a person C who lies on the route by which A is S of B, but not on the route by which A is R of B, will regard A as the S of B. Where a number of relationships holding between two persons lie close together in order of genealogical nearness, the particular relationship chosen by some third person will depend, therefore, on his relationships to the first two persons. As we pass beyond the boundary of genealogical relationship, the scope for differences of view as to what is the relationship between two persons becomes enormously increased, and such factors as locality, the chance friendships between individuals, and so on, become important determinants of the relationship in which two persons regard themselves, and of the relationships in which others regard them. It may also be mentioned in this connection, that the process of collecting pedigrees and asking questions about relationship may elicit new relationships for remoter members of a pedigree; for the informants acquire a certain context which may be unusual, and may state, for example, that A is the R of B on the basis of that context, although A and B may be in some nearer relationship by another route. A good informant when he departs from the context of a given pedigree in stating a relationship will say that he is giving the relationship 'by another road', an expression which will be familiar to those who have worked on relationship in South-East New Guinea.

Formal expression may now be given to the above peculiarities of a classificatory system. Although any two persons are related by every possible classificatory relationship, these relationships fall into an order, so that the complete relationship between two persons may be expressed as the sequence of relationships which hold between them, the shorter the route by which a given relationship holds and the greater the number and the difference of routes by which the relationship holds the *earlier* the relationship in the sequence. In other words, for any given person there is in relation to any other given person a grouping of relationships, the word 'grouping' being used in the way defined in Chap. III.

But we may also look at the same facts from a different point of view, that from which we may reach the important concepts of family and tribal grouping. From this point of view there is a grouping of every person with respect to any given relationship— there is his mother's grouping, his mother's brother's grouping, and so on—and, in the case of classificatory relationships, such a grouping may consist of about half or a quarter of the community. This grouping is, of course, a sequence of persons, ordered by 'nearness' of the given relationship. The grouping of mothers is the sequence 'own mother', 'mother's sisters', 'mother's mother's sister's daughters', and so on, the latest members of the sequence being persons who can be found to be mothers only by the most roundabout routes, which no *one* member of the community may be able to work out.

If two persons have one relationship, which is a close genealogical one, then the difference of intensity between this and the next relationship of the sequence is likely to be considerable for obvious reasons. This is, therefore, naturally taken to be *the* relationship holding between these two persons by the community as a whole. If, however, the first member of the relationship sequence is not calculable by a close genealogical route, then the difference in intensity between this and later members of the sequence is likely to be less, with the result that different relatives may use different terms for this relationship.

Finally, in the case of any two persons who are the most remotely related in the community, we shall naturally find that they are regarded as in every relationship possible by someone or other in the community.

We are now in a position to turn to those other features of existing classificatory systems that Rivers maintains to be the result of certain existing or extinct modes of marriage.

We have already seen that the term 'classificatory relationship' is commonly used in two senses, which ought to be clearly distinguished. It may refer to that classification of genealogical[1] with non-genealogical relatives, which we have both in open and closed class systems and in classificatory systems. It may, on the

---

[1] By 'genealogical' I always mean 'genealogical for someone in the group'.

other hand, refer to that classification under one relationship term of relatives who need not be classified together under a class system. This type of classification can occur equally under a class system, under a classificatory system, and under a system in which genealogical relationships only are recognised. A relationship term may be classificatory in this second sense only; but, if it is classificatory in the first sense, it must also be classificatory in the second sense, for even under an open class system any two given classes are in more than one distinct relationship, as we have already seen (p. 243 *seq.*); under a closed class system classification in the second sense is still further increased (p. 247 *seq.*); and, finally, under a classificatory system there appear to be other classifications in this second sense, which could not occur under a class system. It is proposed to consider these now, owing to the importance they assume in Rivers' theoretical work.

Rivers maintains that where we find a classification of the second kind this is generally to be explained by the existence or former existence of a certain systematic form of marriage. We need not consider here certain other explanations which Rivers suggests for special cases, as, for example, the classification of relatives whom a man was once permitted to marry with relatives whom a man could not marry, owing to the introduction of a new form of marriage and the prohibition of an old form. If the marriage with certain relatives be systematic, it follows that certain relationships will tend to coincide, so that if A is R of B, then A is also S of B, and if B is T of C, then B is also U of C, and so on. It would not, therefore, be surprising to find that only one of these pairs of relationship terms should survive, and that the terms should become classificatory (in the second sense of the term). We cannot, however, put the argument quite in this way if we have a classificatory system, for under a classificatory system all relationships, consistent with exogamy and the sex-relation, coincide. In the classificatory sense of a term (in the first sense of classificatory) any marriage, consistent with exogamy, which we like to name, takes place systematically, under a classificatory system. Therefore, systematic marriages in the classificatory sense are not the cause of classifications (in the second sense) under a classificatory system. We have, however, already seen that with respect to a given relationship of a person there is a grouping of persons; there is always one person towards whom another has a given relationship the most intensely, and this will be the shortest genealogical route by which this person has the given relationship, and this person we can regard as the R (where R is the relationship) of the first. If systematic marriage with the closest relative (by a given relationship) take place, then, and only then, is there any reason why relationship terminology should be affected, for the tendency for marriage with a certain relative to produce the appropriate classifications will depend on the intensity of the relationship. Consider, for example, the effect of systematic marriage with other than the closest mother's brother's wives; since there will also be a closer mother's brother's wife than the one married, there must be a greater number of non-coincidences of the relationship mother's brother's wife and wife than of coincidences of these two relationships; but clearly to produce a classification of mother's brother's wife with wife, the coincidences must be more frequent than the non-coincidences. Therefore, terminology will only be affected by marriage with the mother's brother's wife if systematic marriage with the closest mother's brother's wife is practised.

This argument may be generalised, and we can, therefore, state that relationship terminology can only be affected by systematic marriage, under a classificatory system, if the marriages are between close relatives, a fact which Rivers does not seem to have realised.

This does not, of course, apply to those classifications which could be produced by a class system, if we are prepared to admit the former existence of a class system, and the survival in relationship terminology of the classifications produced by it. If, however, we do not accept this view of the former existence of a class system, then those classifications, consistent with a class system, must also be regarded as the consequences of systematic marriage with close relatives. Where, for example, we have apparent granddaughter and grandmother marriage, we must suppose this to be either the survival of the terminology of a closed class system, or else the effect of systematic marriage of men with their own granddaughters. Since a man must marry a woman who is not his own granddaughter in order to have an own granddaughter, this would involve a state of society in which marriages are systematically dissolved as well as contracted, a gerontocracy far exceeding Rivers' picture of it. We are, therefore, forced to the alternative of the former existence of a closed class system in order to avoid this absurdity.

The necessity of assuming the former existence of a closed class system for one part of Melanesia strengthens considerably the argument for the former existence of class systems throughout Melanesia, the classificatory system in its various forms being a survival of this early system. A complete explanation of the various relationship systems of Melanesia, New Guinea, and

Australia on these lines would probably require the hypothesis of several kinds of closed class systems, themselves perhaps resulting from more than one open class system (although their origin in open class systems is more open to doubt). The large number of classificatory systems resulting from the small number of class systems would depend very largely on the kinds of systematic marriage with close relatives introduced. The time-order and nature of these changes would still be very similar to those worked out by Rivers. The one universally surviving feature of the class system would be the non-genealogical use of relationship terms and almost as universal the classification of mother's sister's children, etc., with father's brother's children, etc. The classifications of alternate generations together, such as we have in Pentecost and elsewhere, would be survivals of a closed class system, and, therefore, earlier than the terminologies produced by marriages inconsistent with a class system, which subsequently developed. Probably later than the development of a classificatory system out of a class system must have been marriage with the mother's brother's wife, due to an influence that did not spread all over the area, and later still, but more restricted, the prohibition of this marriage, associated with avoidances between these relatives. The prohibition of cross-cousin marriage, which occurs in many areas, must also be regarded as late, if the dual organisation be early, since it is the prohibition of a marriage which is fundamental to a class system with two exogamous groups, except for certain 16-class systems (see p. 249).

It is not, however, proposed to enter further into these considerations in this Appendix, the principal object of which has been to make clear the nature of the classificatory system, so that the description of the particular variety of it found on Rossel, and described in Chap. IV, may be intelligible.

INDEX[1]

[1] The Appendices are not indexed.

For EU product safety concerns, contact us at Calle de José Abascal, 56–1°,
28003 Madrid, Spain or eugpsr@cambridge.org.

www.ingramcontent.com/pod-product-compliance
Ingram Content Group UK Ltd.
Pitfield, Milton Keynes, MK11 3LW, UK
UKHW010350140625
459647UK00010B/964